PEOPLE AND ORGANISATIONS

# Managing in a Business Context

## DAVID FARNHAM

Chartered Institute of Personnel and Development

Design by Curve

Typeset by Fakenham Photosetting Ltd, Fakenham, Norfolk

Printed in Great Britain by the Short Run Press, Exeter, Devon

*British Library Cataloguing in Publication Data*
A catalogue record of this book is available from the British Library

ISBN 0-85292-783-5

Chartered Institute of Personnel and Development, CIPD House, Camp Road, London SW19 4UX
Tel: 020-8971 9000   Fax: 020-8263 3333
E-mail: cipd@cipd.co.uk Website: www.cipd.co.uk
Incorporated by Royal Charter. Registered Charity No. 1079797.

# Managing
## in a
## Business
## Context

**David Farnham** is Professor of Employment Relations at the University of Portsmouth and National Examiner for Managing in a Business Context in the Core Management   He is also the author of *Employee Relations*   (with S. Horton) *Managing People in the Public Se*   *in Britain.*

# Other titles in the series:

*Core Personnel and Development*
Mick Marchington and Adrian Wilkinson

*Employee Development*
Second Edition
Rosemary Harrison

*Employee Relations*
Second Edition
John Gennard and Graham Judge

*Employee Resourcing*
Stephen Taylor

*Employee Reward*
Second Edition
Michael Armstrong

*Essentials of Employment Law*
(Sixth Edition)
David Lewis and Malcolm Sargeant

*Managing Activities*
Michael Armstrong

*Managing Financial Information*
David Davies

*Managing Information and Statistics*
Roland and Frances Bee

*Managing People*
Jane Weightman

*Personnel Practice*
Second Edition
Malcolm Martin and Tricia Jackson

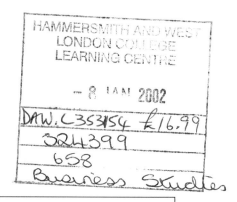
The Chartered Institute of Personnel and Development is the leading publisher of books and reports for personnel and training professionals, students, and all those concerned with the effective management and development of people at work. For details of all our titles, please contact the Publishing Department:

*tel* 020 8263 3387
*fax* 020 8263 3850
*e-mail* publish@cipd.co.uk

The catalogue of all CIPD titles can be viewed on the CIPD website:

www.cipd.co.uk/publications

324399

# Contents

# Foreword

Welcome to this series of texts designed to complement the Core Management syllabus. The role of the personnel and development practitioner has become an important part of the total management of all types of organisation in the private, public and voluntary sectors. A fundamental element of that role is the ability to comprehend and contribute to the overall goals, performance and outcomes of organisations. This is the purpose of the Core Management syllabus: to equip personnel and development practitioners to understand and appreciate complex business and managerial issues and to develop their skills so that they can play a full role in that process.

The awareness of markets, products and services is now a key attribute for personnel and development practitioners. The specialised knowledge that was once confined to 'corporate planners' has become the 'business strategy' that influences and affects every member of the organisation, whatever the sector. This text sets out to examine the nature of the strategy process, to demonstrate its negotiated role and implications for HRM specialists, and to explore how economic, legal, political, technological and international factors form the context in which organisations operate and personnel and development are practised.

Professor Ian J Beardwell
Head, Department of HRM
Leicester Business School
De Montfort University
Leicester

# Acknowledgements

I should like to thank my colleagues at the University of Portsmouth, Sylvia Horton and David Preece, for writing Chapters 4 and 6 respectively. In addition, Sylvia Horton and Dr Alan Rutter each read some of the chapters and other colleagues, Richard Christie and Dr Paul Trott, helped me with relevant references and support. I should like to record my thanks to them all, and to Richard Goff, Chris Jackson and their colleagues at CIPD Publications in producing this text.

Professor David Farnham
University of Portsmouth
May 1999

# Introduction

The overall purpose of this module of the Core Management professional standards is to identify, examine and analyse the major contexts within which private, public and voluntary organisations operate. The module also raises issues of how managements are responding to contextual diversity, continuous change and ethical ambiguities in conditions of uncertainty. As a result of environmental turbulence, managers are having to identify, devise and implement appropriate strategies to ensure survival of their organisations, in response to market and contextual uncertainties. This book describes, analyses and discusses these and related issues. There is considerable emphasis within the module on knowledge and understanding, rather than on skills and competencies. So, in addition to using this text as a source of information, analysis and references, students are strongly advised to keep up to date with current issues and current affairs by regularly reading the quality press, such as the *Financial Times, Guardian, Independent, Daily Telegraph* and *Economist.*

# 1 The strategic framework

This chapter introduces its readers to some basic ideas about strategy, planning and the strategic process. Strategy has a long history and there are many conflicting perspectives of the strategic process, so the approach adopted here is a selective but demanding one. With organisations operating in increasingly complex, unstable external environments, those leading them – in the private, public and voluntary sectors – are increasingly using systems and techniques of strategic management in response to uncertainty, change and market competition. The deterministic view of strategy is a rationalist one. It is concerned with assessing where an organisation is at the moment (and how it got there), analysing the directions in which it might go in order to survive and prosper, determining how it can get there and subsequently evaluating whether it has achieved its objectives. Alternatively, strategy can be 'shaped', without any predetermined objectives, and 'emerges' over time in response to organisational needs. Planning has a number of meanings but can most usefully be defined as the process of establishing intended courses of action (or means) to achieve particular ends.

By the end of this chapter, readers should be able to understand and explain:

- the nature of strategy and the main elements within the strategic process

- the differences between strategic search, choice and implementation

- the ways in which strategy is determined

- types of strategy adopted by organisations and the importance of strategic review, monitoring and benchmarking

- how the external environment impacts on private, public and voluntary organisations

- the concepts of PESTLE and SWOT and the dynamics of the political, economic, social, technological and legal contexts on organisations.

In addition, readers should be able to:

- undertake PESTLE and SWOT analyses

- advise on the opportunities and threats arising from this.

See also the Professional Standards Index (page 345).

## THE NATURE AND ROLE OF STRATEGY AND PLANNING IN ORGANISATIONS

Strategy is a disputed concept, with different meanings for different people at different times. As de Wit and Meyer (1998: 3) put it: 'there are strongly differing opinions on most of the key issues within the field and the disagreements run so deep that even a common definition of the term strategy is illusive'. Originally 'strategy' – from the ancient Greek *strategia*, 'generalship' – was associated with the planning and winning of wars. Nowadays strategy, such as business strategy, marketing strategy or human resources strategy, is mainly linked with the management function in organisations and with those people and groups responsible for planning organisational success in the market place. But the term strategy is also used in a personal sense. Someone might have 'a strategy for developing their career'; another might claim to have a 'strategy for the good life'; and someone else a 'strategy for self-development and personal growth'. More generally, however, strategy is used in the collective sense. Thus people might say that 'the team's strategy for beating its opponents is to base our position on past experience' or 'the company's strategy for recruiting the best staff is to provide career opportunities internally'. In this chapter, strategy is used primarily in this collective sense and, in particular, its relation to the processes and contexts of organisational planning in uncertain, turbulent environments.

Conceptualised in these terms, strategy is a vital part of the management process. It arises as organisations face increasingly uncertain conditions. As a result, those leading organisations seek more structured ways of meeting these challenges in a world dominated by shortages of skills and resources and by market or political competition. The development of relevant 'strategic frameworks' by top business and organisational leaders is one response to these demanding contextual challenges. Yet development of strategic responses is not limited to top people in organisations; it takes place at all organisational levels – corporate, functional or divisional, and departmental. Indeed, the phrase 'strategic framework' implies that there is no single way in which strategic direction, choice, implementation and evaluation may be determined and that strategy operates at a multiplicity of organisational levels. This means that the vocabulary of strategy is a linguistic minefield of competing models, paradigms and values, although one rooted strongly in Anglo-American private sector literature. Public sector strategic management literature is more limited (Elcock 1996, Isaac-Henry 1999). For some observers, the search for an effective strategy is more realistically seen as a pseudo-rational process in which individual, organisational and group attitudes and beliefs play just as important a part in the process as do chosen techniques, apparent logical thinking and sound judgement.

Quinn (1980), for example, distinguishes the words 'strategy', 'objectives', 'goals', 'policy' and 'programmes'. For him, a strategy is the pattern or plan that integrates an organisation's major goals, policies and actions into a coherent whole, while objectives or goals state what is to be achieved, when the results are to be achieved, but not how to achieve them. All organisations have multiple goals within a complex hierarchy of goals, so Quinn defines an enterprise's major goals as those affecting its overall direction and viability. These are its 'strategic goals'. Policies are rules or guidelines expressing the limits within which action should take place, with the major ones being called 'strategic policies'. Programmes, in turn, specify the step-by-step sequence of actions required to achieve major objectives, with strategic decisions being those determining the overall direction of an enterprise and its viability. Quinn also accepts that strategies exist at different levels in large organisations. In distinguishing between 'strategies' and 'tactics', Quinn argues that the primary difference lies in the scale of action or the perspective of the leader. What appears to be a 'strategy' to a departmental head may seem to be a 'tactic' to the chief executive, with tactics being of relatively short-term duration in their impact on the organisation.

Drawing on analyses of military and diplomatic strategies, Quinn goes on to argue that effective formal strategies contain four main elements. First, they incorporate the most important goals to be achieved, policy guidelines for action, and programmes to accomplish defined goals. Second, effective strategies develop around a few key concepts and thrusts, giving them cohesion, balance and focus. Third, strategies deal with not only the unpredictable but also the unknowable, with organisations needing to build a 'strong posture' so that they can achieve their goals despite the external forces acting on them. Fourth, organisations have a number of hierarchic and mutually related supporting strategies. Effective strategies also appear to encompass certain critical success factors such as:

- clear, decisive objectives

- maintaining the initiative

- concentration

- flexibility

- co-ordinated and committed leadership

- surprise

- security.

Mintzberg (1987a) sees the need for eclecticism in defining strategy. He provides five interpretations of strategy, arguing that a good deal of confusion stems from contradictory and ill-defined uses of the term. Mintzberg examines various definitions of strategy to avoid this confusion and to enrich people's ability to understand and manage the processes by which strategies are formed. First, there is 'strategy as plan'. This is defined as some kind of consciously intended course of action or set of guidelines to deal with a situation. Second, there is 'strategy as ploy' where a specific manoeuvre is developed which is intended to outwit opponents or competitors to bring their strategies into the open. Third, there is 'strategy as a pattern' which involves patterns of actions where intended strategies are realised through resulting behaviours that emerge as substantive 'strategy' only in retrospect. Thus, as one business executive has said, 'Gradually the successful approaches merge into a pattern of action that becomes our strategy. We certainly don't have an overall strategy on this' (quoted in Mintzberg, Quinn and Ghoshal 1995: 15). Fourth, there is 'strategy as position' or a means of locating an organisation in its environment. By this definition, strategy becomes a mediating force between organisations and their environment. This definition of strategy is compatible with those obtained through a pre-selected plan or position, aspired to through a plan or ploy, or reached through a pattern of behaviour. Fifth, there is 'strategy as perspective'. Here strategic content consists of not only a chosen position but also an ingrained way of seeing the world. This definition suggests that strategy is a 'concept' and an abstraction, existing only in the minds of interested parties. It is a shared perspective, in the 'collective mind', which unites individuals by common thinking and behaviour. Mintzberg believes, however, that these different definitions of strategy interrelate and each one 'adds important elements to our understanding of strategy, indeed encourages us to address what is really intended'.

Another attempt to provide an understanding of the nature of strategy is suggested by Hax (1990). While agreeing that a simple definition of strategy is not easy, he argues that some elements have universal validity and can be applied to any organisation. His starting point is the assumption that strategy embraces all the critical activities of a firm and that, as a concept, it can be considered separately from the process of strategy formulation. He identifies six critical dimensions to be included in any unified definition of strategy:

- strategy as a coherent, unifying and integrative pattern of decisions

- strategy as a means of establishing an organisation's purpose in terms of its long-term objectives

- strategy as a definition of a firm's competitive domain

- strategy as a response to external opportunities and threats and to internal strengths and weaknesses as means of achieving competitive advantage

- strategy as a logical system for differentiating managerial tasks at corporate, business and functional levels

- strategy as a definition of the economic and non-economic contribution the firm intends to make to its stakeholders.

Since the concept of strategy embraces the overall purpose of an organisation, Hax believes that it is necessary to examine the many facets making up the whole strategic dimension. By combining these, a more comprehensive definition is obtained. In this way, strategy becomes the fundamental framework through which organisations assert their continuity, while at the same time enabling them to adapt to their changing environments to gain competitive advantage. For Hax, then, the ultimate objective of strategy is to address the needs of organisational stakeholders: 'to provide a base for establishing the host of transactions and social contracts that link a firm to its stakeholders'.

The concept of strategy, then, is a problematic one. To provide a precise definition is misleading, since there is widespread disagreement among practitioners, academics and researchers about the boundaries, methods and philosophical underpinnings of the strategic process. Determining and applying strategic processes is a contingent, complex activity, in part rational, in part humanistic and in part value driven. As de Wit and Meyer (1998: 4) concede: 'the variety of partially conflicting views means that strategy cannot be reduced to a number of matrices or flow diagrams that one must learn to fill in'. There is, in short, no simple definition of what strategy is. A number of perspectives, conceptual tools and approaches may be identified, but no definitive answer is possible.

## RATIONAL APPROACHES TO STRATEGY

There are a number of approaches to conceptualising, analysing and describing the strategy process. Each one provides specific ways in which the process and tools of strategic management can be explained and explored. A simple typology suggests a spectrum of models ranging from 'rational planning' approaches, on the one side, to 'natural selection' ones, on the other, with 'logical incrementalism', 'the emergent approach', 'chaos theory' and 'institutional' approaches in between these extremes. The basic dichotomy is between the 'planning' and 'incrementalist' perspectives. In the planning perspective, emphasis is on deliberate strategy, where strategy is intentionally designed. Strategy is formally structured, implementation is focused on programming and strategic change is implemented from the top down. In the incrementalist perspective, emphasis is on 'emergent' strategy, where strategy is unstructured, fragmented, and shaped gradually. Implementation is focused on learning or organisational development, with strategic change requiring cultural and cognitive shifts.

The rational or planning approach to strategy provides 'textbook' models of the strategy process. No single rational model exists; there is a confusing multiplicity of sub-models. In effect, the rational planning approach adopts a 'scientific', rational perspective of strategy. It emphasises the scientific nature of the strategic process which, if properly applied, can improve the effectiveness and growth of organisations in conditions of change. The underlying principle is that strategies are the outcome of objective analyses and planning. It is rooted in the assumption that analytical, logical methods of managing strategy can be prescribed, individuals can be trained to use these methods, and pay-offs can be demonstrated by using them effectively. This approach is predicated in the belief that rational decision-making points to the future direction of the organisation, through formal planning systems.

The rational approach is a prescriptive one, where strategies have objectives defined in advance, although they may be adjusted if circumstances change. The strategic process includes analysis of the environment, analysis of resources and identification of vision, mission and objectives, followed by development of strategic options and choosing among them. The chosen strategy is then implemented and evaluated. The advantages of the prescriptive approach include: the opportunity it provides of giving an overview of the organisation; the possibility of making comparisons with defined objectives; and the ability to monitor what has been agreed, so that evaluation of progress can be made. There are many versions of the rational, planning model of strategy; three are presented here: the 'hopper method', 'recipe view' and 'linear sequential' approaches.

**The hopper view**
Andrews (1987: 28) illustrates the hopper method. This approach 'feeds' or 'funnels' (like a hopper) a number of variables into the strategy process, such as organisational, informational and managerial variables, and integrates them to create organisational responses capable of facilitating corporate purpose. For Andrews, corporate strategy is:

> the pattern of decisions in a company that determines and reveals its objectives, purposes or goals, produces the principal policies and plans for achieving those goals, and defines the range of business the company is to pursue, the kind of economic and human organisation it is or intends to be and the nature of the economic and non-economic contribution it intends to make to its shareholders, employees, customers and communities.

In this method of determining strategy, interdependence of purposes, policies and action is seen to be crucial to any individual strategy and its opportunity to achieve competitive advantage for the organisation. The essential elements of strategy for Andrews are 'formulation' and 'implementation'. Formulation is about deciding what to do, and implementation is about achieving results. Formulation involves identifying 'opportunity and risk', 'determining the company's material, technical, financial, and managerial resources', taking account of 'the personal values and aspirations of senior management', and acknowledging the company's 'non-economic responsibility to society'. Implementation, in turn, necessitates adopting appropriate 'organisational structures and relationships', designing necessary 'organisational processes and behaviour', and drawing on the strategic and personal skills of 'top leadership'.

This method of formulating and implementing suitable strategies for organisations begins by identifying 'opportunities and risks' in the environment and links these with the organisation's 'distinctive competence' and 'corporate resources'. It is the matching of opportunities and resources that results in the schematic development of a viable economic strategy. In undertaking this to determine choice of products and markets, top managers are expected to take account of economic, technical, physical (eg location), political, social and global factors, and match them with the company's competence and resources. The former might include the organisation's financial, managerial and organisational competence, as well as its reputation in the market place. 'In each company, the way in which distinctive competence, organizational resources and organizational values are combined is or should be unique.'

## The recipe view

The recipe view of strategy provides structured procedures for determining strategy, and is illustrated by a major British text by Johnson and Scholes (1999: 11). They define corporate strategy as being 'concerned with the overall purpose and scope of the organisation to meet the expectations of owners or major stakeholders and add value to the different parts of the organisation'. In arguing that strategic management is different from other aspects of management, because of its ambiguity, complexity, organisational impact, fundamental nature and long-term implications, Johnson and Scholes provide a three-dimensional model of strategy. They analyse it in terms of 'strategic analysis', 'strategic choice' and 'strategic implementation'. Strategic analysis is concerned with the strategic position of the organisation 'in terms of its external environment, internal resources and competences, and the expectations and influence of stakeholders' (p 17). In language similar to that of Andrews (1987), they define strategic choice as 'understanding the underlying bases guiding future strategy, generating strategic options for evaluation and selecting from among them'. Strategic implementation translates strategy into organisational action 'through organisational structure and design, resource planning and the management of strategic change' (pp 20–22).

Johnson and Scholes identify at least three different levels of organisational strategy: corporate, business unit and operational. The first is concerned with the organisation's overall purpose and scope; the second with how to compete successfully in the market; and the third with how resources, processes and people can effectively deliver corporate and business level strategies. They also explore the vocabulary of strategy, defining key terms such as: 'mission', 'vision', 'goal', 'objective', 'core competencies', 'strategies', 'strategic architecture' and 'control'. In arguing that different organisations are likely to emphasise different aspects of the strategic management process, Johnson and Scholes conclude that strategic priorities need to be understood in terms of the particular contexts of organisations.

### The linear sequential view

The linear sequential implementation approach is a logical, rationalist approach to conceptualising corporate strategy, using a systems model of 'inputs', 'processes' and 'outputs'. It is epitomised in many basic American texts, such as those of Higgins and Vincze (1993) and David (1997), and British ones such as Bowman (1996). Higgins and Vincze (1993: 5), for example, define strategic management as the process of managing the organisation's mission and the relationship of the organisation to its internal and external environments. They provide a five-stage model of strategic management, with details for determining objectives and formulating strategy. Their five stages are: 'formulation of vision statement, mission statement and goals'; 'determination of strategic objectives'; 'formulation of strategies'; 'implementation of strategies'; and 'evaluation and control of strategies'. The first three stages make up 'strategic policies', with the last two providing 'policies that aid implementation' and 'control policies'. In the determination of organisational objectives and strategy formulation, Higgins and Vincze argue that business leaders take account of organisational mission, internal and external environmental analyses and an assessment of the organisation's 'strengths, weaknesses, opportunities and threats'. This leads on to a set of 'strategic alternatives', an 'evaluation of alternatives', decision-making and a 'hierarchy of strategies'.

David (1997: 4ff) defines strategic management 'as the art and science of formulating, implementing, and evaluating cross-functional decisions' enabling an organisation to achieve its objectives. He sets out three stages in the strategic management process: strategy formulation, strategy implementation and strategy evaluation. Strategy formulation includes: developing a business mission; identifying an organisation's external opportunities and threats; determining internal strengths and weaknesses; establishing long-term objectives; generating alternative strategies; and choosing particular strategies to pursue. Strategy formulation includes 'deciding what new businesses to enter, what businesses to abandon, how to allocate resources, whether to expand operations or diversify, whether to enter international markets, whether to merge or form a joint venture and how to avoid a hostile takeover'.

In David's model, strategy implementation requires organisations to establish annual objectives, devise policies, motivate employees and allocate scarce resources so that formulated strategies can be executed. In his view, this demands developing a 'strategy-supportive culture', creating an effective structure, directing marketing efforts, preparing budgets, utilising information systems and linking employee compensation to performance. This is often the most difficult stage in strategic management and hinges upon the abilities of managers to motivate employees and carry them with them to achieve organisational purpose. He sees interpersonal skills as being especially critical for successful strategic implementation. For David, 'the challenge of implementation is to stimulate managers and employees throughout an organization to work with pride and enthusiasm towards achieving stated objectives'. Strategy evaluation in the David model is the primary means of determining whether or not particular strategies are working. This involves reviewing external and internal factors that are bases for current strategies, measuring performance and taking corrective actions.

In this model, strategy formulation, strategy implementation and strategy evaluation take place at three hierarchical levels in large organisations. He classifies these as corporate, divisional or strategic business unit, and functional levels. In his view, by fostering communication and interaction among managers and employees across hierarchical levels, strategic management helps firms and organisations work as a team. This model of the strategic process is based on the belief that organisations 'should continually monitor internal and external events and trends so that timely changes can be made as needed', so as to adapt to change (p 7). In his view (p 22), 'it is a known and accepted fact that people and organisations that plan ahead are much more likely to become what they want to become than those who do not plan at all'.

Lynch (1997) regards corporate strategy as important because it deals with the fundamental issues affecting the future of an organisation. It does this by integrating an organisation's functional areas and activities to ensure its survival and growth. In his view, strategy develops out of considering the resources of an organisation in relation to its environment, with the prime purpose of adding value to it and then distributing the added value among its stakeholders. He identifies five key elements of strategy, which are principally related to the need to get competitive advantage in the market place. These are sustainability, distinctiveness, competitive advantage, exploitation of linkages between the organisation and its environment, and vision. He identifies three 'core areas' of corporate strategy: 'strategic analysis', 'strategy development' and 'strategy implementation'. Strategic analysis is concerned with the organisation's environment, its resources and its vision, mission and objectives. Strategic development focuses on the strategic options available to the organisation, rational selection of the ways forward, finding the strategic route ahead and considering strategy, structure and style. Strategy implementation enables selected options to be put into operation, although there may be practical difficulties in motivating staff and from external pressures such as legislation, regulation and market forces.

Lynch identifies the major environmental factors impacting on corporate strategy as:

- increased global competition

- consolidation and development of trading blocks

- cheap telecommunications and computer technology

- the collapse of the command economies of eastern Europe

- the emergence of the Asian 'Tiger' economies

- a better-educated workforce.

As a result, corporate strategy becomes international in scope and has moved out of being the preserve of north American and European countries. Markets have become more international, thus making it necessary to balance global interests with variations in local demand. In describing the essential elements of what he describes as 'prescriptive corporate strategy', he identifies these as: developing and defining the organisation's objectives; analysing the external environment; reconsidering the organisation's objectives; developing strategy options; selecting the option against the likelihood of achieving the objectives; and implementing the chosen option. For Lynch, the advantages of the prescriptive approach are that it provides: an overview of the organisation; the possibility of comparing objectives; a summary of the demands on an organisation's resources; a picture of the choices that the organisation may need to make; and the possibility of monitoring agreed plans. Drawing on Mintzberg (1994), however, he also highlights six difficulties with the prescriptive strategic process:

- the future may not be predicted accurately enough to make rational choices

- it may not be possible to determine the long-term good of an organisation

- the strategies proposed may not be capable of being managed in the ways expected

- top management may not be able to persuade others to follow their decisions

- strategy decisions may need to be altered because circumstances change

- implementation is not necessarily a separate and distinctive phase, and comes only after a strategy has been agreed.

## LOGICAL INCREMENTALISM

Logical incrementalism is where strategic management is seen, not as a formal planning process, but as a series of sub-processes by which strategies develop on the basis of the experiences of managers and their sensitivity to changes in their environments. It is the process of developing strategy by small, incremental and reasonable steps rather than by macroscopic 'grand plans'. Incrementalists do not question the value of planning and control as means of managing organisational processes, but claim that strategy formation is not one of them, since planning is less suitable for non-routine activities such as innovation and change.

Quinn (1978) is widely credited with being influential in developing the incrementalism perspective and as being one of the most important pioneers of 'emergent strategy'. In his view, 'when well-managed major organizations make significant changes in strategy, the approaches they use frequently bear little resemblance to the rational–analytical systems so widely touted'. The processes that are used to arrive at total strategy are typically fragmented, evolutionary and intuitive. He criticises both the formal systems planning approach, which underemphasises power-behavioural factors, and the power-behavioural approach because studies of these have been conducted in settings far removed from the realities of strategy formation. His research into 10 major companies in the 1970s provided several important findings:

- neither the formal systems planning nor power-behavioural models adequately characterise the ways in which successful strategic processes operate

- effective strategies tend to emerge from a series of 'strategic subsystems', each of which attacks a specific strategic issue in a disciplined way, but blended incrementally and opportunistically into a cohesive pattern that becomes the company's strategy

- the logic behind each subsystem is so powerful that it may serve as a normative approach for formulating these key elements of strategy in large companies

- because of cognitive and process limits, almost all these subsystems – and the formal planning activity itself – are managed and linked together by an approach best described as 'logical incrementalism'

- incrementalism is not muddling through: it is purposeful, effective, proactive management for improving and integrating both the analytical and behavioural aspects of strategy formulation.

According to Quinn, strategic decisions do not lend themselves to aggregation in a single, massive decision. Successful managers link together and bring order to a series of strategic processes and decisions. They proceed incrementally to handle urgent issues. In his view, logic dictates that managers proceed flexibly and experimentally from broad concepts towards specific commitments. Managers make the latter concrete as late as possible in order to narrow the bands of uncertainty and to benefit from the best available information. This is the process of logical incrementalism. It is logical in the sense that it is reasonable and well considered, and incremental in the sense that it is structured on a piecemeal basis. Properly managed, logical incrementalism allows executives to bind together the contributions of rational systematic analyses, political and power theories and organisational behaviour concepts, thus allowing them to attain cohesion and focus.

Mintzberg's (1987b) 'crafting strategy' complements Quinn's analysis. For Mintzberg, the crafting image of strategy captures the actual process by which effective strategies are made, rather than the rational planning image. Using metaphor, Mintzberg argues that 'managers are craftsmen and strategy is their clay. Like the potter, they sit between the past of corporate capabilities and a future of market opportunities.' To manage strategy is to craft it and this involves dedication, experience, involvement with the material, the personal touch, mastery of detail, a sense of harmony and integration by practitioners. This process incorporates:

• managing stability, not change

• programming a strategy which has already been created, not actually creating it

• detecting subtle discontinuities that might undermine a business in the future

• knowing the business, on the basis of personal knowledge and understanding

• managing emerging patterns of strategy and helping them take shape, which requires creating a climate within which a variety of strategies can grow

• reconciling both change and continuity.

Ultimately, for Mintzberg, the crafting of strategy, like managing a craft, requires 'a natural synthesis of the future, present and past'.

## THE EMERGENT APPROACH

The emergent approach to strategy is one where the final objective is unclear and whose elements are developed as strategy proceeds. This approach derives from the observation that human beings do not always react rationally and logically to situations, and that strategy emerges over time in adaptation to human needs. According to de Wit and Meyer (1998: 151), 'the distinction between deliberate and emergent strategy goes to the heart of the debate on the topic of strategy formation. While theorists disagree on many points, the crucial issue is whether strategy formation should be deliberate or more emergent.' The key principle of emergent strategy is that it does not have a single, definitive objective and that strategy develops over time. The test for emergent strategy is to examine how strategy has developed in practice over a defined period. The emergent approach identifies corporate vision, mission and objectives, analyses the environment and its resources and out of these processes strategy is developed, implemented and evaluated.

According to Lynch (1997), the advantages of the emergent approach are:

- it accords with organisational practice

- it takes account of people issues, such as motivation, that make the rational approach unrealistic in some cases

- it allows strategy to develop as more is learnt about the strategic situation

- implementation is redefined so that it becomes an integral part of the strategy development process

- it provides opportunity for the culture and politics of an organisation to be included in the strategic process

- it provides flexibility to respond to changes, especially in fast-moving markets.

Concerns about the emergent approach include:

- in multi-functional or multi-divisional organisations, resources need to be allocated between the demands of competing units and this requires some central strategic overview

- in some industries where long-term issues are involved, decisions have to be taken and adhered to by direction from the centre

- management control is simpler where the basis of the actions to be taken has been planned in advance.

Emergent strategies develop, then, when strategies emerge from situations rather than being prescribed in advance. They came to the fore in the light of market turbulence in the 1970s, when some researchers argued that the basis of rational, prescriptive strategy was false. Three sets of emergent strategy are distinguished: 'survival-based theories', 'uncertainty-based theories' and 'human resources-based theories'. Survival-based theories are rooted in the belief that strategy is decided primarily in the market place, hence the optimal strategy for organisational survival is to be efficient. As Williamson (1991: 75) writes: 'economy is the best strategy'. If organisational survival is paramount, survival-based theorists argue, the most appropriate strategy is to pursue a number of strategic initiatives at any one time and let the market decide the best one (Whittington 1993).

Uncertainty-based theories use mathematical probability to show that development of corporate strategy is complex and uncertain, thus making accurate predictions of the future impossible. Because the environment is turbulent and uncertain, only limited strategies are possible. Miller and Frieson (1984) found, for example, that sudden shifts in strategy and in the organisational structures of companies occurred before they had reached a steady state. It is possible to provide mathematical models of such systems and show that they oscillate between stable and turbulent states. Stacey (1993) suggests that the environments of many businesses, such as computer firms, are inherently unstable, so business strategy has to emerge rather than aiming at the false certainties of the prescriptive approach.

Human resources-based strategies stress the importance of people in strategy development. They highlight the motivation of people, politics and cultures of organisations, and desires of individuals in developing strategy. The ways in which people act and interact in strategic development is vital, and a process of trial and error can be used to devise acceptable strategies. These theories particularly emphasise the difficulties arising as new strategies are introduced which confront people with the need to change. Recently, there has been discussion on the learning aspects of strategic development. In his conceptualisation of the learning organisation, Senge (1990) suggests, for example, that there are five learning disciplines, crafted to enable individuals and organisations to learn, where learning is creative activity aimed at developing new strategies and opportunities. These are:

• personal mastery that creates an organisational environment encouraging groups to develop goals and purposes

• mental models that reflect upon the images that managers and workers have of the world, and how these influence actions and decisions

• shared vision that builds commitment to achieve group aims by agreeing what these aims are

• team learning that uses group skills to develop individual abilities and competencies

• systems thinking that enables groups to understand the major forces influencing them.

Other ways at looking at strategy include 'complexity and chaos theory', the 'institutional' and 'natural selection' approaches. Those adopting the 'complexity and chaos' perspective argue that organisations exist in complex and unstable worlds which are difficult to understand, let alone manage. However, it is possible for people to experience particular contexts so that they become sensitive to the complexities and uncertainties around them. When there are deviations from these established patterns, they sense them intuitively. Strategic management is to do with building upon the capacity to be intuitive and to take action based on that capacity.

Institutionalists, such as Scott (1995), argue that managers can choose what strategies to develop because these arise from similarities in institutional settings. These enable them to see how their organisations operate within a particular environmental context. Managers can understand these institutionalised assumptions, such as how a university 'works' or how a retail firm operates, and the ways in which things are 'done' within them. Ways of seeing things and behaving become institutionalised, so that organisational strategies tend to develop within institutionally similar cultural parameters.

An approach far removed from the idea that managers can control their organisations is that of 'natural selection' theorists, such as Hannan and Freeman (1989). Drawing on the views of population ecologists, they argue that the success of organisations depends on how doing things coincides with the needs of the environment. Where they coincide, organisations prosper; where they do not, organisations wither away. Some organisational cultures are suited to their external environments; others are less so, and the extent to which managers are able to influence this is overstated.

## VISIONS, MISSIONS AND STRATEGIC OBJECTIVES

Like all the terms and concepts used in describing and analysing strategy, 'vision' has a number of meanings. Basically, vision is the strategic intent or desired future state of an organisation, as defined by its leading strategists, normally the chief executive. Johnson and Scholes (1999) state that there are a number of ways in which strategic vision may be determined. It might be formulated deliberately, as part of the planning process. It might be associated with the founder of a business. It might be derived from external forces, such as privatisation, market testing or compulsory competitive tendering in the public services. It might even be related to intuition. The crucial point is that vision encapsulates a view of a realistic, credible and successful future for the organisation. For Bartlett and Ghoshal (1989), building a shared corporate vision gives context and meaning to every manager's roles and responsibilities and it helps individuals understand the company's stated goals and objectives. In their view, such a vision must be crafted and articulated with clarity, continuity and consistency because:

- clarity of expression makes corporate objectives understandable and meaningful

- continuity of purpose underscores those objectives' enduring importance

- consistency of application across business units ensures uniformity throughout the organisation.

Vision is not the same as an organisation's mission and objectives. It is an awareness of where the organisation is and how it and its competitors will be competing in the future, while mission and objectives are concerned with current issues facing the organisation. Vision underpins the purpose and strategy of an organisation. Hamal and Prahalad (1994) have put forward five criteria for judging the relevance and appropriateness of an organisation's vision: foresight, breadth, uniqueness, consensus and actionability.

The mission of an organisation is a general expression of its overall purpose and the broad directions that it seeks to follow. It derives out of its leaders' vision and takes account of the values and expectations of its leaders and major stakeholders. Some would claim that corporate mission is an organisation's reason for existence. Others view corporate mission as encompassing the basic points of departure that direct an organisation in a particular direction. Corporate mission can be articulated in a 'mission statement', though there is disagreement among strategists over exactly what a mission statement is and what it should include. Some have questioned the sometimes lengthy nature and content of mission statements, while others have indicated that companies should concentrate on short, concise statements of 'strategic intent' (Hamal and Prahalad 1989). The sorts of items included in mission statements, although the list is neither exclusive nor exhaustive, are:

- the direction of the organisation

- organisational purpose

- its values

- points of departure for the strategy process

- the nature of the business on which the company intends to focus

- the organisation's competitive ambitions.

Whatever is in the mission statement, and whatever form it takes, it has a number of functions for the organisation. One is to point the organisation along a stated pathway, by defining the boundaries within which strategic choices and actions take place. Second, the mission statement conveys to its stakeholders that the organisation is pursuing valued activities affecting their interests. Third, by specifying the fundamental principles driving organisational actions, the mission statement can inspire individuals to work together co-operatively. In formulating mission statements, those responsible take account of factors such as:

- the nature of the business which the organisation is in

- the importance of customer interests

- the basic values and beliefs which the organisation stands for

- the need to address its market niche and competitive advantage

- the reasons for adopting its choice of approach.

Strategic objectives, in turn, state more precisely than mission statements what is to be achieved and when the results are to be achieved, but are distinguished from functional and business unit objectives. The purpose of strategic objectives is to focus the tasks of management on specific outcomes and provide means of assessing whether the outcomes have been attained. In the past, writers like Ansoff (1965) were keen to stress the importance of setting quantifiable objectives, but nowadays it is generally recognised that some strategic objectives cannot be easily quantified. In developing corporate objectives, those responsible normally recognise that overall strategic objectives need subsequently to be translated into objectives for different functions and, in larger organisations, for different business units. Further, in larger organisations, strategic objectives need to be adjusted to take account of the circumstances and business conditions of different parts of the organisation. Strategic objectives commonly relate to overall financial, marketing and other targets. Financial targets relate to issues such as profitability, costs relative to key competitors, financial stability, earnings on capital invested, revenue growth, dividends, cash flow, and share price. Marketing targets include market share, products or service diversity, growth opportunities, ability to compete in international markets and quality issues. Other strategic objectives cover customer relations, customer service, product/service leadership, research and development, investment in human resources, training and development, and operational costs.

## STRATEGIC ANALYSIS AND CHOICE

### Analysing the environment

The external environment of organisations is complex, because it is concerned with everything outside an organisation affecting its prospects and activities. This includes the industry and markets in which it operates, the competitors with which it competes, the customers it aims to satisfy and the general political, economic, social, technological, legal and global environments over which it has little control. Analysing the environment is therefore a difficult and challenging task for strategists. First, as discussed above, there is fundamental disagreement about the nature of the strategic management process. Prescriptive strategic actors, for example, are more likely than those of the emergent school to argue that uncertainties of the environment can be readily predicted. Emergent strategic actors, on the other hand, argue that the environment is so turbulent and unstable that prediction serves little purpose. Second, because the environment is dynamic, strategies have to be developed against a backdrop of continual change. Third, since the environment contains so many external influences affecting the strategic direction of organisations, only selected ones can be explored.

PESTLE analysis provides a useful starting point for analysing the general environment of an organisation. PESTLE stands for the 'political', 'economic', 'social', 'technological', 'legal' and 'environmental' contexts impinging on an organisation. PESTLE produces a checklist for examining the factors most likely to influence an organisation's market and business prospects. The political ones include party alignments at local, national and European levels. The economic ones include energy and communication costs, consumer spending, government spending, interest rates, currency fluctuations, exchange rate policy, inflation and investment spending. The sorts of social issues affecting demand for an organisation's goods or services and its labour supply include education, health, demography, attitudes to work and leisure and general social trends. Technological factors include the impact of computers and information technology on working life, rates of technological change and levels of research and development spending in an organisation. The main environmental factors affecting an organisation cover pollution, resource conservation, the 'social costs' of given policies and other 'green' issues.

A conceptual tool used in analysing the industry environment of organisations is Porter's (1980) five forces model, which has the purpose of analysing competitive advantage for firms in the market place. The five forces are the bargaining power of suppliers; bargaining power of buyers; threat of potential new entrants; threat of substitutes; and extent of competitive rivalry. According to Porter, suppliers are particularly strong when they command a price premium for the products they sell and when their delivery schedules or quality affects the final product. Customers are strong when they have substantial negotiating power or other leverage associated with price, quality and service. New entrants pose threats when they are able to compete strongly through lower costs. Substitutes normally pose a threat as a result of technological or low cost breakthroughs. Competitive rivalry is seen to be central to such an analysis and firms build defences against competitive threats. Criticisms of the five force model include the following:

• it assumes the organisation's interests come first

• it assumes that customers are not the drivers of competitive strategy

• it largely ignores the human resources aspects of strategy.

The industry life cycle, also discussed by Porter, charts the development of markets from their commencement, through growth, maturity and decline. As an analytical tool, it is useful in identifying the factors shaping an industry's development and it helps identify relevant customer research and development, and competitor strategies, and the impact on profitability, at different phases in the life cycles of industries. Life cycle analysis examines the advantages of early entry, the fragmentation of market share as markets mature, the incidence of cycles and their effect on demand in mature markets. What appears to be significant in mature markets is the importance of the company, not the industry. Even where industries seem to be mature, companies need to generate new growth opportunities by looking beyond existing markets to maintain their competitive position.

The main reasons for analysing competitors are to enable organisations to develop 'sustainable competitive advantage' (Porter 1985). Competitive advantage involves every aspect of the ways in which an organisation competes in the market place. Possible sources of advantage include: product differentiation; low cost production; niche markets; high performance; quality and customer service; and the culture, leadership and style of an organisation. The main tests for sustainable competitive advantage appear to be that: they are sufficiently significant to make a difference; they are sustainable against environmental change and competitor attack; and they are recognisable and linked to customer benefits. Competitor analysis seeks to explore the differences between the organisation and its competitors in terms of: market share; growth and profitability; cost structures; competitor objectives; and current and past strategies.

## Analysing resources

Having the necessary resources, including human and capital resources, is a necessary condition for achieving corporate purpose. In his analysis of the resources of organisations, Kay (1993) identifies 'architecture', 'reputation' and 'innovative ability' as being important in strategy development. He argues that organisations have a series of contracts and informal relationships with employees, suppliers, distributors, and collaborating firms inside and outside the industry. Resources add value to organisations, by taking inputs from suppliers, finance from the capital market, human resources from the labour market and converting them into finished goods and services. Effective resource analysis enables an organisation to determine the core skills and competencies it requires in order to be successful.

Product portfolio analysis, based on the Boston Consulting Group (BCG) matrix, provides a means of examining the balance of an organisation's product portfolio, by considering relative market shares and market growth rates. The portfolio is divided into four categories: 'stars' (high market share, high growth), 'cash cows' (high market share, low growth), 'problem children' (low market share, high growth) and 'dogs' (low market share, low growth). This model enables consideration to be made of the contribution of each to the organisation, and comparisons with the competition. It indicates that the key strategy is the creation of a balanced portfolio of products, comprising some low risk but slow growth, and some higher risk with future potential. Due to its weaknesses in defining markets and relative market share, however, it is now accepted that the BCG matrix is useful only as a starting point in the analytical process.

There are five sources of finance for strategic activities:

• equity finance, ie issuing new shares to existing or new shareholders but with the disadvantages of cost and loss of business control

• long-term debt finance, which is simpler and cheaper, but with limits to amounts available and difficulties if the organisation defaults on paying interest charges

- leasing of plant and machinery, with tax benefits and lower costs, but the equipment remains the property of the lessor at the end of the period

- savings from reducing short-term debts, which can normally be made only once

- selling existing assets to fund development elsewhere.

When assessing new strategic proposals, it is usual to undertake a financial appraisal, and 'discounting' techniques are often used to do this, even though there are difficulties in producing accurate financial projections.

Analysis of human resources is important because people are a vital resource in contributing to added value and, because strategy development often involves change, some people resist it. The areas which human resources analysis covers include human resources audits, training and development, and the implications of strategic change for managing people. Analysis of sources of finance also needs to be explored, such as retained profits, which are the largest and cheapest source of funds. Other sources include equity finance, long-term debt finance, leasing of plant and machinery, savings from cost reductions and selling assets.

According to Johnson and Scholes (1999), 'stakeholder mapping' is a means of identifying stakeholder expectations and power in organisations, and helps to establish political priorities when carrying out strategic analyses. In classifying organisational stakeholders in relation to the power they hold, and the extent to which they are likely to show interest in the organisation's strategies, the power/interest matrix indicates the type of relationship that an organisation needs to establish with each stakeholder group. This is done in terms of 'minimal effort', 'keeping informed', 'keeping satisfied' and 'identifying' key players. Typical stakeholders include: management; shareholders or the 'electorate' or 'members' of the organisation; employees; suppliers; government as regulator and tax collector; and the local community.

A SWOT analysis is useful in bringing together the

environmental analysis of an organisation, its resource/competence analysis and its strategic capacity for dealing with them. SWOT stands for Strengths, Weaknesses, Opportunities and Threats. Strengths are internal, positive attributes of organisations, helping them to gain advantage in order to achieve their strategic objectives. Some organisations define their strengths by benchmarking them through comparing their own processes, products, service or activities with those of 'best practice' organisations. Weaknesses are internal negative attributes of organisations that may result in them failing to achieve their strategic objectives. Weaknesses, too, can be identified and possibly remedied by benchmarking and following 'best practice'. Opportunities are external factors that substantially assist organisations in their efforts to achieve their strategic objectives. Threats are external factors that may result in organisations failing to achieve their strategic objectives.

## Strategic choice

Strategic choice is about generating options that are likely to achieve an organisation's goals and objectives, costing them and choosing the best or optimum solution. There are a variety of ways in which strategic options are determined within the strategic process. Johnson and Scholes (1999) argue that strategic choice is at the core of the strategic management process, because it focuses on decisions about the organisation's future direction and intent. They believe that strategic choice decisions need to be made at both corporate and business unit levels, and they identify three bases upon which strategic choice is built. These are 'corporate purpose and aspirations', 'strategic business unit strategy' and 'enhancing single business unit strategy' (or 'corporate parenting'). Ownership of the organisation, its mission and strategic intent, its scope and diversity and, in some cases, 'the global dimension', all influence corporate purpose and aspirations. The bases of strategic business unit strategy, in turn, encompass the achievement of competitive advantage, price-based strategies, differentiation strategies and focus strategies (see below). Enhancement of strategic business unit strategy is concerned with portfolio management, financial strategy, the role of parent companies and the parenting mix.

Other ways of determining strategic options are on a resource basis and a market basis. Resource-based strategic options look for sources of added value in organisations and make use of core competencies within them. They utilise the concept of the 'value chain', or supply chain, to link the value of the activities of an organisation with its functional parts and to assess the contribution each makes to the added value of the business and to the 'value' as perceived by the customer. According to Porter (1985), the primary activities of a company are:

- inbound logistics (ie receiving, storing, handling and transporting goods within the company)

- operations

- outbound logistics (ie how final products are delivered to customers)

- marketing and sales

- service.

The organisation's support activities are:

- procurement

- technology development

- human resources management

- firm infrastructure (ie the planning and control systems).

Both sets of activities provide added value to organisations, but assessing them quantitatively is difficult.

Value can be added 'early' in the value chain or 'later'. The organisation is one 'link' in the value chain, which stretches right back to the raw materials, and also includes the distribution chain. Examining where and how organisational resources add value generates strategic options. Early activities, such as inbound logistics, operations and procurement, add value by processing raw materials into standardised products, and resource options concentrate on lower costs. Later activities, such as outbound logistics, marketing and sales and service, use intermediate products to produce differentiated items targeted at specific customer needs. Here resource options focus on research, development and marketing, including:

• increased standardisation of products/services

• investing to reduce production costs

• capital investments to add value

• varied products/services targeted at particular markets

• research, development and product innovation.

Resource-based strategies examine the range of capabilities present in organisations such as people, finance, patents, information technology and core competencies. Core competencies are those skills and technologies enabling an organisation to provide particular benefits to its customers. These are important in developing strategic options because they deliver sustainable competitive advantage to firms. Options not addressing core competencies are less likely to contribute to strategy than those that do. Renewed emphasis has been given to resource-based strategic options by the concept of core competencies developed by Hamel and Prahalad (1994). Developing these, and the firm's resource capabilities, is concerned with issues such as technology, value added, people skills, financial resources, benefits to customers and new skills and competencies needed by the firm in the future.

Market-based options are those arising from market opportunities and market constraints. They build on analyses of customers and competition. Generic industry-based strategies are a means of generating basic strategy options in the market place and are concerned with seeking competitive advantage for the firm. Porter (1985) identifies three generic strategies that explain sources of competitive advantage and the competitive scope of targeted customers. The strategies are 'low-cost leadership', 'differentiation' and 'focus'. Low-cost leadership aims to make the organisation among the lowest-cost producers in the market. Differentiation occurs when the products of an organisation meet the needs of some customers in the market place better than other producers do. Underlying it is the concept of market segmentation, that is the identification of specific groups who respond differently to other groups to competitive strategies. Essentially, particular groups of customers are likely to pay more for a differentiated product when it is targeted towards them. Focus strategy (or niche strategy) involves targeting a small segment of the market, by using either a low-cost focus or a differentiated one. With a differentiation strategy of cost focus, firms seek cost advantage in their target segments; with a strategy of differentiation focus, firms seek differentiation in their target segments only. One criticism of Porter's generic strategies is that they are supply-based rather than demand-based, thus largely ignoring the market.

Another market-based option is the 'market options matrix' (Kotler 1994). This distinguishes between markets, defined as customers, and products defined as items sold to customers. By examining the market place and products available, it is possible to structure options that organisations can adopt. Such options include moving to new markets based on increasing new customers, and new products based on increasing technical innovation. Developing these options may involve organisations diversifying from their original markets. The main reason for such diversification is synergy, which is a concept associated with linkages in the value chain. Although the marketing matrix option is a method of generating options, it provides no guidance on choosing them.

## STRATEGIC IMPLEMENTATION AND EVALUATION

Strategic implementation is concerned with the activities required for putting strategies into practice. It requires the setting of general objectives, formulating specific plans, providing the necessary finances and resources to carry these out, and monitoring and controlling the system to ensure that the agreed objectives are being met. Implementation may be comprehensive, incremental or selective. Comprehensive implementation programmes are employed when organisations have a clear-cut strategic direction, based on a prescriptive, rational approach. Incremental implementation occurs in conditions of uncertainty, which requires a flexible emergent approach to strategy. Selective implementation is used where neither of the above circumstances exists.

**Objective setting and planning**

The relationship between strategic development and implementation is the subject of some academic debate. Pettigrew and Whipp (1991), for example, argue that implementation is best seen as a continuous process, rather than as one with distinct stages such as strategy formulation and implementation. They argue that strategy is not a linear process, with distinct stages, but an experimental, iterative process where the outcomes of each stage are uncertain. The empirical evidence supporting this view is quite strong. Hrebiniak and Joyce (1984) suggest, in contrast, that implementation is governed by two principles: 'intended rationality' and 'minimum intervention'. Intended rationality means that managers are likely to act in rational ways but they reduce the task of implementation to a series of small steps to make it manageable. It also suggests that individuals include in the implementation process their own personal goals, which are not necessarily those of the organisation. Minimum intervention means that managers need to change only what is necessary and what is sufficient to produce a lasting solution to the problems being addressed. Emergent approaches, on the other hand, imply that implementation needs to be considered as both a single event and a series of activities, the outcomes of which may shape the strategy itself.

In setting targets and objectives, decisions have to be made about who is to implement the strategies and what objectives and tasks need to be accomplished. How this is operationalised depends on in what ways strategy was determined (ie by central direction or by full consultation with any stakeholders involved) and who was involved in developing it. In essence, disseminating the main objectives and activities for implementation can follow a 'cascading' process, from the top of the organisation downwards. In functionally organised businesses, for example, this requires corporate strategic objectives being translated into functional objectives, such as those of marketing, operations, human resources, finance, and research and development, and these in turn being translated into marketing, operations, human resources, finance, and research and development action plans. In fast-changing environments it is not necessary to have rigid objectives because they might be overtaken by outside events. Communication and co-ordination are vital to satisfactory implementation, especially where organisations are seeking benefits from corporate synergy or value chain linkages.

The purpose of strategic planning is to use formal planning to develop and implement strategies related to the mission and objectives of the organisation. The basic process covers background assumptions, long-term vision, medium-term plans and short-term plans. Plans integrate the activities of the organisation and specify the timetable for completing each stage. Historically, there were three approaches to strategic planning: top down, bottom up and integrated, where the latter combined elements of both the top down and bottom up approaches. In undertaking strategic planning, many leading it believe that it is important to establish the background assumptions and basis upon which the business is conducted. The organisation can then explore its long-term vision and broad strategic direction. A medium-term plan can be developed for the next two or three years and a short-term annual plan developed subsequently. De Geus (1988) argues that an effective planning process can aid organisational learning by providing organisations with desired new behaviours, explaining the contexts making these behaviours essential, and visibly rewarding the desired behaviours. Effective planning incorporates business plans, covering such issues as finance, personnel, markets and operations.

During the 1970s, 1980s and 1990s, critics argued that strategic planning had become too bureaucratic and rigid in its application (Lenz and Lyles 1985; Hamel and Prahalad

1993). The reasons why certain forms of strategic planning had failed included poor direction from top management, the need for greater flexibility, political difficulties and inappropriate corporate cultures. More specific criticisms were:

- strategic thinking had been replaced by formulaic planning

- inadequate resources had been allocated for strategic planning

- annual budgets took priority

- overemphasis was placed on procedures and form filling

- planning was controlled by specialist staff, not by line managers

- too much emphasis was put on financial results

- there was lack of risk-taking and entrepreneurialism in organisations.

For Mintzberg (1994) the main role of strategic plans is to make plans operational, after basic strategic thinking has been undertaken. Planning is about analysis; strategic thinking is about synthesis. He suggests three ways in which strategic planning assists organisations. First, it contributes to the communication process. Second, it identifies new strategic insights by posing the right sorts of questions in organisations. Third, it presents alternative ways of viewing strategic issues.

There are a number of ways in which strategic planning is conducted, depending on the environment, product range and management style of the organisation. Campbell and Goold (1987) distinguish different styles of strategic planning, according to 'planning' and 'control' influences. Where corporate centre helps shape the plans of a business, this is 'planning influence'. Where the centre controls the process as the plans are being implemented, this is 'control influence'. Four main styles of strategic planning were identified:

- strategic planning where the centre is involved in formulating plans, with an emphasis on long-term objectives during the control process

- financial control where the centre exercises strong short-term financial control, with individual units being able to operate as they wish

- strategic control, which lies between the strategic planning and financial control approaches

- a centralised style where all major strategy decisions are made at the centre, with day-to-day implementation being delegated to business units.

The main conclusions of this research were: strategic planning style should be matched to the circumstances of the business; some styles (such as financial control) demand greater understanding of a business than do others; and shared commitment to implement agreed strategies by working together is vital.

## Organisational structure and people issues

Building appropriate organisational designs and structures is an important response to strategic implementation, if organisations are to deliver their missions and objectives effectively. Factors taken into account in developing appropriate organisational designs include: the age of the organisation, its size, degree of centralisation/decentralisation, the technical content of the work, the different tasks in different parts of the organisation, leadership style and its dominant culture. Four main types of organisational structure are distinguished:

- functional structures, based on an organisation's managerial functions (eg operations, finance, marketing, personnel, and so on)

- multi-divisional structures, based a corporate headquarters with separate divisional units linked with products or geography, each with their own functional sub-structures (the 'M-form' structure)

- holding company structures, based on a central holding company, with a number of subsidiaries, whose role is to act as the central shareholder and to allocate funds to the most attractive profit opportunities (the 'H-form' structure)

- matrix organisational structures, based on dual responsibilities such as for products (horizontally) and geographical areas (vertically).

Where innovation is important, other structures have been noted. In Kanter's (1984) study of the structures and processes most conducive to innovation, she demonstrates the importance of matrix structures, problem-solving 'parallel' organisations looking for innovative solutions to problems, and participative styles of management.

The sorts of criteria taken into account in developing appropriate organisational structures include: simplicity, least-cost solutions, motivating staff, and adopting a pertinent culture. Environmental factors, such as market changes, market complexity and competition, impact on structure. Generally, change and complexity indicate the necessity for flexible, decentralised structures, while standardisation and mass production require more centralised structures. In modern technical systems, which rely on specialised controls and expert knowledge, decentralisation is recommended, since there is little point in having such knowledge without decision-making power to use it. Since staffing issues such as recruitment, rewards, appraisal and training are all affected by strategic implementation, formal procedures have to be built into those systems in order to develop revised human resources management (HRM) policies and procedures.

Some writers assert that a strategic approach to managing people is largely, if not wholly, associated with the emergence of HRM (Guest 1987; Keenoy 1990), on the assumption that no distinctive human resources strategies existed prior to HRM. Here it was asserted that business strategies merely defined the nature of competition in the market place, leaving the personnel management contribution to be secured pragmatically. Thomason (1990) rebuts this view by arguing that historically the acquisition and utilisation of human resources in organisations have been approached in a number of different ways at different times. He identifies four historical approaches, delineating particular periods where 'typical' organisations tended to adopt a distinct approach to labour acquisition and utilisation in broadly comparable conditions. He is not arguing that market conditions solely determine the approach adopted, but that they impose limits on available options, as well as predisposing enterprises to adopt one approach in preference to others.

For Thomason, all organisations need strategies to decide how to survive in their business environments. Private firms are likely to express business strategies in terms of how they can compete in the market place; public services in terms of how they can secure their revenues in the face of competing calls on the public purse. 'In any organisation, the answers to this question can be given only by taking some account of both the opportunities and threats offered by its product/service markets and the strengths and weaknesses of its own combination of resources, and not just the one' (Thomason 1990: 3). Decisions relating to opportunities and threats in product or service markets suggest that they have tendencies to one of four main types of business strategy:

- low-cost leadership, aiming to supply mass production goods or services more cheaply than competitors

- differentiation, emphasising a superior product or service commanding a premium price

- focus, relying upon either differentiation or low-cost leadership to supply a niche market

- asset parsimony, which depends on high entry costs as protection against competitors, or flexible use of limited assets to generate high output performance.

The second set of decisions takes account of whether the markets for the organisation's resources are capable of meeting these demands, and determines whether the preferred competitive strategy will be facilitated or frustrated by availability of the resources needed. As Porter (1985) argues, competitive advantage depends not only on conditions in product or service markets but also on the availability of factors of production.

Thomason identifies at least three historical shifts in business strategy. The first was associated with the onset of the industrial revolution; the second with industrial rationalisation in the late nineteenth century; and the third with 'new wave rationalisations' from the 1960s. In the first period, typical business strategy was one of differentiation; in the second period, cost leadership; and in the third period 'focus', where competitive advantage was secured by paying attention to customer needs and emphasising quality, reliability, delivery and teamwork. Currently, enterprises can be found following any one of these strategies, although the strategy of asset parsimony is losing ground as a source of competitive advantage because cheapness of modern technologies allows freer entry by competitor firms into many markets.

The approaches to labour acquisition adopted by typical enterprises varied, depending on what the business strategy required of its workforce or on labour force capacity in the labour market. The differentiation strategy was dependent upon the availability of a core workforce of skilled labour, which in industrialising Britain was satisfied by its apprenticeship system and flow of workers from countryside to towns and cities. The low-cost strategy in the period of mass production needed a workforce capable of doing short-cycle tasks for relatively low wages. This was secured by recruiting workers from the external labour market, subjecting them to close supervision and linking their pay to output. When enterprises had to develop new customer relationships, in the face of global competition, the strategic remedy lay in developing internal labour markets, because most skills were job-specific and non-transferable between firms and industries. Firms needed to train and develop their employees, to assure the future supply of labour, and retain them until they had recouped their investment from the flexible performance of employees. In terms of labour utilisation, work during the first period was organised by putting it in workshops and factories, and in the second period was fragmented. In the third period, work is characterised by being flexible, versatile and multi-skilled, with workers being expected to achieve quality, reliability and delivery in their job tasks.

This indicates that labour acquisition and utilisation varies with business strategy and the capacity of the external labour market to supply the necessary labour that firms want. In the first historical period, labour acquisition of the core workforce was paramount. In the second period, acquisition was important, but the emphasis switched to labour utilisation. And in the latest, third period, two distinct developments associated with creation of internal labour markets are discernible. In one, the criteria to be satisfied in labour acquisition are related to trainability, with provision of learning opportunities becoming a salient feature of labour utilisation. In the other, the criteria are extended to embrace broader personality traits, related to capacity for handling change and personal learning from opportunities created by 'learning organisations'.

Thomason concludes that different human resources strategies are necessary for different circumstances, and serve different business strategies. The 'pre-personnel management' approach, still extant in the small firm sector, depends on the ability of firms to recruit skilled labour in external labour markets in response to business needs. Effective labour utilisation uses a 'selection strategy' as the main mechanism of labour control. With mass production, 'traditional personnel management' depends on the ability of firms to draw on the external labour market to supply the workers they need. A 'supervision strategy' of labour control is adopted, where company rules are policed in order to secure targeted levels of performance. In modern niche-market enterprises, in contrast, labour supply is guaranteed by developing internal labour markets, through appropriate training and development programmes. However, the strategy of labour control differs according to whether business strategy relies on price leadership or differentiation. In the former case, a 'development strategy for staff flexibility' may be most appropriate. In the latter case, a 'partnership strategy for worker commitment', with problem-solving and creative skills, may be appropriate.

### Information, monitoring and control
Monitoring and control systems are important because information can be used to assess resource allocation choices,

monitor progress in implementation, evaluate performance, assess the environment for significant changes from the planning assumptions, and provide a feedback mechanism. Strategic control systems monitor the main elements of strategy and its objectives. These may involve financial measures, customer satisfaction, quality measures and market share. Financial monitoring examines cash flows, earnings per share, and so on, while strategic controls have a broader perspective. Strategic controls can be improved by:

• concentrating on key performance indicators and factors for success

• distinguishing between corporate, business and operational levels of information, monitoring only those that are relevant

• avoiding over-reliance on quantitative data

• creating realistic expectations of what the control system can achieve.

All rely on having simple, cost-effective information about the organisation and its environment.

For Johnson and Scholes (1999), resource allocation and control can be undertaken in a number of ways, depending on the need for innovation and change, and whether decisions are centralised or decentralised. The practical choices on how resources should be allocated and controlled are planning systems, direct supervision, performance targets, social and cultural control, market mechanisms and self-control. Information is a key resource that can determine the success or failure of strategies and 'recent advances in the speed and lower cost of information processing should – in principle – improve the capability of control systems to measure performance against targets' (p 476).

## CONCLUSION

This chapter has shown that there are a variety of ways of conceptualising strategy, exploring it and examining the strategic process. There is no single definitive approach or framework. The most basic one is the 'reactive', unplanned approach, commonly found in many small or even medium-size organisations, where strategic decisions, if they are taken, are made on an *ad hoc* basis, normally by the chief executive/managing director in response to some immediate external or market contingency. There may even be practical constraints on managing strategically in some organisations, which may be the result of the inadequacies of the actors involved, uncertainty, unwillingness by those in authority to take risks, or poor human judgement. At the other end of the strategy spectrum, there are the different philosophies and practical implications, underpinning the rational, logical incrementalist and emergent approaches to strategic analysis, search, choice, implementation, monitoring and control. The reality is that any particular strategic approach taken by those in leadership roles in contemporary organisations, how they convert strategy into practice, how links are made between corporate and functional strategies and how strategy and policy are integrated, are contingent upon time, place, circumstances and personalities. It is also noticeable that most contemporary models of strategy come from the private sector, with the result that approaches to strategy in public organisations are often based on those imported from the private sector. Yet local government had adopted 'corporate management' in the 1970s, while 'planned, programme, budgeting' and 'policy analysis review' were common in the civil service at around the same time. The search for an 'ideal' framework for analysing and determining strategy is an ongoing and challenging one.

# 2 The economy

The central economic problem facing humankind is how to satisfy the infinite wants of an ever-growing population within the constraints of the finite resources available. With the economic demands of people virtually unlimited, and the supply of economic resources to satisfy those demands fixed in the short term, conscious economic choices have to be made to determine economic priorities. Economic goods and services are those human-made commodities whose production requires the use of scarce resources to create, exchange and distribute them. They include finished goods and services, capital goods and raw materials. Although there are a limited number of 'non-economic' goods, such as fresh air and sunshine, which are normally freely available according to 'need', they are increasingly the exception rather than the rule. More generally, economic goods are commodities for which people's demands exceed the availability of scarce resources to produce them. It is the task of any economy to solve the economic problems associated with this universal feature of resource scarcity. This chapter outlines some of the main problems facing the UK economy and how the economy has changed, particularly over the past 20 years.

By the end of this chapter, readers should be able to understand and explain:

• how the external economic environment impacts on private, public and voluntary organisations

• the main features of the market economy, its structures and processes and their implications for organisations

• interactions between political and economic systems, including the European dimension.

In addition, they should also be able to:

- assess current economic and market changes and their impact on organisations

- advise managements on the possible effects of government economic policies, legislation and European directives on organisations and their activities.

See also the Professional Standards Index (page 345).

## ECONOMIC PROBLEMS AND ECONOMIC SYSTEMS

In modern economic systems the fundamental economic units are households, firms and government agencies. These actors are units of consumption in using the goods and services produced in an economic system, with households also supplying key resources, such as labour and finance, to the production process. It is firms, in turn, that are agents in transforming and converting the scarce resources available into the goods and services demanded for consumption and investment purposes. Investment is the flow of expenditure channelled into activities producing new resources not intended for immediate consumption. Through planned investment, production capacity becomes possible. Government's economic role is a complex one, acting as a provider of services to taxpayers, collector of taxes from households and firms and manager of the macro-economy.

The scarce resources used by firms and government in creating new economic goods and services for consumption and investment are 'the factors of production', usually defined as land, labour and capital. Land incorporates those natural resources such as oceans, forests, minerals and soil fertility used in production. Labour is the sum total of human resource skills, knowledge and competencies that are available. And capital is those human-made aids to production, such as advanced technology and communication systems, which raise economic productivity and real output per worker over time. Capital is also used to describe money (ie finance capital) as a commodity, available for investment. The total output of all the commodities produced by a country over a given period, normally a year, is its gross national product (GNP).

The issues of scarcity and choice mean that all economic systems have a number of common problems to resolve. These are:

- What goods and services are to be produced and in what quantities, including the balance between consumption and capital goods?

- How are these goods and services to be produced, given current resources, technology and productive capacity?

- Who is to get the goods and services produced, or how is GNP to be divided among a country's economic and non-economic participants?

- How efficient are the methods being used in the production and distribution processes?

- Are existing resources being fully utilised or are some unemployed or underemployed?

- In monetary economies, are prices stable or are they rising out of line with productivity?

- Is the economy growing and increasing its capacity over time?

Three types of economic system have provided institutional frameworks for solving these economic problems. These are free market economies, command or planned economies, and mixed market economies. In free market economies, economic decisions about allocation of resources, and production of goods and services, are made through money prices, generated by voluntary economic exchanges among producers, consumers, workers and owners of factors of production. Decision-making is largely decentralised, with mainly private ownership of the means of production and some limited forms of social ownership. The market mechanism (or the price system) allocates resources, adjusts production and consumption decisions, distributes incomes to those owning factors of production, and paves the way for economic growth. In this case:

- individual economic units decide what, how, where and when to produce and consume

- they do so with reference to money prices

- prices respond to the forces of demand and supply for individual goods or factors of production

- the outcome is a balance of demand and supply, with co-ordination of the economic activities of individual units and agents.

Command or planned economies are where economic processes are determined not by market forces but by planning agencies which implement society's economic goals. Such systems characterised the countries of eastern Europe and the former Soviet Union until the breakdown of communism in the late 1980s and early 1990s. They have been replaced by 'economies in transition', as these states shift towards free enterprise and market-based economic systems.

It is mixed economies, combining private enterprise with varying degrees of government intervention, that dominate the world economy today. Resource allocation between alternative uses is determined largely by the actions of individual firms, with governments establishing either the level of aggregate output and/or the efficient use of factors of production through appropriate monetary and fiscal policies. They also influence distribution of incomes by taxation and welfare policies. In some cases, governments nationalise and operate key industries such as electricity, gas, railways and other 'commanding heights' of the economy. Over the past 20 years, however, most Western governments have privatised large proportions of their public industries, thus shifting the balance to the market or private sector (Coates 1995).

## DEVELOPMENT OF THE MODERN UK ECONOMY

The UK economy is a mixed economy but Britain's historical legacies influence the country's economic activities today.

Britain was the first country to industrialise, from the mid-eighteenth century onwards, and to experience a significant shift from a predominantly agrarian economy to an industrial one. Changes in the techniques and organisation of production resulted in increases in investment, productivity and output, enabling Britain to feed a rapidly growing population and penetrate expanding overseas markets. By the mid-nineteenth century, Britain had become a largely urban and industrial economy, a net importer of food, the world's leading producer of manufactured goods and a major exporter of goods and services. Her staple industries were coal, textiles, cotton, engineering and iron and steel. And, by this time, the benefits of the 'Industrial Revolution' were beginning to 'trickle down' to the 'lower orders'. This prosperity was achieved in a free market, private enterprise, *laissez-faire* economy, where the state's role was the limited one of providing national defence and a framework of law and order. A central feature of the international trading system was the 'Gold Standard', where national currencies were exchanged for gold at a fixed exchange rate (Pollard 1969).

The late nineteenth century was an economic watershed for Britain. There was an economic depression, with rising unemployment, caused by increased competition in world markets from a newly unified Germany and the United States (US). Britain's policy of 'free trade' and no restrictions on imports and exports resulted in cheap agricultural products coming in from the 'New World', which led to a crisis in arable farming. This was followed by a brief period of rapid economic growth in the early twentieth century and renewed expansion in the staple trades in terms of output, exports and employment. But rising prices and downturns in the economy followed. During the First World War (1914–18), markets were lost, new international rivals such as Japan emerged, and national capital was consumed. Britain suspended the Gold Standard in 1914 and there was a decline in Britain's stock of capital and a significant decline in her holdings of overseas assets (Aldcroft 1993).

The inter-war years (1919–39) were generally a period of slump, depression and high unemployment although, because of falling prices, those in employment enjoyed rising living standards. Britain's staple industries, upon which the economy had relied, declined but new industries expanded such as chemicals, electrical goods and motor vehicles. Britain's economic problems, however, were aggravated by three main factors:

- restoration of the Gold Standard between 1925 and 1931, when sterling was overvalued, thus raising the prices of British exports relative to their major competitors

- financial orthodoxy, where governments sought 'balanced budgets' and cuts in public expenditure so as not to 'crowd out' the private sector

- until 1931, continued commitment to free trade.

Following the Wall Street crash in the US in 1929, abandonment of free trade and creation of import controls internationally, there was a world-wide slump between 1931 and 1934. It was not until the late 1930s, with military rearmament, that the UK economy experienced renewed growth and falling unemployment, but the Second World War (1939–45) led to further capital consumption and loss of international markets. During the war, production and 'manpower' were centrally directed, prices controlled by government and basic goods such as food and clothing rationed, according to need. In order to maximise output and promote efficient use of scarce national resources, the UK had shifted to a planned, closed, command economy.

The period from 1945 to the mid-1970s has been described as the 'post-war consensus'. The UK economy was slowly freed from its wartime constraints, industry rebuilt and the pre-war private enterprise system replaced by a mixed, market economy operating in an international economy of fixed exchange rates. The post-war Labour government (1945-51) nationalised the Bank of England, the coal, gas, electricity, telecommunications and railways industries and extended the modern welfare state. Higher public expenditure, through increased taxes and government spending, funded this. The state created the National Health Service (NHS), provided 'free', tax-funded secondary, technical and university education, and supported other universal, social services (Booth 1995).

For over 30 years, successive governments – both Conservative and Labour – intervened in the management of the economy through the use of appropriate fiscal and monetary policies based on the economic theories of John Maynard Keynes (1936) or 'Keynesianism'. These aimed to maintain simultaneously full employment, price stability, balance of payments equilibrium and economic growth. There were, however, both technical and practical problems in doing this. The outcome was a 'stop-go' cycle of economic expansion, falling unemployment and rising prices followed by economic contraction, rising unemployment and slower price rises. Further, by the mid-1970s, 'stagflation' had taken root, where unemployment and prices rose together. This coincided with a breakdown of the fixed exchange rate mechanism, determined at the Bretton Woods conference in the USA in 1944, a quadrupling of oil prices and balance of payments problems for the UK. In 1976, the Labour government turned to the International Monetary Fund for help. Government, in return for a loan to support sterling, adopted strict monetarist policies involving tight control over money supply and tight fiscal policy to contain aggregate demand. The net result was a slowdown in price rises but rising unemployment.

The succeeding Thatcher administration (1979-90) continued initially with a monetarist policy (monetarism) but also adopted what became known as supply-side economic policies (Oulton 1995). Monetary theory or monetarism, in distinction from Keynesianism, contends that controlling inflation is the most important policy goal, because employment can best be stimulated by price stability. Demand management is self-defeating because public spending crowds out private spending. Hence growth of money supply should be geared to the expected growth rate of real output in the economy, while the exchange rate is allowed to float freely, thus protecting the balance of payments. This means that public spending must balance tax revenues and be kept under tight control to prevent inflation. Supply-side economics links with monetarism, since it rests on the assumption that market supply must be created before demand, if non-inflationary growth is to be sustained. It is the level of supply which ultimately determines the level of employment not, as Keynes argued, the level of aggregate demand. Supply-side economics and monetarism, it is claimed, allow taxes to be cut, leave more income to be spent by households, provide incentives to work and generate real growth. Growth, in turn, provides additional jobs in sectors where there is genuine private demand by households and consumers for new products or services. This 'genuine' demand is distinguished from the 'artificial' demand generated by government spending, which is seen as keeping uncompetitive and technologically backward industries and firms in business when they should be left to go into liquidation. These theories reflected a resurgence of classical economic orthodoxy, which emphasises individual responsibility in the market place and denies government a major role in providing relief to the weak in the economy. Economic efficiency supersedes social equity as the guiding principle of public policy (Britton 1991).

During the Thatcher and Major (1990–97) administrations, control of inflation was the main policy goal and governments relied upon interest rates as their primary means of regulating demand. Exchange rate policy presented ambiguities, however, since rates were never permitted to float as freely as advocates of monetarism argued. There were testy debates about whether the UK should become a committed member of the European Exchange Rate Mechanism (ERM) and whether she should sign up to European economic and monetary union (EMU). There were attempts to deregulate markets, by allowing the free interplay of supply and demand (Beatson 1995). Governments transferred important public assets, such as gas, electricity, telecommunications, water and railways, back to the private sector, through privatisation, but unemployment rose and continued at high levels throughout the period.

The Blair administration, elected to office in 1997, claims that it has adopted a 'third way' in economic policy. In its project to renew 'social democracy', the New Labour government argues that it is integrating the need for economic efficiency (associated with neo-liberal market freedoms) with that for social justice (associated with protecting the economically weak). New Labour's approach is said to be a third way, because the party has moved 'beyond an Old Left preoccupied by state control, high taxation and producer interests; and a New Right treating public investment, and often the very notion of "society" and collective endeavour, as evils to be undone' (Blair 1998: 1). According to Giddens (1998: 26), the third way transcends 'both social democracy and neoliberalism' and is presented as an alternative to both state socialism, associated with the post-war Labour party, and market-liberalism advocated by the Conservatives in the 1980s and 1990s.

## CHANGING STRUCTURES OF THE NATIONAL AND INTERNATIONAL ECONOMIES

The developed countries of the international economy are the 15 members of the EU, the small European states of Iceland, Norway and Switzerland, the US, Canada, Japan, Australia and New Zealand. These 23 industrialised countries account for about 75 per cent of world output, of which the UK's share is some 4 per cent. For 30 years after the end of the Second World War, these countries were simultaneously able to sustain both relatively high levels of economic growth and full employment. From the mid-1970s, however, due largely to the quadrupling of oil prices, triggered by war in the middle east, inflation and unemployment began to rise. With further rises in the price of oil in 1979 and 1980, these countries shifted from Keynesian policies to monetarist ones and interest rates rose sharply. From the mid-1980s, when oil prices collapsed, the influence of the Organisation of Petroleum Exporting Countries waned. The economies of the developed countries grew rapidly again and inflation once more became an economic problem. The response of the political authorities was another attempt to tighten monetary policies and raise interest rates. These curbed inflation but again resulted in rising unemployment. With the collapse of communism in eastern Europe between 1989 and 1991, the international economic consensus appeared to be one supporting the mixed economy model, with reliance on market forces and some government intervention, as the most realistic economic system in current circumstances (Artis 1996).

## De-industrialisation in the UK

The structure of the UK economy has changed significantly over the past 50 years. In 1950 manufacturing accounted for over a third of national GDP; now it has declined to about a fifth. Manufacturing covers a wide range of goods including engineering, machinery and equipment, vehicles, textiles, foodstuffs, wood and metal, chemicals, pharmaceuticals, paper, plastics, rubber and electrical goods. There is some debate about the causes and consequences of the relative (but not absolute) decline of manufacturing output in the UK, since real output in manufacturing continues to rise slowly due to capital investment, rising productivity and improved production systems. One reason for the relative decline of manufacturing is that as households and individuals become richer, demand for manufactured goods declines and rising incomes are spent on services including leisure, financial products and health care. De-industrialisation, however, is not limited to the UK; it is common to all developed economies (Ferguson and Ferguson 1994).

In reality, the UK is facing keen competition from other Organisation for Economic Co-operation and Development (OECD) countries and is losing her share of world markets in manufactured goods to countries like Germany, France, Sweden and Spain. She lacks competitive edge in terms of both price and quality. It is in service industries where growth is now located. The UK's exports of services such as finance, insurance and information technology continue to expand, compared with other economies, with some three-quarters of her workforce employed in the service sector. In this sense, the UK is in transformation from an industrial to a post-industrial economy. Some commentators argue that a main reason for the relative decline of UK manufacturing is competition from the newly industrialising economies of

South-East Asia – the so-called 'Tiger Economies' of Malaysia, Thailand, Singapore, Korea and Taiwan. Malaysia, for example, aims to be fully industrialised by 2020. Because firms in these countries pay lower wages, have lower social security costs and invest heavily in new plant and machinery, they have a competitive advantage over manufacturers in developed countries. It is these socio-economic conditions and higher levels of productivity which encourage Western multi-national companies to locate in the Far East, so as to raise profits and get higher returns on their capital investments. Yet while these countries export manufactured goods, they also import them and their share of exports into developed countries remains fairly low. Indeed, most trade of developed countries is with other developed countries. Only about a fifth of manufactured imports into the UK are from developing countries.

Some, however, take a less sanguine view of de-industrialisation. They argue not only that it results in job losses, deskilling and rising unemployment but also that a strong manufacturing base is crucial for economic growth, technological innovation and export potential (Blackaby 1979). Whether de-industrialisation can be accounted for by import penetration, low investment, low productivity or uncompetitiveness is the subject of debate. During the 1970s and 1980s, Keynesians argued that the UK's problem was that she could not get economic growth without suffering import penetration, and what was needed was reflation and economic protectionism to prevent import penetration. Writers like Bacon and Eltis (1976), in contrast, attributed the decline of manufacturing to growth of the non-market sector. They argued that public-sector spending was crowding out the private sector, which was unable to expand for lack of sufficient resources. Further, such spending is seen as 'taxing' the private sector, which has less money to spend in the market place. It is evident that this was the view that influenced the Thatcher government in the 1980s but de-industrialisation continued none the less.

Another important 'industrial' sector of the economy is energy and water supply. The share of output provided by this sector to GDP has remained fairly constant over the past 50 years at around 5 per cent, although it went up to over 10 per cent during the mid-1980s. Energy and water supply cover capital-intensive industries such as oil, gas, water and coal. The importance of coal supply has declined significantly during this period, while that of oil has grown. Other sectors remaining fairly stable over the past 50 years are: construction, public administration and defence, the wholesale and retail trades, hotels and restaurants, and transport and communications.

The largest relative decline to UK GDP has been agriculture, forestry and fishing. They accounted for about 5 per cent of GDP 50 years ago but now constitute only 2 per cent. Again, agricultural and related output have not fallen absolutely over this period, only relatively, and at a much slower rate than the rest of the economy. The differential decline of agriculture can be explained in terms of more intensive farming methods, greater competitiveness, and the impact of the Common Agricultural Policy (CAP) on the supply of agricultural products in the market place, resulting in overproduction (Jewell 1993).

The sectors demonstrating the most significant rises in their shares in GDP over the last 50 years, as indicated above, have been services. The share of financial and business services has increased from some 3 per cent to about a fifth, while that of education, health and social work has increased from about 3 per cent to 12 per cent. Clearly, the UK is now largely a 'service' economy, where manufacturing industry plays a less significant and strategic role than it did 50 years ago (Cairncross 1992).

**Europe and the world economy**
With the development of the EU, patterns of trade within Europe have changed substantially over the past 40 years. The evidence indicates that trade between member states of the EU has grown substantially, with the big four – Germany, France, Italy and the UK – exporting about 50 per cent of their total exports to other EU countries. In the cases of Belgium, the Netherlands, Portugal and Ireland, it is nearer

70 per cent. In terms of imports by member states, over 50 per cent of imports are now from EU member states, compared with just over a third in the late 1980s. At EU level, the European economy is probably as 'closed' as those of the US and Japan, since it is a regional economic grouping. The world economy has also changed radically over the past 50 years (Van der Wee 1987). With the breakdown of colonialism and imperialism, there are now almost 200 independent countries in the world, ranging from rich, developed countries, on the one hand, to poor developing ones, on the other. Some countries, in turn, have regional economic links such as those of the EU, North American Free Trade Agreement and Association of South East Asian Nations. However, there are wide differences in economic power, political constitutions, size, language, culture and wealth among these countries, and it is estimated that about one billion (or one fifth) of the world's population still lives in poverty (World Bank 1998).

In the developing economies of post-communist eastern Europe and Russia, the task has been to create modern market economies based on private enterprise and foreign investment. In the diverse regions of Latin America, which are already market economies, countries have accumulated huge international debts, which consume over 50 per cent of their GNP in interest and capital repayments. Bringing down inflation and reducing public debt rebound in high unemployment and slow growth. Liberalisation of their economies and privatisation of their state sectors are typical responses to these problems. It is the south-east Asian Tiger economies that have achieved the highest rates of economic growth during the 1990s. By 1995, both Hong Kong and Singapore had *per capita* GDPs higher than that of the UK. A major feature of economic growth in this geographical area is that it is rooted in manufacturing and exporting. Despite its financial crisis in 1998, Malaysia is now showing signs of recovery and renewed growth, and only in Indonesia, with its corrupt economic and political systems, are there continued signs of economic and overt political instability.

India, Bangladesh and Pakistan are among the 10 most

populous nations in the world, and the poorest. Agriculture still accounts for between 25 and 35 per cent of output, with much of it produced by small-scale farmers. These countries have also introduced measures of liberalisation, reductions in protectionism, privatisation, tax and financial reforms and encouragement of foreign investment to stimulate growth. The Middle East is another diverse area of economic activity. Some countries, with small populations and large oil reserves, such as Saudi Arabia and Kuwait, have high standards of living. Others, like Egypt, are backward and economically retarded. Only Israel has the economic status of a developed country, with acceptable rates of annual growth.

The continent of Africa, divided into northern and sub-Saharan Africa, has a mixture of economies. Those in the north include oil-rich states such as Libya and Algeria and some unstable ones such as Sudan. More than half the economies in sub-Saharan Africa have contracted over the last decade, due to civil war, corruption and endemic tribalism. Many suffer from political instability, heavy debt to Western governments and international aid agencies, and ineffective economic policies. Only South Africa has achieved modest but continual *per capita* economic growth during the past decade.

## PRIVATE BUSINESSES, PUBLIC ORGANISATIONS AND VOLUNTARY ASSOCIATIONS

The UK economy operates within a capitalist, mixed economy and it is private and public enterprises that dominate the production, distribution and exchange of goods and services. These organisations have a number of functions including:

- producing and selling goods and services demanded by individuals and organisations

- employing and rewarding the owners of the capital and human resources employed within them

- trading with one another, nationally and internationally

- setting the economic pace of the nation.

Private organisations are created by individuals or groups for market or, less usually, 'not-for-profit' purposes, and are ultimately accountable to their owners or members. Government creates public organisations primarily for political (ie non-market) purposes and these bodies are ultimately accountable to political representatives and the law for achieving their objectives.

Private organisations may be unincorporated associations, partnerships, companies or voluntary bodies, but are normally commercial businesses aiming to make profits and a return on their finance capital for shareholders, although they can also be non-profit-making ones such as voluntary associations. Businesses vary widely in size and scope, from small-scale local enterprises to large multinational corporations operating across continents, and they provide a wide range of goods and services in the primary, secondary and tertiary sectors of the economy. Private not-for-profit organisations are even more heterogeneous, not only in size and ownership but also in function, ranging from trade unions and friendly societies, to sports clubs and self-help groups. The criteria of success by which business organisations are judged are primarily market and economic ones (Horton and Farnham 1999).

The criteria for success by which the performance of public organisations is assessed are less easy to define and measure than for private organisations, since they include social and political measures as well as market ones. Public organisations are involved in a wide range of activities and encompass all those public bodies involved in making, implementing and applying public policy throughout the UK. They include central government departments, departmental agencies, non-departmental agencies, the National Health Service (NHS), public corporations and local authorities.

In practice, when it comes to providing a dividing line between private and public organisations, the distinction is blurred. Tomkins' (1987) spectrum of organisational types illustrates the interdependence and interrelationships between the private and public spheres:

- fully private

- private with part state ownership

- joint private and public ventures

- private regulated

- public infrastructure, operating privately

- contracted out

- public with managed competition

- public without competition.

Ultimately, the relative configurations of private and public organisations reflect political and economic choices in society. For the purposes of analysis here, however, a distinction is made between what are primarily described as private businesses, public organisations and voluntary associations.

### Private businesses

Private businesses dominate agriculture, manufacturing, distribution, many service enterprises and the financial sector such as the banks, insurance, pension funds and Stock Exchange, and are profit-oriented organisations. The private sector now includes a large number of former nationalised industries that were transferred from public ownership during the 1980s and 1990s, by either 'public offers' to the general public or 'trade sales' and management buyouts. Examples of public offers include: British Aerospace, British Airways, British Gas, British Steel, British Telecom, Cable and Wireless, regional electricity companies, Rolls Royce and the water companies. Examples of trade sales or buyouts include: the assets of the National Enterprise Board, National Freight Corporation, British Rail hotels, shipbuilding yards, National Bus, Scottish Bus, Royal Ordnance factories, Unipart, Short Brothers and the Trust Ports. Only a handful of nationalised industries remain, such as the Bank of England and the Post Office (Hughes 1995).

Transfer of ownership of public corporations to private shareholders has both supporters and critics. Arguments in favour are political and commercial, and include:

- reducing the role of the state in economic activity

- diminishing political control of the economy

- fostering a share-owning democracy by expanding personal share ownership

- facilitating workers' share-holding in their own companies to improve employment relations

- reducing the public-sector borrowing requirement, ie the amount that government borrows yearly to balance its income and expenditure

- removing civil service interference to enable managers to manage freely

- benefiting consumers by increasing competition and providing better services to customers.

The commercial arguments include:

- promoting new business opportunities for investment and expansion

- meeting international competition

- facilitating efficiency and productivity improvements

- cutting unit costs

- adopting a market orientation to customers and clients

- lowering prices and removing state subsidies.

Opponents of privatisation argue that the selling of public assets results in lost revenue to government, as well as weakening its influence in economic and industrial affairs. More substantively, since nationalised industries are monopolies, they need to be controlled centrally by political means rather than by private-sector monopolists with commercial aims. Another argument is that because they are public utilities they should meet citizen need rather than market demand based solely on ability to pay. Also, as major players in the economy, public utilities need to be planned by central authorities to ensure that efficiency, investment, and research and development are not simply profit led.

The most common form of private business is the registered company or business corporation. There are about a million registered companies in the UK. The Companies Acts provide the basic legal regulation of these enterprises and facilitate the legal incorporation of private businesses by creating a legal entity, or corporate body, which is separate and distinct from the personality and existence of any individual who is an owner of the organisation. This legal fictional body employs people, holds and owns property and enters into commercial contracts. The Companies Acts lay down rules for the constitution, management and dissolution of such organisations, though they leave their internal management to be determined by the company's directors, subject to specific safeguards for shareholders. The Registrars of Companies for England and Wales and for Scotland issue certificates of incorporation and record changes of name. They are also responsible for company registrations and safe custody of documents required by law.

There are two types of registered company: the private limited company (Ltd) and public limited company (Plc). There are many more Ltd companies than Plcs, which have far larger financial resources per company than do private companies and their shares are bought and sold on the Stock Exchange. Plcs are sometimes multinational corporations, private companies rarely so. Plcs are normally employers of large numbers of people, while private companies employ fewer people per enterprise. More generally, both types of joint stock or limited company have a number of commercial advantages:

- incorporation makes financial capital available, normally as shares where each contributor needs to provide only a small proportion of the total paid-up capital

- transfer of capital ownership is possible, through buying and selling shares

- further financial capital can be raised

- limited liability is provided for shareholders, so if a company goes out of business, financial liability is limited to the amount of the original shareholding.

## Public organisations

Central and local government organisations provide public services, which are funded largely from tax revenues, although there is a trend for some charging to individual users to be introduced. However, public services are generally provided collectively for individual consumption as citizen rights, not according to ability to pay. The services include: national defence, law enforcement, fire protection, environmental health, health care, personal social services, education, public transport and roads, recreational facilities and consumer protection. Central government has overall responsibility for public services and deciding policy on how services are to be provided, funded and administered. But there is no rational explanation for the current distribution of responsibilities between central and local government, which has evolved in a pragmatic fashion (Horton and Farnham 1999).

Central government is responsible for a range of services and encompasses all those bodies for whose activities a minister of the Crown is directly or indirectly responsible to Parliament. It includes the armed services, government departments, departmental agencies and non-departmental agencies. There are some 20 major government departments such as Defence, Education and Employment, the Treasury and Agriculture, but most central government services are provided by agencies. In 1988 the Efficiency Unit of the Cabinet Office (1988) published a radical report entitled *Improving Management in Government: The next steps*. It is widely known as the Ibbs report and pointed to improvement in the managing of government business which it claimed had been achieved since 1979. Ibbs proposed changes in the structure and management of the civil service, so as to secure better value for money for taxpayers and improved services to clients. It stated that the civil service was too large and diverse to be managed as a single entity. The report recommended that free-standing agencies should be created to carry out the executive functions of government. This was to be done within a policy and resource framework set by a small core of policy makers in central departments. Government accepted Ibbs' proposals and implemented them.

There are now over 130 Next Steps Agencies, employing some 380,000 civil servants or about 80 per cent of the total civil service workforce. Next Steps are departmental agencies and include the Benefits Agency (responsible for social security and income support), Employment Agency (responsible for unemployment support and helping people find jobs) and Child Support Agency (responsible for ensuring absent parents support their children financially). There are also a number of non-departmental public agencies, of which there are several hundred, which are not headed by a government minister, such as the Arts Council and Botanical Gardens at Kew (Cabinet Office 1998).

The largest public organisation is the NHS, which was created by the National Health Service Act, 1946. It is based on the principle that medical care and comprehensive health services should be readily available and supplied, largely free of charge, to anyone normally resident in the UK. Major reorganisations took place in 1974 and 1990 and the New Labour government, elected in 1997, is introducing further NHS reforms. In 1990, the Conservative government created an internal market in the health service, with district health authorities and family practitioners becoming purchasers of services and entering into contracts with hospitals and community care units as providers. Hospitals and community care services became public corporations (see below), with self-governing 'trust' status, and had responsibility for managing their own budgets and determining which services to provide to patients. General practitioners (GPs) were encouraged to seek self-funded status and manage their own budgets. The aims of these changes were to:

- delegate as much decision-making as possible to where patient care was delivered

- give providers of health services self-governing status to determine patient-care policies

- introduce an internal market in the NHS to encourage hospitals and other units to compete for patients and provide better patient care at lower cost.

The general thrust of the changes was to encourage greater economic efficiency and effectiveness by using 'pseudo' internal market mechanisms and private-sector business management methods. These initiatives reflected similar changes in other parts of the public sector, with increasing emphasis being placed on market values rather than welfare values. New Labour's policy, set out in its white paper (Cm 3807, 1997), retains the internal market and contracts between purchasers and providers. And primary care units, consisting of GPs and community health practitioners, are being created which will become both major providers and purchasers of hospital services.

More than 400 local authorities provide the remaining public services in the UK. In England, for example, there are non-metropolitan counties, non-metropolitan districts, metropolitan districts, London Boroughs, unitary authorities and the City of London. Local authorities consist of elected councillors, working in co-operation with professional officers. Their joint task is to ensure the efficient provision of the wide range of services, laid down by law, that authorities are required or choose to provide. These services include consumer protection, fire services, roads and traffic, and personal services, such as education, libraries, social services and housing. Other local services are cemeteries, development control, environmental health, art galleries, museums and provision for physical recreation.

The provision of local public services was transformed during the 1980s and 1990s, as some were privatised (such as bus services and the compulsory sale of council houses) and others were deregulated and exposed to market competition (such as the compulsory competitive tendering of local authority building and maintenance work). The remaining services were subjected to internal market structures and requirements to operate as if they were commercial businesses (Painter and Isaac-Henry 1999). Although local public organisations continue to exist, differences between public and private organisations have narrowed, as the boundary between the public and market sector has become blurred (Horton and Farnham 1999).

Public corporations, which include the remaining but few nationalised enterprises such as the Post Office and Bank of England, have a number of features:

- they are publicly owned and publicly accountable organisations

- they are separate legal bodies, created by statute or royal charter, which can enter into contracts, sue and be sued, and now include NHS trusts

- some are managed by boards, appointed by ministers, which are accountable to Parliament for the efficient running of their corporation; others have boards appointed in accordance with statutory requirements

- they are financed either directly by central government or by revenue obtained by sales of goods and services they provide. Capital expenditure is financed by borrowing from the Treasury, the general public or their own reserves

- they are exempt from normal parliamentary control exercised over government departments, although they are ultimately accountable to Parliament

- their employees are not civil servants.

**Voluntary associations**

Voluntary associations include professional bodies, trade unions, pressure groups, political parties, employers' associations, charitable trusts, the churches and other religious organisations. They tend to be relatively small bodies, normally employing fewer resources than private businesses and public organisations. Their goals are welfare and community-oriented, with private assets. In some cases they are democratically controlled bodies, run by their members on collegiate and participatory lines. Some voluntary bodies have become much more important in recent years, as they increasingly provide services to the public, under contract to public organisations.

## MARKETS, PRICES AND MARKET REGULATION

A market is where the buying and selling of goods or services takes place, but it does not need to have a physical presence. Markets may be local, regional, national or international. Although most economists regard markets as primarily economic phenomena, they are social constructs that enable buying and selling to take place within certain rules and conventions. In Far Eastern cultures, for example, there is often no 'fixed' market price for a particular good (say a suit) or a service (say a haircut), since it is expected that the parties will bargain the price at which the commodity is actually bought and sold.

Markets consist of producers and consumers or sellers and buyers, who may be individuals, households, business corporations or government agencies. In modern advanced market economies, business corporations and government agencies dominate the supply side of markets, with households and individuals buying commodities. A free market is one in which the forces of supply and demand are allowed to operate without interference of third parties or institutions. In free markets, it is the pressure produced by the interplay of market forces, or market supply and demand, which induce adjustments in market prices and/or the quantities traded in the market place. Prices are normally measured in monetary values, with equilibrium or market prices being where the quantity that consumers are prepared to buy equals the quantity that producers are prepared to sell. Prices act as signals which co-ordinate the economic actions of individual decision-making units and provide a mechanism whereby changes in supply and demand affect the allocative efficiency of resources in the economy as a whole.

### Market supply

The quantity of a commodity supplied by a producer is the amount the producer is prepared to sell at a particular price at a particular time. It is influenced by four main factors:

• the price of the commodity

- the costs of the factors of production

- the goals of the producer

- the current state of technology.

It can be hypothesised that the higher the price of a commodity the greater the quantity that the producer is willing to supply, because more profit is made in doing this. Conversely, the lower the price of a commodity, the smaller the quantity that the producer is willing to supply. Similarly, the lower the costs of factors of production, the greater is the quantity the producer is willing to supply, while the higher the costs of the factors of production the smaller is the quantity that the producer is willing to supply. Quantity supplied also changes according to the producer's goals – whether it is aiming to maximise profits, maximise sales, enter a new market or maintain an existing market position. Technological developments affect quantity supplied, because they lower unit costs of production and ensure higher output at lower cost.

Market supply increases when there is a rise in the quantity supplied at each price. It decreases when there is a fall in the quantity supplied at each price. Factors causing an increase in market supply include: falls in the prices of other commodities; falls in the costs of factors of production; changes in the goals of producers; and technological improvements. What causes a decrease in market supply is rises in the costs of factors of production, and changes in the goals of producers.

**Market demand**
The quantity of a commodity demanded by a consumer is the amount the consumer wishes to buy at a particular price at a particular time. It is influenced by a number of factors. These include:

- the price of the commodity

- the prices of other commodities

- the size of consumer income

- consumer tastes

- social factors.

It can be hypothesised that the lower the price of the commodity the greater the quantity the consumer is willing to buy. Conversely, the higher the price, the smaller the quantity the consumer is willing to buy. Where commodities are substitutes for one another – butter and margarine for example – a fall in the price of one causes a fall in the quantity demanded of the other. Conversely, a rise in the price of one causes a rise in the quantity demanded of the other. Where commodities are complementary, such as pipes and tobacco, a fall in the price of one causes a rise in the quantity demanded of the other, while a rise in the price of one causes a fall in the quantity demanded of the other. Where commodities are unrelated, a change in the price of one does not directly affect the quantity demanded of the other.

Normally a rise in consumer income results in a rise in the quantity demanded of a commodity. Similarly, a fall in consumer income results in a fall in demand. This is usually the case with consumer goods. In other cases a rise in consumer demand results in a rise in the quantity demanded up to a certain level; then it falls away. Consumer demand for basic foods, for example, is not infinite. Quantity demanded may decline above a certain level of income, as consumers transfer income to more expensive foods. In other cases, quantity demanded rises to a certain level of income and then remains unaffected. Social factors such as sex, age, social class, educational attainment and occupation affect quantity demanded, while changes in consumer tastes have similar effects.

Market demand increases when there is a rise in quantity demanded at each price, and decreases when there is a fall in quantity demanded at each price. The factors causing an increase in market demand include: rises in the prices of substitutes; falls in the prices of complements; rises in consumer income; and changes in consumer taste. Decreases in market demand are caused by: falls in prices of substitutes; rises in prices of complements; falls in consumer income; and changes in taste.

## Prices and market regulation

In free markets, prices are determined by the interplay of supply and demand, and market equilibrium is reached where, in aggregate, consumers and producers are satisfied with the current combination of price and quantity of units bought and sold per period of time. There are few 'perfect' or 'free' markets in the real world, however, since oligopoly (few producers), monopoly power (single producers), monopsony (a single buyer) and lack of full knowledge of the market by consumers, lead to market imperfections. Other criticisms of the free market model are their adjustment dislocations, hidden social costs and inequalities in income and wealth distribution. Markets are also based on demand, not on need, and can operate at below optimum use of available resources. For these reasons, governments find it necessary to intervene in markets for economic, social and moral reasons. One form of intervention is regulation of markets. Since the 1960s, there have been many examples of market regulation, covering: employment protection; equal opportunities; health and safety at work; controls on prices, wages and profits; regulation of financial markets; and competition policy through control of monopolies and mergers. Since the 1980s, new forms of regulation have been introduced, including industry-specific regulatory bodies linked with the privatisation of gas, water, electricity, railways and telecommunications (Waterson 1988). At the same time, extensive deregulation has occurred, allowing markets such as bus transport and financial services to expand (Veljanovski 1991).

Various forms of state regulation exist. These include general regulations, such as competition policy, or specific regulations, such as those relating to particular firms, industries or commercial behaviour. Some argue that regulation provides a means for correcting market failures – such as controlling the monopoly powers of private businesses. A contrary view argues that government regulation benefits producers not consumers, because firms lobby government to introduce policies favourable to their own interests. Moreover, since regulation takes various forms – including licensing, certification, inspection and price and profit controls – it involves high transaction costs for businesses and the state, such as negotiating, monitoring and enforcing regulatory rules.

Competition policy is an example of general regulations, and seeks to influence or change the industrial structure within which firms operate and/or the behaviour of firms to customers or other firms. It covers monopolies, mergers and restrictive practices and dates back to the Monopolies and Restrictive Practices Act 1948. Other legislation has been passed since then including: Restrictive Practices Acts 1956, 1968 and 1976; Resale Prices Act 1964 and 1976; Monopolies and Mergers Act 1965; Fair Trading Act 1973; and Competition Act 1998. The 1998 Act, for example, gives the Office of Fair Trading (OFT) and industry regulators powers to combat anti-competitive practices and abuse of dominant positions in the market place. Articles 85 and 86 of the Treaty of Rome (1957 – strictly the Treaty Establishing the European Community – TECU) deal with restrictive practices and monopolies, and the EU merger regulation 1989 covers business 'concentrations with a Community dimension'. These legislative measures lay down rules covering monopolies, mergers, restrictive agreements, consumer protection and anti-competitive practices.

A number of agencies have been set up to monitor this legislation. The main ones are the Monopolies and Mergers Commission (MMC), Restrictive Practices Court, Office of Fair Trading (OFT) and Directorate General for Competition in the European Commission. A firm can be referred to the MMC, for example, where its market share is thought to be excessive. In conducting its investigation, the MMC must have regard to efficient production and distribution, a balanced distribution of industry and employment in the UK, increases in efficiency and encouragement of new enterprise. The OFT, in turn, has a duty to collect information on commercial activities, so that trading practices affecting consumer interests adversely may be exposed. The OFT can initiate procedures leading to the banning of specified trade practices and has powers to refuse, grant or suspend licence applications in particular areas of business and trade. Following the Competition Act 1998, the OFT has powers to:

• enter premises and demand the production of documents

• order termination of an offending agreement or conduct

- impose financial penalties of up to 10 per cent of turnover

- take action against companies failing to co-operate in an investigation.

To evaluate the impact of competition policy in the area of monopoly, for example, it is necessary to examine indicators such as the effects of policy on market structure, the conduct of firms and market performance. Other influences, such as international trade, technical progress, the EU and technology, also need to be taken into account. In its judgements, the MMC assesses monopolies in terms of their policies and effects on prices, new entrants and profitability. With typical inquiries taking about two to three years to complete, critics claim that the MMC is a slow and ineffective body. It is also argued that governments are often reluctant to take effective remedial action against monopolists, preferring instead to rely on informal undertakings with targeted organisations. Additionally, the remedies secured after investigations normally apply solely to the firms involved, thus having limited impact on firms in other industries and markets. As a result, monopoly policy has not achieved any major changes in the structure or conduct of the monopolies investigated. The evidence indicates that current policies against companies engaging in anti-competitive practices are weak and fail to act as deterrents on monopolistic activities.

Regulation of the privatised public utilities, whose monopoly market positions remain largely intact, is an example of industry-specific regulation. Here again the impact of regulation has been mixed. The major regulatory agencies are the Office of Water Services, Office of Telecommunication, Office of Electricity Regulation and Office of Gas Supply. Two main problems have arisen in regulating these industries effectively. One is that in some public utilities, such as electricity, the industry has not been privatised as a single unit but vertically disintegrated into production and distribution sectors. Thus, a natural monopoly may exist in some parts but not in others. Second, although competition has been introduced into many regulated utilities under the scrutiny of the regulators, the extent of new entrants has been limited. In the water industry, for example, there have been no new competitors. Thus, the expectations of promoters of privatisation, who regarded it as a temporary measure leading to dominant monopoly positions being undermined by new entrants to these industries, have not been fulfilled. Transfer of ownership has occurred, however, with foreign companies taking control of water companies and electricity generating companies.

## NATIONAL INCOME AND INTERNATIONAL TRADE

A country's national income, normally described as its gross national product (GNP), measures the money value of the goods and services available to that country from economic activity over a given period, normally a year. As can be seen from Figure 2.1, GNP can be measured in three ways, by adding up the sum of outputs of the country's industries, the sum of expenditures or the sum of incomes. Figure 2.1 indicates that in a simple two-sector economy, comprising businesses and households, the business sector produces the total goods and services making up national output, using factor inputs from the household sector to do this. The household sector is paid factor incomes by the business

*Figure 2.1* Output, income and expenditure in a two-sector economy

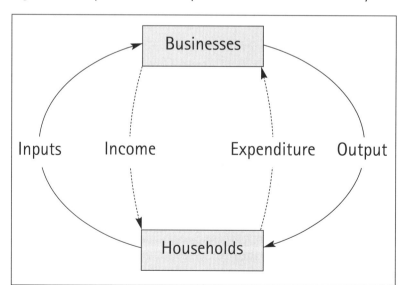

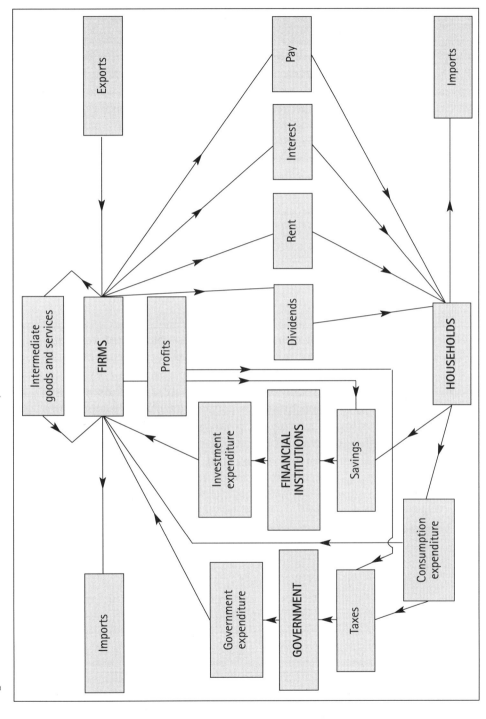

*Figure 2.2*   The circular flow of income in the UK economy

sector for the services they provide, and then it spends them on the output generated.

The output approach to measuring GNP aggregates the sum of value-added at each stage of production by all industries in the country. The sum of these added values gives gross domestic product at factor cost, which, after net property income from abroad, gives GNP. The expenditure approach aggregates consumption and investment expenditures to obtain total domestic expenditure at market prices. It aggregates only the value of final purchases and excludes all expenditure on any intermediate goods or services involved in the production process. Since final expenditures at market prices include the effects of taxes, subsidies and expenditures on imports, while excluding the value of imports, these have to be taken into account in measuring GNP by this method. Net national income or net national product is GNP adjusted to take account of capital consumption, the annual reduction in value of a country's national assets.

Figure 2.2 shows in more detail the flows of income resulting from the buying and selling of goods and services in the UK economy. Gross revenue received by firms, for example, comes from a number of sources. These are: consumption expenditure by households; investment or capital expenditure by the corporate sector via financial institutions, firms or households; government or public expenditure; expenditure received from overseas sales; and expenditure from other firms buying intermediate goods and services used in the production process. Payments made by firms, government, overseas companies and households take the forms of: wages paid to workers; interest on loans; rent on property; dividends to shareholders; corporate savings through retained profits to companies; taxes to government; revenues to overseas firms paid for imports; and incomes to other firms selling intermediate goods and services. Household income, in turn, goes on consumption spending, personal savings, taxes and payments for imported goods and services such as consumer products, holidays abroad or overseas investments.

National income not only indicates general living standards but is also the primary determinant of level of employment.

To understand how the level of national income is determined, it is necessary to outline the determinants of each of the main aggregate components of national expenditure. These are: consumption, investment, the government sector and overseas sector. Consumption expenditure is aggregate spending on goods and services satisfying current demand in the economy. Its major determinants are: level of national income; changes in national income; expectations based on this; and taxes on factor incomes. Other determinants include national wealth, interest rates, availability and cost of credit, and social expectations. Other things being equal, aggregate demand increases when there is a rise in consumption expenditure, and falls with a decrease in consumption spending.

Investment is defined as the flow of expenditures devoted to economic activities producing goods not intended for immediate consumption. At aggregate level, investment spending depends on factors similar to those determining investment at the level of the firm. These are: expected future demand in the economy; its spare capacity; wages and material costs; interest rates; and company profits. There are likely to be two stages in determining fixed investment. The first is deciding what the optimum level of capital capacity is, given demand and financial considerations. The second is influenced by technological and operational considerations and by financial factors. A rapid rate of investment is more likely to need high-cost external finance than a slower rate. Other things being equal, rises in investment spending induce increases in aggregate demand, with falls in investment leading to falls in aggregate demand.

The government (or public) sector comprises central and local government. The public sector raises revenue through taxation and sales of any marketed products. Tax revenues consist of direct taxes on incomes and indirect taxes on capital, goods and services for sale. Expenditure by public authorities falls into three categories: current expenditure on goods and services, mainly wages to public employees; capital expenditure on infrastructure such as roads, hospitals and schools; and transfer payments to pensioners, the unemployed and other social security benefits. Tax revenue and public expenditure need not balance. A government deficit can be met by borrowing from the private sector or general public, primarily through issuing gilt-edged government bonds and securities. Similarly, a government surplus can be used for repaying past debts. Other things being equal, aggregate demand is increased by a rise in public expenditure, either directly through a rise in current and capital spending, or indirectly through a rise in transfer payments to individuals, thus raising their capacity for consumption spending. Aggregate demand is also increased by cuts in taxation. It is decreased when public expenditure is cut or taxes are raised. The latter is done either by reducing private incomes through higher direct taxation or by reducing real incomes by raising indirect taxes.

The overseas sector affects aggregate expenditure through exports, which are purchases abroad of goods and services produced domestically, and imports, which are supplies of goods and services from abroad to meet domestic demand. Other things being equal, a rise in exports increases aggregate output, while a rise in imports decreases it. Demand for exports and imports are determined by the preferences of purchasers, relative prices and incomes. Demand for UK exports, for example, depends upon world demand and the prices of UK goods relative to those of her competitors. Similarly, demand for imports into the UK depends on level of domestic demand, prices of imported goods relative to those produced domestically, consumer taste, quality and demand for raw materials. In general, the level of exports is determined autonomously outside the UK economy, while imports depend essentially on the level of domestic demand.

In the elementary income–expenditure model of the macro-economy, it is aggregate expenditure, or aggregate demand, which determines both volume of national output and the associated level of employment. This is where supply of national output equals quantity of output that people wish to buy with their incomes. Aggregate expenditure equals the total spent on consumption, investment, government and exports, while national income equals the total volume of consumption, savings, taxes and imports. Since aggregate expenditure equals national income at equilibrium, this means that investment plus government spending plus exports equals savings plus taxes plus imports. In this model, the equilibrium level of national income is established when total leakages from the economy – savings plus taxes plus imports – equal total injections – investment plus government spending plus exports. This model of the macro-economy concentrates exclusively on the demand side. There is no reason to expect that the equilibrium eventually reached will be associated with full employment. On the contrary, this simple representation of the Keynesian system indicates that an unemployment equilibrium is possible. Even if wages and prices are fully flexible, the economy need not necessarily return to full employment when, after adjustments, total leakages equal total injections.

Trade among countries in global markets is an extension of the principle of economic specialisation in the international sphere. Domestic economic specialisation concentrates production capacity into those areas in which individuals, organisations and geographical regions have some natural or acquired advantage. This promotes economic efficiency and, accompanied by trade, raises standards of living beyond those that might be achieved had each individual, organisation or region remained self-sufficient. Nation states, however, differ from geographical regions in a number of respects. First, factors of production are able to move more freely within countries rather than between them. Second, each country has its own national currency. Third, there are variations in taxation, economic policy and social policy among countries, resulting in practical economic and political barriers to international trading between them.

Nation states nevertheless find that they are better suited to participate in some types of economic activity than others. Hence international trade affects the exchange of one nation's products against those of others when it is economically advantageous to do so. Some of this exchange takes place because most countries are incapable of satisfying all their economic wants from their own natural resources.

This is due to the uneven distribution of minerals, agricultural products and other resources throughout the world. These commodities can be obtained only by one country importing them from another in exchange for the goods or services it produces domestically.

Another economic factor promoting international trade is that although many nations can produce a wide range of commodities, they are better at producing some kinds of goods (or services) than others produce. These differences tend to be reflected in relative prices. It becomes profitable, therefore, for one country to concentrate on producing the goods and services for which it is best suited, and exporting any surpluses to other countries in exchange for commodities in which others have a comparative advantage. It is international differences in the skills and costs of labour, agricultural fertility and capital investment which are the principal factors making international specialisation feasible and profitable.

## THE STATE AND ECONOMIC MANAGEMENT

If the immediate post-war decades were the heyday of Keynesianism and demand management policies (Dow 1964), then the period since the mid-1970s has witnessed a sea change in the nature of economic policy. Governments have abandoned demand management policies, and the policy objective of full employment, and are now primarily concerned with control of inflation. This is associated with the re-emergence of monetarism and supply-side economics as the dominant orthodoxies guiding economic policy. While Keynesianism was linked predominantly with social democracy and the Welfare State, monetarism and supply-side economics in the UK, the US and other Western states have been particularly associated with the New Right in politics during the 1980s and 1990s (Curwen 1994).

The origins of the monetarist and supply-side counter-revolution emerged in the early 1970s. They derived from the growing concern of some politicians, business leaders and the electorate over the combination of rising inflation and rising unemployment. 'The nightmare of stagflation – simultaneous sharply rising prices and unemployment – had arrived' (Smith 1987: 45). It needed a combination of conditions to advance the cause of the 'new economics': an intellectual reassessment of economic theory, economic recession and political opportunity. Intellectual revisionism came from commentators such as Friedman (1963 and 1970). Economic recession followed the oil price shock of 1973–74 and the Conservative Party, which now contained a strong monetarist element, won the 1979 UK general election. Monetarism rests on pre-Keynesian principles and is commonly employed to describe the school of economic thought which holds that inflation results from excessive growth of money supply. Monetarists argue that, to be effective, government policy needs to adhere to the 'fixed monetary growth rule' which allows money supply to grow at a constant rate approximately equal to growth in output. Monetarists also argue that expanding aggregate demand results, in the long run, in higher prices. Both monetarists and Keynesians are concerned with level of demand for the economy's output but they differ over how government should seek to influence it. They also disagree about the consequences of their approaches. Monetarists contend that changes in the quantity of money are the only important sources of change in the level of national income. Keynesians attribute a larger role to fiscal policy in determining the level of aggregate demand.

In its earliest form, monetarism was based on an elaborated version of the simple 'quantity of money' theory. This states that in the long run changes in the money stock have minimal effect on the quantity of output or employment. The central propositions of monetarism as it emerged in the late 1960s were, first, that the demand for money function is more stable, and better defined statistically, than many of the components of aggregate demand. Second, the unique properties of money are emphasised, such as its role as a commodity which is substitutable for a wide range of other commodities and financial assets. As a result, monetary policy is seen as likely to have a direct impact on aggregate demand. Keynesian analysis emphasises that the initial impact of monetary policy falls on financial assets, with only a weak and uncertain impact on aggregate demand.

One of the more important aspects of modern monetarism is its concern with the role that expectations play in economic decision making. Rational expectations, in particular, have become associated with extreme monetarist views and suggest that individuals do not make systematic forecasting errors. On the contrary, their guesses about the future are often correct. If this is the case, the outlook for the efficacy of any macro-stabilisation policy is bleak, because households and firms learn to interpret economic events. The result is that they anticipate government action and take measures in advance to offset or evade it. The implication is that only unanticipated policy is likely to have any effect on real output, even in the short run. This contrasts with Keynesianism, which makes no allowance for private-sector anticipation of government action.

Revival of interest in monetarism since the 1970s has done much to clarify the issues separating monetarists from their critics. The chief area of disagreement concerns the principal sources of instability in the economy. Monetarists argue that the private sector of the economy is basically stable and that fixed policy rules are necessary to insulate the economy from ill-conceived government actions. It is the latter, monetarists argue, which are the principal source of economic instability. Non-monetarists, on the other hand, claim that the principal source of economic instability is the private sector. They emphasise the instability of private investment decisions and support an active counter-cyclical policy to achieve macroeconomic stability.

Two important policy implications follow from monetarism. First, stimulating aggregate demand is harmful, since it results in serious inflation. Second, money supply is crucial to economic stability and governments are expected to pursue a fixed level of money supply increase, departing from it only with great caution. In contrast with Keynesianism, monetarism implies three things: a less active fiscal and monetary policy, a greater concern with inflation than with unemployment, and a focus on the long rather than short term. Monetarists thus disapprove of fine-tuning the macro-economy through the use of Keynesian policy instruments, including adjustment of government spending. For monetarists, increased government spending involves two unacceptable measures: increasing the money supply and public-sector borrowing.

If sound money is the first major precept upon which monetarist analysis is based, two related principles follow: the need to reduce government borrowing and overall public spending. Sound money is supposed to keep inflation down, with the other two policy goals intended to make the economy more efficient by replacing public spending with private spending. A public sector deficit is financed by the sale of securities to the non-bank private sector, borrowing from overseas, bank lending to the public sector, and increases in currency. According to monetarists, the effects of public-sector borrowing are likely to be inflationary where the financing takes the form of new currency in circulation, but not where genuine borrowing takes place from the non-bank private sector. Reducing government borrowing and overall public spending is also favoured by monetarists on the ground that the requirements of the public sector otherwise 'crowd out' the private sector. Public-sector borrowing, it is argued, raises interest rates through increased sales of government bonds, making borrowing by the corporate sector more expensive. And this may have adverse effects on private investment.

New classical macroeconomics, while developing out of monetarism, essentially restates, in a more rigorous form, orthodox classical economics. This rests on the notion of rational expectations combined with a natural rate of unemployment which emerges as a result of efficient clearing of the market. According to classical economists, the prices of products are derived from the 'natural' rates of reward of the factors of production. The reward to labour is determined by the long-run cost of subsistence of labour, while profit is residual. The natural rate of unemployment is that determined by structural and frictional forces in the economy and cannot be reduced by raising aggregate demand. Attempts to hold unemployment below its natural rate result in accelerating inflation. The natural rate of unemployment, in other words, is that level remaining when the economy is in equilibrium.

New classical economists, in rejecting the idea that economic growth is achieved by manipulating aggregate demand, see the solution to the problem of growth lying in two directions. First, inflation has to be squeezed out of the economy by monetary discipline. Second, the economy has to be freed from obstacles inhibiting the efficient working of the market. Supply-siders emphasise that the principal determinant of growth is the allocation and efficient use of labour and capital. They focus on impediments to the supply of, and efficient use of, factors of production. Chief among these is believed to be disincentives to work and invest. These are claimed to result from the level and structure of taxes, institutional restrictions and customary barriers to the efficient allocation of resources. The policy prescriptions following from this are lower taxes and facilitating competition in labour and product markets.

Like monetarism, supply-side economics is a conservative economic doctrine which views capitalism as a natural economic form, deriving from the individualist nature of society. Individualism is seen to be the central feature of human society, with capitalist economic activity allowing it to be manifested in its purest form. In capitalist free markets, it is believed, entrepreneurs pursuing profit opportunities provide the creative element of capitalism. Supply-side economics focuses on the level of taxes and their consequences for economic activity. Its advocates believe that individuals respond to one key incentive – the money return on their labour and efforts. According to King (1987: 142), 'all individuals are considered to be calculating utility-maximisers'. This implies that 'they will work harder for higher pay and lower taxes; and the lower taxes are, the fewer will work in the black economy'.

## THE SINGLE EUROPEAN MARKET AND ECONOMIC AND MONETARY UNION

UK entry into the European Economic Community in 1973 marked a fundamental change in her economic relations. By participating in the policy-making institutions of the EU and through the process by which the EU budget is set, the UK government exerts influence on both the processes and outputs of the EU. The EU budget, for example, is determined annually and is very important to all 15 member states: Austria; Belgium; Denmark; Finland; France; Germany; Greece; Ireland; Italy; Luxembourg; the Netherlands; Portugal; Spain; Sweden; and the UK. It is classified under six main budget headings: Agriculture; Structural Operations; Internal Policies; External Action; Administration; and Reserves. Agricultural policy expenditures are the largest category of spending, especially farm price support (the CAP), which accounts for about half of total expenditure. Other large items of expenditure are the EU's three main structural funds: the European Regional Development Fund; the European Social Fund; and the Guidance Section of the European Agricultural Guidance and Guarantee Fund. Overall, the UK remains a net contributor to the EU budget, with her contributions being dominated by customs duties and value added taxes (VAT) paid to the EU (Artis 1996).

In its early days, the EU raised its revenues largely from contributions by member states. Since 1970, the EU has its own resources which are obtained from levies on agricultural imports, import duties on other goods, a share of VAT receipts and, since 1988, a contribution based on size of GNP. The EU budget continues to be a source of disagreement among member states, because of overspending on agricultural policy, problems of fraud, and the potential costs of extending the EU into central and eastern Europe. Nevertheless, the EU budget amounts to just over 1 per cent of the combined annual GDP of the whole EU, which means that it is dwarfed by the taxes raised and expenditure made by individual governments of member states. In terms of output, the EU's is smaller than that of the US, by about

4 per cent, but larger than that of Japan's. Within the EU, the GDP of the UK is the fourth largest behind those of Germany, France and Italy. However, because of the UK's relatively large population, a comparison of GDP per head shows that she is well down the EU league table, with a GDP per head which is just below the average for the other member states. The highest GDPs per head are found in Luxembourg, Denmark, Belgium, Austria, France and Germany; the lowest in Greece, Portugal and Spain.

## The single market

The Single European Act (SEA) 1986 marked an important step in realising the objectives of the Treaty of Rome (TECU). Under the Treaty, member states agreed a timetable for removing tariff barriers and fixing a common external tariff for goods and services. The aims of the SEA 1986 were to bring about freer trade within the Community by removing the large number of remaining non-tariff barriers and taking steps to ensure the free movement of persons, capital and goods. The Act was a response to the perception that the European market was still fragmented and, as a result, that European industry was not as competitive as it could be. Key elements in the SEA were completion of the 'single' or 'internal' market by 1 January 1993 and qualified majority voting in the Council of Ministers. The benefits of the single market were expressed in terms not only of freer trade and more competition but also of increasing consumer welfare by:

• eliminating inefficient producers

• eliminating monopoly power

• reducing prices

• increasing *per capita* national incomes.

The single market initiative was designed to eliminate (non-tariff) physical, technical and fiscal barriers impeding trade between member states. Physical barriers are lengthy delays at border crossings and documentation associated with movement between member states. As long as frontier, customs and immigration controls exist, trade among member states will be different from trade within member states. Technical barriers cover regulations about product specifications, including different regulations among member states on safety or pollution controls that impede transnational trade. Other technical barriers relate to public sector procurement, since governments have traditionally discriminated in favour of domestic suppliers, with the result that high proportions of national expenditure by member states were blocked to non-nationals within the Community. Under the SEA 1986, such discrimination is prohibited and public-sector announcements for tendering have to be placed within the EU's Official Bulletin. Fiscal barriers arise from different rates of expenditure taxes, notably VAT and excise duties, resulting in discrimination against producers of other member states (Jewell 1993).

The original Schengen Accord in 1985 aimed at eliminating internal border controls for the five member states signing it. This was followed by the Schengen Agreement 1990, agreed by all member states except the UK and Ireland. This led to the effective elimination of internal border controls on people travelling between these states, common visas, more stringent external border controls and a Schengen information system. A range of subjects was included in the single market programme, much of which is now completed. These covered: control of goods; veterinary control provisions; food, ethical drugs and chemicals; motor vehicles; banking, credit institutions and insurance; and transactions in securities, capital movements, company law and direct taxation. Other subjects covered: people; standards and general technical barriers; intellectual property and new technology; transport; and public procurement. New provisions are continually being introduced, although their number has dropped dramatically, as existing measures are scrutinised and examined. The impact of the single market measures vary from sector to sector. In some areas, non-tariff barriers remain high.

A continuing area of controversy is fiscal reform, since to complete the single market some degree of harmonisation in the taxation systems of member states is necessary, particularly concerning VAT and excise duties. The general approach has been to try to seek consensus where possible, but the practical and economic difficulties are considerable. However, the rights of national governments to decide when and how to collect revenues, and how to use them, are jealously guarded. Common tax proposals, whether relating to pollution, information technology or consumer goods and services, always raise concerns with the business community, on the grounds this could lead to extra burdens on firms as well as posing a threat to competitiveness (Artis and Lee 1994).

Measures also exist to promote fair competition in the EU. The objectives of market integration are to ensure efficient use of resources through competition, to stimulate best use of know-how, to encourage innovation and promote research. Thus, the European Commission has powers to enforce competition law, impose fines, declare void anti-competitive practices and demand information. State aid to firms or industry is also regarded as discriminatory where it benefits specific undertakings at the expense of others. It is acceptable only where it:

- promotes economic development areas which have low living standards or serious unemployment

- promotes important projects of common European interest, or remedies serious disturbances of a member state's economy

- facilitates development of economic activities or certain areas.

Such aid corrects regional imbalances, accelerates industrial growth and neutralises distortions in competition. Euro-policy also allows certain industries to be run down without excessive social distress. However, this aid must be part of reorganisation, and investment assistance must not expand capacity.

### Economic and monetary union

Following the post-war economic order of western Europe, the US and Japan created at the Bretton Woods Conference, the Treaty of Rome 1957 had little to say about monetary issues. It was assumed that stable currencies would remain the norm and that economic reconstruction in Europe would be based on achieving a common market, through progressive removal of barriers to free movement of goods, services and capital. By the late 1960s, however, a new era of currency instability threatened. The Commission first favoured fixed exchange rates and Franco-German support ensured that economic and monetary union (EMU) became a formal goal of heads of state at the Hague in December 1969. They set up a group, led by the Prime Minister of Luxembourg, Pierre Werner, to report on how EMU could be achieved. The Werner group submitted its report in October 1970, with a three-stage plan to achieve full economic and monetary union within 10 years.

In 1971, the six member states agreed to implement the policy but, with the collapse of Bretton Woods and the floating of the US dollar, the EMU project came to an abrupt halt. A year later, member states created the 'snake', which was a mechanism for managing floating currencies within narrow margins of fluctuation against the dollar (the 'tunnel'). Because of the oil crisis of the early 1970s and the weakness of the dollar, the snake lost its members and was reduced to a Deutschmark area after two years. EMU did not come to the fore again until France and Germany pushed for a European Monetary System (EMS) in the late 1970s. This was based on fixed but adjustable exchange rates, and all member states, except the UK, initially participated in the Exchange Rate Mechanism (ERM). ERM was based on the principle that exchange rates of member states were linked to central rates against the European Currency Unit (ECU), which was a weighted average of participating currencies. Currency fluctuations had to be contained within a margin of 2.25 per cent either side of bilateral rates.

From 1980, ERM did much to reduce exchange rate fluctuations and achieve currency stability. With the introduction of the single market and moves towards greater integration, it was acknowledged that the full potential of the single market could not be achieved as long as high transaction costs and exchange rate fluctuations remained. In April 1989, the President of the European Commission, Jacques Delors, submitted a report proposing the introduction of EMU in three stages. Recognising that full monetary union necessitates capital market integration, exchange rate union, harmonisation of monetary policy, a single currency and a central bank to manage the exchange rate, the report stressed three things:

• greater co-ordination of member states' economic policies

• rules on the size and financing of national budget deficits

• establishment of a new independent institution responsible for monetary policy.

In 1989, an intergovernmental conference identified what needed to be done to attain full EMU and led to the Treaty on European Union (TUE), formally adopted by heads of state at Maastricht in December 1991, signed on 7 February 1992.

Maastricht provided for EMU to be completed by 2002, in three successive stages. Stage 1 began in 1990, with member states adopting the following measures:

• prohibiting restrictions on capital movements

• prohibiting overdrafts by central banks to public authorities and public undertakings

• prohibiting privileged access of the latter to financial institutions.

Stage 2 began in January 1994. Precise but non-binding rules on public financing were adopted and a new type of monitoring of public finances was introduced, carried out by the Commission. The European Monetary Institute (EMI) was established to strengthen co-operation between national central banks.

Stage 3 started on 1 January 1999. Common budgetary rules became binding on member states and a single monetary policy was introduced. This was entrusted to the

European System of Central Banks, made up of national central banks and the newly created European Central Bank (ECB) in Frankfurt. It also saw the launching of the 'Euro' in which 11 participating currencies were locked together at irrevocable fixed conversion rates (but not the pound sterling, Irish punt, and Danish and Swedish Krone). The convergence criteria for currencies joining the Euro were: price stability; the ratio of public deficit to GDP to be not greater than 3.5 per cent; public debt not to exceed 60 per cent of GDP; convergence of interest rates; and participation in ERM. During the transitional phase from January 1999 to July 2002, national currencies continue to be legal tender but, at the beginning of 2002, they will be phased out and the Euro phased in. Since 1 January 1999:

- new issues of government bonds have been in Euros

- the equity markets of Europe have operated in Euros

- the UK and other excluded countries have no fixed exchange rates with the Euro and face the usual foreign exchange risks

- one 'Euroland' interest rate exists.

Some of the claimed benefits of EMU are:

- price transparency

- stimulus to trade

- savings in conversion and transaction costs

- efficient allocation of resources

- economising on foreign currency reserves

- low inflation and price stability

- lower interest rates

- precondition for future integration

Some of the claimed costs of EMU are:

- loss of autonomy over national economic policy

- loss of exchange rates as a policy instrument

- reduces the ability of government to inflate taxes

- reduces the real value of public debt

- differential impact on regions, ie 'winners' and 'losers'.

UK exclusion from EMU is controversial, with economic and political undertones. The government has declared that the UK will join the Euro but not until the economic climate is 'right'. The final decision is to be based on a public referendum and five economic tests:

- Are business cycles and economic structures compatible so the UK can live with Euro interest rates?

- Is there sufficient flexibility to deal with any problems that might arise?

- Will joining EMU create better conditions for firms making long-term decisions to invest in the UK?

- What impact will entry have on the competitive position of the City?

- Will joining the Euro promote higher growth, stability and a lasting increase in jobs?

## CONCLUSION

The UK economy has undergone significant changes over the past 20 years. It is now a more open and deregulated economy than it was then and, at the same time, the national economy has become more integrated with the other member states of the EU, through the single European market. The structure of the economy has changed too. The UK's manufacturing base has shrunk and its economic structure is now dominated by a large services sector. Another significant development has been the large-scale privatisations that have taken place, albeit paralleled by the creation of new regulatory bodies to oversee the now privately owned utilities. State economic policy has changed too, from one strongly rooted in post-war Keynesian principles to a more market-based, supply-side and monetarist approach. There have also been significant changes in the ways in which central and local government organisations are funded, structured and managed. These sorts of structural and economic policy changes continue to impact on private, public and voluntary organisations. It is these and related developments, such as the potential issues associated with EMU, which require constant assessment and appraisal by those leading and managing organisations in the dynamic, increasingly international market place in which private and public enterprises operate.

# 3 The political system

For many people, 'politics' denotes activity about which they 'feel a combination of cynicism, scepticism and mistrust.) It is experienced as something distant and remote from everyday life' (Leftwich 1984: 138). This is surprising, since politics is about the ability of those with power to influence or ultimately enforce changes of behaviour in others. All activity involving humans collectively is political, since politics exists whenever there are disagreements or conflicts over resources, decisions or ideas. The purpose of political solutions is to resolve or accommodate conflicts between competing interests to achieve stability and social peace. Politics is not the cause of human conflicts, it reflects differences of interest between individuals, organised groups and nation states. If political disputes are not settled peaceably, social disorder or physical violence can result. It is through the machinery and processes of politics that such conflicts are identified, contained and resolved.

Politics is also about the factors influencing and reflecting the distribution of power in society, as well as the effect of power on use of resources and how these are allocated. Politics is ultimately about 'the "transformative" capacity of social agents, agencies and institutions: it is not about Government or government alone' (Leftwich 1984: 144). Crick (1964: 22) defines macro-politics as the activity by which differing social interests 'are conciliated by giving them a share in power'. It is 'a way of ruling divided societies without undue violence – and most societies are divided, though some think that this is the very trouble'. Politics also takes place in families, social clubs, trade unions, work organisations and between nations. These are called micro-politics and international relations, respectively.

At the end of this chapter, readers should be able to understand and explain:

- how the external political environment impacts on private, public and voluntary organisations

- interactions between political and economic systems, including the European dimension.

In addition, they should also be able to:

- provide examples of how organisations are affected by political institutions and processes, and how organisations can influence the policy-making process

- advise management on possible effects of government policies, legislation and European directives on organisations and their activities.

See also the Professional Standards Index (page 345).

## FORMS OF GOVERNANCE AND THE DEMOCRATIC PROCESS

There are various ways of classifying political systems. Ball (1993) identifies four: authoritarian, communist, post-communist and liberal democratic. In authoritarian systems, limitations are placed on 'open' politics and competition for power. Coercion is used to enforce obedience to the political authorities, civil liberties are weak and there is no independent judiciary. Autocracies are dominated by traditional or military élites, often in modernising third-world countries. These regimes tend to be unstable and range from conservative monarchies and dictatorships, on the one hand, to civilian military regimes or direct military rule on the other.

Communist regimes are those characterised by:

- an ideology reflecting the ideas of Karl Marx

- a political system dominated by a single party

- state ownership and control of the economy, which is centrally planned

- central control of communications, limited civil liberties and extensive censorship

• limited judicial independence, and power concentrated in the dominant party.

Until recently, communist regimes included eastern Europe and the Union of Socialist Soviet Republics (USSR). Today the remaining Communist regimes include China, Cuba and North Korea.

Post-communist regimes are new and resulted from the overthrow of communism in eastern Europe post-1989. The collapse of the USSR in 1991 resulted in 15 successor states, while the break-up of Czechoslovakia and civil war in Yugoslavia had similar consequences. These states have the following political characteristics:

• weak government, paralysed in part by lack of political legitimacy

• multiparty systems

• limited civil liberties

• extensive state ownership, gradually moving towards market economies.

All are inherently unstable and whether they will eventually move towards authoritarian populist regimes or full liberal democracy is uncertain.

The political systems of Western countries are typically liberal democracies. In essence, they are systems of representative government by majority rule, where individual rights are protected from state interference and cannot be restricted even by electoral majority. A central problem in liberal democracy is how to reconcile the economic liberties associated with freedom of contract and free market exchange, based on overt inequalities, with individual political and social rights, embodied in the law, based on equal citizenship. The ideas underpinning modern liberal democracy derive partly from those of 'classical liberalism' and partly from the concepts of democracy and equality before the law stemming from the American and French revolutions at the end of the eighteenth century.

Classical liberalism emerged from two main intellectual

sources: (political theories of civil society and social contract and economic theories of market capitalism. This is why liberal democracy is rooted in capitalist societies, based on private ownership of capital and the market economy.) The political theories of classical liberalism originate from the writings of Hobbes (1651, pub. 1946) and Locke (1690, pub. 1947), who were social contract theorists. Although their theories of human nature differ substantially, as do their analyses of political authority, both agree that the lawful state is instrumental to peace, prosperity and human welfare. Hobbes's view of humankind is pessimistic and based on fear, where the state of nature is one in which people are selfish, aggressive and acquisitive and life is nasty, brutish and short. In this war of each against the other, the strongest rule and might is right. To overcome this condition of social anarchy, people contract to surrender their right to govern themselves by giving power to the sovereign body within the state. For Hobbes, absolute government is the necessary condition for creating law and order, with political obligation by the citizenry being unconditional – except in the case of defending one's own life. Hobbes, in short, is the apologist of the absolute state, but one based on a social contract.

Locke, in contrast, believed humankind to be rational, moral and social. In his view, (individuals are born free, with certain fundamental human rights such as personal autonomy, freedom from tyranny and freedom to own property. For him, the state of nature is one of relative peace and harmony, where everyone is responsible for enforcing the moral law. In entering into a social contract with one another in society, and handing over the right to make and enforce civil law to the state, citizens consent to being ruled by limited, neutral government. Government's role is to uphold personal freedoms, including the right of 'life, liberty and estate'. Political obligation under this social contract depends upon government (providing the political conditions for protecting property, defending individual freedoms and enforcing legal contracts.)

Economic theories of market capitalism are associated with the writings of the classical economists, starting with Adam

Smith (1776, pub. 1976). Classical economic theory is based on the assumption that individuals are the best judges of their own economic interests and holds that individual pursuit of economic self-interest, in a competitive market economy, results in aggregate economic benefit to all. For classical economists, it is market capitalism, where the 'invisible hand' of the market co-ordinates the diverse activities of producers and consumers through the price mechanism, which ensures the most efficient use of scarce resources, without the need for a state bureaucracy to manage the economy.

Neither Hobbes nor Locke was a democrat, and market liberals like Smith and his successors were political economists, not political theorists. They emphasised the virtues of free markets and possessive individualism. Like economic liberals, political liberals focused on individualism as the motivating force behind human action. If humankind is rational, moral, born free and equal, and endowed with certain natural rights, it was argued, then humans were the best judge of their political interests. However, only in an ordered society can individuals exercise their human rights and develop their full potential. Logically, people should govern themselves but this is not possible in large-scale modern societies. It fell to democrats such as Rousseau, (1776, pub. 1972) and the American federalists, Paine (1791, pub. 1984) and John Stuart Mill (1851, pub. 1972) to provide the democratic and egalitarian ideas embodied in modern liberal democracy. Since direct personal involvement is not possible in the large modern state, citizens delegate to representatives the power to govern themselves democratically. Political sovereignty remains with the people, who participate in choosing government, and government is representative and responsive to the wishes of the people, with political obligation being conditional upon government meeting popular demands.

By the mid-nineteenth century the fundamental principles and tenets of liberal democracy had been established in both the political and economic spheres, even though they were not practised universally. They included ideas of:

- free market economics and the invisible hand of the market

- popular sovereignty, with ultimate power resting with the people

- basic human freedoms such as free speech, freedom of association and holding property

- political equality before the law

- the principle of majority rule, with the need to protect minority interests from abuse of power

- the principle of government as trustee of delegated power from the people it represents.

If the ends of liberal democracy were to provide legitimate government for its citizens, then it was to be the means of facilitating civic progress and civilising society.

Modern liberal democracy, then, has emerged in Western industrialised countries out of the ideas associated with social contract theory, market capitalism and representative democracy. In its modern form, liberal democracy is characterised by a number of features:

- inter-party politics, with more than one party competing for power

- open competition for political power, with established procedures for political debate

- relatively open recruitment to positions of power

- representative systems, with periodic elections of representatives, based on universal suffrage

- pressure groups outside government influencing policy

- individual freedoms, such as freedom of speech and from arbitrary arrest, upheld by an independent judiciary

- a free mass media willing to criticise government and its policies to facilitate free speech and ideas.

Above all, liberal democratic states have governments with limited, not absolute, powers. Governments are circumscribed constitutionally in what they can do and how they exercise their authority. There are also private areas of social and economic life in which the state does not intervene.

## THE MACHINERY OF GOVERNMENT IN THE UK

Figure 3.1 provides a simple systems model of the UK political system. It provides a framework for identifying and analysing the 'inputs', 'processes' and 'outputs' of the political system. Inputs are the 'demands' and 'supports' of the system, demands are what individuals and groups want the system to achieve; its supports are the resources required for achieving them, including public willingness to participate as voters, activists and taxpayers. The political process begins with individuals who are influenced by public opinion and the mass media and, to be effective, this activity has to be channelled into collective action through parties, pressure groups and elections as political demands and supports. Demands and supports are fed into the machinery of government, where some are accepted, others accepted in part, and the rest rejected. The policies and decisions of the machinery of government are the outputs of the system which feed back into it, helping to generate further demands and supports.

Since many demands on the political system are incompatible with one another, thus reflecting social and political conflicts in democratic societies, constitutional machinery has been created, aiming to manage these conflicts. The elements of the machinery of government are: the legislature, consisting of the monarch, House of Commons and House of Lords; an executive consisting of the cabinet and ministers of the Crown, led by the prime minister; and government departments and an administrative system. There is also an independent judiciary, which interprets and applies parliamentary statutes and common law.

### Parliament

Parliament is the supreme legislative authority that operates within a pluralist political system, incorporating external

*Figure 3.1* A basic model of the UK political system

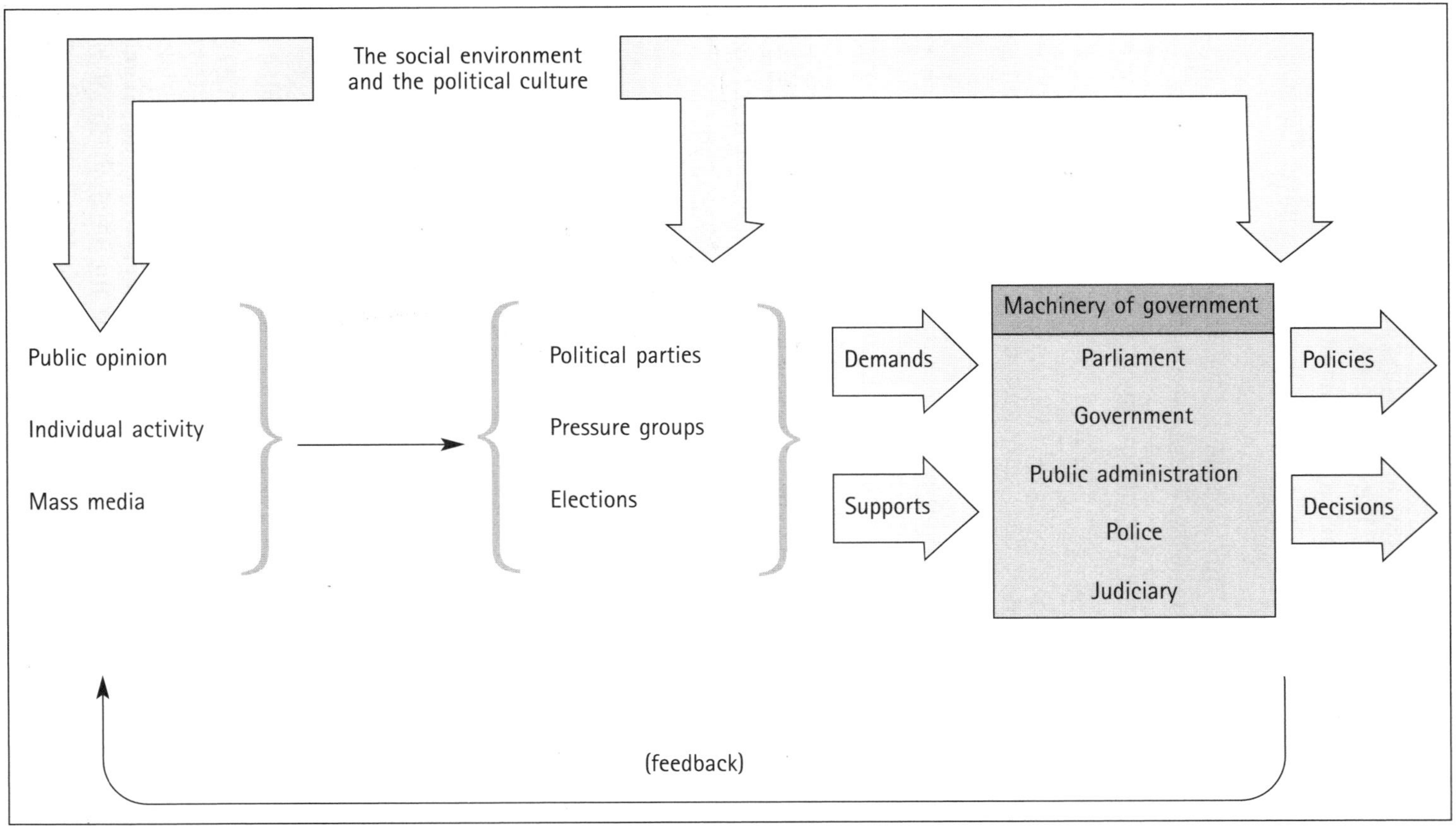

The social environment
and the political culture

Public opinion

Individual activity

Mass media

Political parties

Pressure groups

Elections

Demands

Supports

Machinery of government

Parliament

Government

Public administration

Police

Judiciary

Policies

Decisions

(feedback)

pressure groups and an organised opposition, within and outside Parliament. Each element of Parliament – Commons, Lords and the monarch in Parliament – is outwardly separate and based on different constitutional principles. Parliament has four main functions:

- establishing the laws of the land (or statutes), regulating those aspects of life within the sphere of government

- voting taxes and public funds, as means of carrying out government policy

- holding government and public administration accountable, by scrutinising their activities through questions, debates and select committees

- acting as a channel of representation through which the views of the electorate can be communicated to government through Members of Parliament (MPs), ministers and political lobbying.

A Parliament sits for up to five years, though in practice it is normally dissolved before the five-year period elapses. Every Parliament has a number of sessions, beginning in October or November, which continue, with adjournments, until the summer recess, in July or August. At the end of each session, Parliament is suspended, or prorogued, and at the end of the life of a Parliament the monarch orders its dissolution by royal proclamation, on the advice of the prime minister. The proclamation orders the issuing of writs for an election and announces the date on which the new Parliament is to assemble. Within Parliament, the Commons is the dominant chamber. It is a representative assembly elected by universal adult suffrage. For electoral purposes the UK is divided into 659 electoral constituencies, each of which returns one MP to the House of Commons. At the 1997 general election, there were 530 contestable parliamentary seats in England, 40 in Wales, 72 in Scotland and 17 in Northern Ireland. Election is by secret ballot. All British subjects and citizens of the Irish Republic living in the UK are entitled to vote, provided they are over 18, registered electors, not legally barred from voting and not 'Peers of the Realm'. Similarly, most British subjects are eligible to stand for election to the

House of Commons, unless they are undischarged bankrupts or certain categories of clergy. Judges, civil servants, some local government officers, members of the armed forces and police service, and members of boards of public corporations may stand only if they resign their posts.

By convention, the leader of the majority party in the House of Commons is appointed prime minister by the monarch, with some 100 members from both Houses, but largely from the Commons, being appointed ministers of the Crown. In both Houses, party whips maintain control, by keeping MPs and peers in touch with party business, maintaining party voting strength and informing the leadership of back-bench opinion. The party system is central to the role of Parliament. At every election, the parties lay their policies before the electorate in their manifestos and put candidates up for election. The candidate polling the greatest number of votes in each constituency, not necessarily with an absolute majority of votes, is elected and the party with the majority of seats in the Commons normally forms the government, even if it has not obtained a majority of the votes cast nationally. The distribution of seats by political party after the 1997 general election is shown in Table 3.1.

*Table 3.1*  Distribution of seats in the House of Commons, and percentage votes cast, by political party, at General Election, 1997

| Party | number of seats | per cent votes |
|---|---|---|
| Labour Party | 418 | 44.4 |
| Conservative and Unionist Party | 165 | 31.5 |
| Liberal Democrats | 46 | 17.2 |
| Scottish Nationalist Party | 6 | 21.9* |
| Plaid Cymru | 4 | 9.7** |
| Ulster Unionist Party | 10 | 32.7*** |
| Social and Democratic Labour Party | 3 | 24.1*** |
| Sinn Fein | 2 | 16.1*** |
| Democratic Unionist Party | 2 | 12.3*** |
| UK Unionist Party | 1 | 1.6*** |
| Others | 2 | n/a |

Source: Kessling Archives 1997
*       as per cent of vote in Scotland
**     as per cent of vote in Wales
***   as per cent of vote in Northern Ireland

The impact of the party system on the Commons makes the formal theoretical model of a supreme legislative assembly in the parliamentary system unrealistic. The Commons has all the potential powers implied in the formal model. It can use its legislative powers, hold government and administration accountable and act as the sovereign body. But exercising these powers depends on party composition in the House, because the Commons is divided on party lines and the forces keeping the parties apart are normally stronger than those drawing them together. The Commons therefore does not act as a central body willing to limit and control the power of the executive and, since government normally has a clear majority in the House, the opposition is reduced to ineffectiveness.

The key relationship is between the cabinet and majority party in the Commons. Majority-party MPs are under pressure to support the government, even where they disagree with some policies. In most cases they support government policies, since they have fought hard to secure the election of their party to office. Those having doubts are normally reluctant to criticise government publicly, since it might harm the party's standing in the country and cause them difficulties with local party activists or party headquarters. Few majority-party MPs press their differences with government as far as voting against it on important issues. Also, party discipline in the Commons is very strict. Unless a substantial number of majority-party MPs is prepared to challenge the government, the legislature is subordinate to the executive. While not necessarily ignoring its backbenchers' views, government is the dominant force in the relationship between ministers and majority-party MPs. Nevertheless, MPs have influence by putting pressure upon government behind the scenes. Their work on specialist scrutiny committees is especially important, when there is some cross-party agreement. MPs also play important roles in standing committees by improving and amending parliamentary Bills.

Under the Parliament Acts, 1911 and 1949, the formal powers of the House of Lords are strictly limited, especially regarding the passing of legislation. It has no power to veto or delay money Bills, though it can impose a temporary veto of one year on other Bills. It does, however, have the right to amend Bills, subject to closure in the Commons. The most striking feature of the Lords is that its members are not elected, although proposals are in hand by the Labour government elected in 1997 to reform the House of Lords, although how this is to be done is not yet clear. In the first instance, it will remove most of the 1,000 hereditary peers from the Lords.

## Government

The government consists of approximately 100 ministers appointed to executive posts in the cabinet or as junior ministers. The prime minister provides the leadership of the government, the majority party in the Commons, and heads the cabinet. Most senior ministers are heads of major departments with the title secretary of state, with others holding office as ministers without portfolio. The size of the cabinet varies and is determined by practical and political considerations, but it normally has around 20 members. Certain office holders such as the law officers of the Crown, including the Attorney General and the Scottish counterpart, the Procurator Fiscal, are not cabinet members but attend cabinet meetings for particular issues.

The main function of the cabinet is to take decisions on policy and matters to be submitted to Parliament, especially issues relating to public expenditure. It also oversees and co-ordinates government administration and arbitrates between ministers or departments failing to agree among themselves. The cabinet undertakes these duties through a system of committees, assisted by the Cabinet Office. The cabinet would clearly not be able to fulfil its wide-ranging tasks without the complex committee structure. One purpose of cabinet committees is to co-ordinate decisions between different departments of state concerned with common policy issues. As long as ministers hold office, they share the collective responsibility of all ministers, requiring them neither to criticise nor dissociate themselves publicly from government policies. Collective responsibility reinforces the principle of the indivisibility of the executive and serves a number of political purposes by:

- reinforcing party unity in Parliament and strengthening the party in power against the opposition

- helping maintain government control over legislation and public spending

- minimising public disagreements among departments, such as the Treasury and spending departments

- helping maintain the authority of the prime minister

- reinforcing the secrecy of government and cabinet decision-making.

The role of the prime minister, like that of the cabinet, has evolved by political practice and constitutional convention since the eighteenth century. Today the office is of central importance in the system of government. As leader of the majority party in the Commons, appointed by the monarch, the prime minister has to have a firm hold over party loyalty inside and outside Parliament, and command of the Commons. The power of the office derives from the dominant influence it exercises in the cabinet. As Benn (1980: 126) writes: 'The premiership in Britain today is, in effect, an elected monarchy. No medieval monarch in the whole of British history ever had such power as every modern British Prime Minister has in his or her hands.' It is the prime minister who effectively makes all appointments to ministerial office, since Crown ministers are appointed by the monarch on the recommendation of the prime minister.

By presiding over cabinet meetings, the prime minister is able to control discussions and decision-taking within it. Although a secretariat services the whole cabinet, it has a special relationship and allegiance to the prime minister, who determines which departments are to be abolished or created and has the constitutional right to recommend to the monarch that Parliament be dissolved and a general election held. Compared with other ministers, the prime minister has far more opportunity to present and defend governmental policies to Parliament and the public, including control over what information and communications go to the media about cabinet business and government affairs. The prime minister also takes certain political decisions, without waiting for full cabinet meetings. When a cabinet committee looks at a particular policy, the prime minister may take the chair and report back to a later cabinet meeting on the action taken. This led Crossman (1963) to conclude that:

> The post-war epoch has seen the final transformation of Cabinet Government into Prime Ministerial Government ... [the Prime Minister's] powers have steadily increased, first, by the centralisation of the party machine under his [sic] personal rule, and secondly by the growth of a centralised bureaucracy.

Prime Ministers must, however, retain the support of their cabinet colleagues and parliamentary party, if they are to remain in office. If prime ministers lose the confidence of their supporters, as Margaret Thatcher did in 1990, they can be removed from power.

## Political devolution in Scotland, Wales and Northern Ireland

The New Labour government supports political devolution in Scotland and Wales. Referendums were held on creating a law-making Scottish Parliament and a Welsh Assembly, with more limited powers, in September 1997. Seventy-three per cent of voters supported a Scottish Parliament, with 63.5 per cent wanting it to have tax raising powers, in a turnout of 60 per cent. In Wales, devolution received 50.3 per cent support of voters in a 50 per cent turnout. The Scottish Parliament was established in July 1999 and deals with matters formerly devolved to the Scottish Office, such as health, education, local government, law and order, economic development, roads, the environment and the arts. It has tax-raising powers of plus or minus 3 per cent over national taxes but Westminster retains sovereignty over the Edinburgh Parliament and has responsibility for defence, foreign policy, social security and macroeconomic policy. Of 129 Scottish Members of Parliament (MSPs), 73 are elected on a 'first past the post' basis in existing Westminster constituencies, and 56 through party lists of candidates in eight Euro-constituencies, under proportional representation (PR). The Welsh National Assembly handles matters formerly devolved to the Welsh Office: education, health, agriculture, roads and planning. It has 80 members, 40 elected on a 'first past the post' basis in Westminster constituencies, and 40 on a PR basis from party lists. The future of the Northern Ireland Assembly, resulting from the 'Good Friday' Agreement 1998, is uncertain, following continued political difficulties between Unionist and Nationalist groups in the province.

## LOCAL GOVERNMENT

In liberal democratic theory, a strong case is made for local government. John Stuart Mill (1851) argued that local democratic self-government is fundamental to any national democratic system. It is a means of political education, popular participation and training for future national leaders. It also acts as a counterweight to central government, diffuses political power and accommodates local and minority interests, thus ensuring that government is responsive to popular demands. Local government is also justified on administrative grounds as the best means of providing public services at local level. Different communities have different needs and a system of local elected bodies enables those needs to be identified and prioritised locally. Traditionally, local government has a dual role: exercising a political function by managing conflicts over the provision of public services at local level; and administering local public services.

In the UK, local government consists of local authorities, with different systems in England and Wales, Scotland and Northern Ireland, which are elected bodies providing local public services over defined geographical areas. They have the following characteristics:

• a distinct legal status

• a degree of autonomy and decision-making power

• local tax-raising powers.

Constitutionally, local authorities are subordinate governmental bodies and creatures of statute. Parliament enacts legislation determining the structure of local government, its powers and functions and sources of finance. Unlike local government in other countries, there is no constitutional protection for local government and no general powers to provide good government of the community. It operates within a legal framework determined by central government and is subject to a variety of administrative, financial and political controls.

In England and Wales, the main types of local authorities are unitary authorities, district councils, county councils and London Boroughs, where councillors are elected to serve for fixed terms of four years. Many unitary and district council elections are held in three out of every four years, with one third of the council being elected each time. County council elections are held once every four years. Although 44 million people are eligible to vote, only 40 per cent normally do so. Electoral turn-out is low in the UK compared with most other western European countries, where it is often 80 or 90 per cent. Local councillors have to be local residents or work in the area, and usually stand for a political party. Currently, about 85 per cent of local councillors represent the Conservatives, Labour or Liberal Democrats, with 5 per cent representing ratepayers or nationalist organisations. The remaining 10 per cent are political independents.

Political parties play an important part in local elections and running local authorities. Majority parties control most authorities. In other cases there are 'hung' leaderships, operating in coalition. One view is that party politics has no place in local government, but there is general consensus that political parties are indispensable in ensuring that local councils are responsible to their electorates. They formulate policies presented to their electorates, enable councillors to co-ordinate activities, prioritise issues and apply party principles to specific problems. Political parties are also significant in central–local relations and this is often a cause of friction when different parties are in power centrally and locally. Local leaders may resist the attempts of central government to impose new policies or constrain local authority expenditure. Throughout the 1980s and 1990s, the relationship between central and local government was tense. Successive governments, committed to fundamental changes in the role of the state and restructuring society, demanded radical changes in local government. Unable to get the co-operation of many local authorities, central government used a range of strategies to compel or circumvent local government.

Almost 90 major statutes affecting local government were enacted between 1979 and 1997. Some imposed new responsibilities on local authorities but many removed their powers or compelled them to carry out national policies. The main effect was to change the role of local authorities from principal providers of public services to enablers and facilitators. Now the voluntary and private sectors play an important role in meeting community needs, with local authorities funding or regulating service provision. Central government has also taken control of local authority expenditure. Less than 20 per cent of local government tax revenue is derived from the council tax, with between 80 and 90 per cent coming from central government grants and a nationally determined business rate.

## THE EUROPEAN UNION

The European Union (EU) is a unique political system combining elements of supra-nationalism and inter-governmentalism. Its origins lie in the aftermath of the Second World War, when there was a need for rapid reconstruction and the reintegration of Germany into the community of western European states. Anxious to assist Europe in becoming a strong buffer against the threat of Communist expansion from the Soviet bloc, the US provided Marshall Aid and encouraged international co-operation within Europe. Proposals for a United States of Europe with a federal structure met with little support from post-war states. But six countries – Belgium, Luxembourg, France, the Netherlands, Italy and West Germany – agreed to co-operation in restructuring their coal and steel communities, when signing the Treaty of Paris 1951. Six years later, they signed the Treaty of Rome 1957, which created the European Economic Community (EEC) and the European Energy Community. The EEC committed its members to creating a 'common market', by removing internal tariff barriers and adopting common external tariffs. The benefits of economic co-operation led other countries to seek entry subsequently. Denmark, Ireland and the UK joined in 1973 and Greece in 1981, followed by Portugal and Spain in 1986. The EU was further enlarged in 1995, when Austria, Finland and Sweden became members.

The founding fathers of the EU always had a vision of a politically united Europe but saw economic integration as the best means of achieving that. But there was always ambivalence about political union by their political leaders, because power was – and is – based on the nation state, not Europe. Their strategies have been essentially pragmatic and based upon national interest. Between 1956 and 1986, there was some progress, but integration was impeded by the need to get unanimous agreement on every issue. The 1980s and 1990s have seen greater political will for further integration, prompted partly by the reunification of Germany and end of the Cold War. The Single European Act 1986, the Treaty of Maastricht 1992 and Treaty of Amsterdam 1997 have transformed the EU, with its 300 million citizens, and this period is likely to be seen as a watershed in the development of this political experiment.

The political institutions of the EU are shown in Figure 3.2. These are the Council of Ministers, European Commission, European Parliament and European Court of Justice. Other institutions include the Committee of Permanent Representatives and Economic and Social Committee. The European Council, formerly recognised by the Single European Act 1986, consists of government heads of state, assisted by their foreign ministers, together with the President of the European Commission (Roney 1998). It meets twice yearly to discuss major political issues and policies and the decisions of each meeting are reported to the European Parliament.

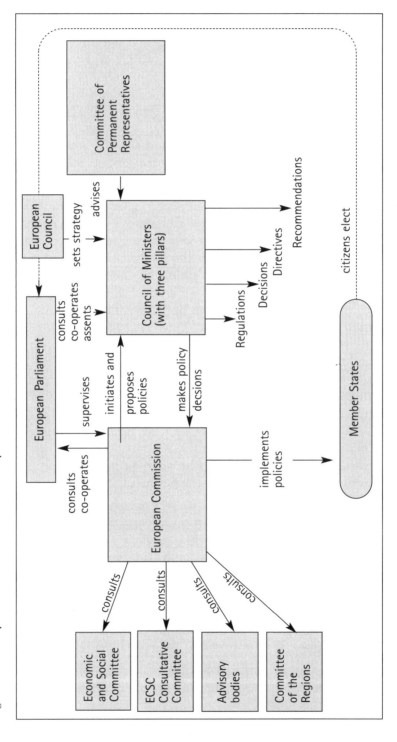

*Figure 3.2* The political institutions of the European Union

## Council of Ministers

The Council of Ministers meets in Brussels and is made up of representatives of governments of member states. Each government normally sends one minister. Composition of the Council varies with the subjects being discussed. The foreign minister is regarded as a main representative but ministers of agriculture, transport, economic and financial affairs, social affairs, industry and the environment also meet for specialised Council meetings. Presidency of the Council rotates among member governments at six-monthly intervals. When decisions are taken by majority, France, Italy, the UK and Germany have 10 votes each, Spain eight, Belgium, Greece, the Netherlands and Portugal five each, Sweden and Austria four each, Denmark, Ireland and Finland three each, and Luxembourg two. Where there is a qualified majority (QMV), it requires 62 votes out of a total of 87. All other decisions are taken unanimously.

## European Commission

The Commission, which is based at Brussels, is the EU's executive body. It consists of 20 members, appointed by agreement between the member governments, for a four-year period. Currently there are two commissioners from each of France, Italy, Spain, the UK and Germany, with one from each of the remaining 10 countries. Members of the Commission must remain independent of governments and the Council of Ministers. The Council cannot remove members but Parliament can pass a motion of censure compelling the Commission to resign as a body. After a controversial report claiming lax management at the highest levels, all Commissioners resigned in March 1999. The European Union Treaties assign a wide range of tasks to the Commission, whose role is to act as guardian of the Treaties, serve as the executive arm of the Communities, initiate EU policy and defend Union interests in the Council of Ministers.

The Commission has to ensure that provisions of the Treaties and decisions of the institutions are effectively implemented. It investigates any presumed infringement of a Treaty either on its own initiative or because of complaints from governments, companies or individuals. If, after investigation, the disputed practice continues, the Commission may refer the matter to the European Court of Justice. The Court's judgement is binding. Since most EU law is directly applicable, any individual or firm can invoke EU law in a national court. This complements the supervision carried out by the Commission.

The Treaties directly invest the Commission with wide executive powers. Additionally, extra powers have been conferred on it by the Council of Ministers to secure implementation of secondary legislation. Under the Single European Act (SEA) 1986, the conferring of executive powers on the Commission is now the general rule. One set of powers is the issuing of 'decisions' and 'regulations' implementing Treaty provisions or Council acts. *Decisions* are binding in their entirety on those member states, companies or individuals to which they are directly addressed. *Regulations* are of general application, binding in their entirety and applicable to all member states, applying directly as EU laws. A second set of powers enables the Commission to apply Treaty rules to specific cases involving governments and firms, such as agriculture and the environment. Third, the Commission administers safeguard clauses in the EU Treaties allowing Treaty requirements to be waived in certain circumstances. Another responsibility of the Commission is to administer appropriations for the Union's expenditure and its four major funds:

• the European Social Fund

• the European Agricultural Guidance and Guarantee Fund

• the European Regional Development Fund

• the European Cohesion Fund.

Effective working arrangements between the Council and European Commission are essential for formulating and implementing EU policy. The most commonly used procedure, in dealings between the institutions, is laid down in the Treaty of Rome. Once a proposal is lodged, dialogue begins among ministers in the Council, who put their national points of view, and the Commission. The Commission draws up the proposal that the Council is to discuss. The Council can adopt the Commission's proposal as it stands by a majority; it can depart from the proposal if there is unanimity; or it may fail to come to a decision. The tendency to use majority voting in the Council was reinforced by the SEA 1986, and later Maastricht, which has substantially extended the Council's scope for taking majority or QMV decisions, particularly regarding the internal market.

**European Parliament**
The Parliament is located at Strasbourg. In 1999, it had 626 members (MEPs): Germany 99; France, Italy and the UK 87; Spain 64; the Netherlands 31; Belgium, Greece and Portugal 25; Sweden 22; Austria 21; Denmark and Finland 16; Ireland 15; and Luxembourg six. MEPs form political groupings rather than national ones. Before the Euro-election in June 1999, the centre-left had a majority in the Parliament with 214 Socialists, 42 Liberal Democrats, 34 United Left and allies and 27 Greens. The centre-right consisted of 202 European People's Party (mainly Christian Democrats), 37 non-attached, 35 Union for Europe, 20 European Democratic Alliance and 15 independent Europe of the nations (European right). The evolution of support for the main political groupings in the European Parliament is shown in Table 3.2.

It is Parliament's role to keep constant watch on the Commission's activities, ensuring that it faithfully represents the Union interest. It has to be ready to call it to order at any time if the Commission gives the impression of yielding to the lobbying of member governments. Parliament normally sits for one week a month, except in August, and for shorter periods in between to discuss special items such as the EU budget. It also has meetings set aside for parliamentary committees. It is to these bodies that members of the Commission report to give account of decisions taken by the Commission, proposals presented to the Council of Ministers, and the position adopted by the Commission towards the Council. It is questions from MEPs to the Commission, and to the Council and Conference of Foreign Ministers, which provide a much-used means of control. The

*Table 3.2* Main political groupings in the European Parliament, 1979–94

| Group | 1979 | 1981 | 1984 | 1987 | 1989 | 1994 |
|---|---|---|---|---|---|---|
| Socialists | 112 | 124 | 130 | 166 | 182 | 221 |
| European People's Party | 109 | 117 | 110 | 113 | 106 | 173 |
| European Democrats | 64 | 63 | 50 | 66 | 48 | 19 |
| United Left and allies | 44 | 48 | 41 | 48 | 42 | 31 |
| Liberal Democrats and Reformists | 40 | 38 | 31 | 46 | 44 | 52 |
| European Democratic Alliance | 22 | 22 | 29 | 29 | 19 | 26 |
| Rainbow/Greens | 11 | 12 | 20 | 20 | 23 | 25 |
| European right | – | – | 16 | 16 | 16 | 19 |
| Non-attached[a] | 10 | 10 | 7 | 14 | 38 | 31 |
| Forza Europa | – | – | – | – | 30 | 29 |

*Note*
*a* MEPs not associated with a political group.
*Source: Trade Union Information Bulletin,* (No. 3/87), Brussels Commission of the European Communities, 1987. *Times Guide to the European Elections 1994.*

European Parliament also holds urgent debates on current issues to bypass lengthy alternative procedures.

The European Parliament has the last word on 'non-compulsory' expenditure, that is, expenditure that is not the consequence of EU legislation. Its budgetary powers cover the institution's administrative costs and certain operational expenditure such as the social and regional funds. Parliament has the power to not only reallocate but also increase this expenditure, within limits. It can also propose modifications to the EU's 'compulsory' expenditure on the Common Agricultural Policy, provided it does not increase the total amount of such spending. It also has the right to reject the budget as a whole, as it has done in the past. It is the president of the Parliament who is responsible for declaring that the budget has been finally adopted, once all procedures have been completed. Parliament thus holds a strong position in the budgetary process. Dialogue between Parliament and the Council of Ministers has increasingly come into play and, where it has not been possible to resolve differences, Parliament has imposed its point of view.

Parliament, however, is not a full legislative body. Under the Treaty of Rome 1957, its involvement in the legislative process was restricted to giving its opinion on certain Commission proposals. In addition, provision was later made for optional consultation at Parliament's request, with the result that it makes its voice heard in the legislative process whenever major legislation is involved. The Single European Act 1986 did not give the Parliament all the legislative powers it wanted, but conferred a power of assent – essentially a joint decision-making power – in relation to limited areas. It also introduced a co-operation procedure applicable to qualified majority voting (QMV) decisions bearing on the internal market, social policy, economic and social cohesion and research. While the Commission remains the driving force behind the drafting of EU legislation, the co-operation procedure enables Parliament to have direct influence on decisions, even though the final word still rests with the Council of Ministers.

The European Parliament, like the UK one, performs the traditional parliamentary functions of scrutiny, representation and public debate. It enjoys limited budgetary powers and powers to delay, amend and initiate legislation but, unlike the UK Parliament, it does not sustain an executive. Nor is it elected to carry out a political mandate. It is unable to provide full democratic control over EU decision-making bodies, though it has powers to remove the commissioners of the European Commission. It did this, albeit reluctantly, in 1999, after a condemning report on the activities of some of the commissioners who resigned *en bloc*, thus causing something of a constitutional crisis in the EU.

### European Court of Justice

The European Court of Justice of the EU (ECJ) has judges appointed for six years by agreement among member governments, assisted by six advocates-general. They are charged with ensuring that implementation of Union Treaties is in accordance with the rule of law. The ECJ also gives preliminary rulings on questions referred to it by national courts. EU law, made up of the Treaties and secondary legislation based on them, is becoming more interwoven with the national law of individual member states. Its implementation is attracting more attention of national courts.

## Other EU institutions

Another important institution is the Committee of Permanent Representatives (COREPER) which prepares work for the Council of Ministers. It is made up of ambassadors to the community of member states, plus their deputies and advisers, assisted by committees of national civil servants. COREPER is useful for lobbying and provides up-to-date information on specific matters and liaises with directorates within the EU. It is involved with behind-the-scenes negotiating and horse-trading, which is the hallmark of EU decision-making (Nugent 1999). The Economic and Social Committee (ESC) is a representative body of employers, professional bodies and trade unions, generally known as the 'social partners'. Although only a consultative body, the ESC is important in acting as a pressure group, by bringing about degrees of harmonisation through 'social dialogue'. Where the policy process reaches stalemate, ESC members often continue talking. The Committee of the Regions, created by the Treaty of Maastricht, has to be consulted on regional policies, economic and social cohesion, transnational European networks, education, vocational training, public health and cultural policies. It is made up of representatives of local and regional authorities, appointed by the Council of Ministers.

## The Single European Act 1986

The SEA, passed in 1986, brought about major amendments to the Treaties of Rome, preparing the way for further developments over the next decade. In particular it:

- changed the way in which decisions were made in the Council of Ministers, replacing the need for unanimity with qualified majority voting (QMV) on all but the most important issues. QMV is where each country is allocated a number of votes in proportion to its population, and a proportion of votes is required for adopting the decision:

- increased the powers of the European Parliament, replacing its consultative status with power to amend or reject proposals by the Council when made by qualified majority

- led to comprehensive reforms of the structural funds of the Community

- created an administrative framework for European co-operation in foreign policy

- adopted 31 December 1992 as the deadline for completion of the internal market.

The Act marked a major step in the direction of economic and monetary union, and the beginnings of a process leading to greater political union.

**Treaty on European Union**

The SEA 1986 was always seen as a stage in the process leading to closer union among member states of the Community. In 1990, the Community convened two intergovernmental commissions, one on monetary union and the other on political union. The commissions culminated in a summit meeting of heads of state at Maastricht in the Netherlands, in December 1991. There the heads of state reached agreement on a range of issues forming the basis of the Treaty on European Union (TEU), which revised the Treaty of Rome. The Treaty of Maastricht identified three pillars. The first related to extending co-operation among member states on immigration, asylum, combating organised crime and drugs, and a range of law and order, policing and security issues. The second pillar covered foreign and security policy, with provisions relating to defence and protection of Europe. The third pillar related to existing treaties, especially the Treaty of Rome, which was extended and amended to include articles on European economic and monetary union. During negotiations over Maastricht, the UK found herself frequently isolated. She supported further intergovernmental co-operation, was generally hostile to closer political union and was strongly opposed to a federal state of Europe. She also opposed a single European currency and central bank, arguing that loss of economic sovereignty would lead to a loss of political sovereignty to Europe.

Apart from political and monetary union, the issue of greater social union was also discussed at Maastricht. The Treaty of Rome had no direct social objectives, although it was committed to raising living standards. In a speech in Bruges, in 1989, Jacques Delors, then President of the European Commission, argued that economic integration and social integration could not be separated. At the same time, the British Prime Minister, Margaret Thatcher, vehemently opposed any regulation of social affairs, arguing that it would undermine the competitiveness of British firms and place financial burdens on British business. All other 11 member states signed the Community Charter of Fundamental Rights for Workers, which did not have the force of law, in the form of a solemn declaration. The Community Charter enshrined the following rights and freedoms for all workers and former workers in the EU, whether employed or self-employed, except, at that time in the UK:

- freedom of movement, emphasising the right to move to other member states and take up occupations on the same terms as nationals

- employment and fair remuneration for that employment

- improved living and working conditions, emphasising the idea that completion of the internal market should be accompanied by harmonisation of social conditions

- adequate social protection

- freedom of association and collective bargaining

- vocational training, with all workers having the right to continue vocational training through their working lives

- equal treatment for men and women, extending beyond pay and giving access to jobs, education, training, career opportunities and social protection

- worker information, consultation and participation

- health and safety protection at the workplace

- protection of children and of adolescents, including a

minimum working age of 16 years old and rights to vocational training after leaving school

- retirement pensions for elderly persons providing a decent standard of living, with those not entitled to a pension having a minimum level of social protection

- measures for the disabled, especially in the fields of training and occupational and social integration and rehabilitation.

The Treaty of Maastricht marked a new stage in the process of creating an ever-closer union among the peoples of Europe. It provided for 'citizenship of Europe' to the peoples of member states and gave their citizens the right to residency anywhere in the Union and to vote in local, national and Euro-elections. The Treaty incorporated an agreement and commitment to European economic and monetary union by January 1999, although the UK and Denmark signed opt-out protocols. Provision was also made for greater political co-operation on foreign policy, policing and security issues. Further powers were given to the European Parliament. The Treaty also committed the EU to reviewing structural funds and creating a Cohesion Fund to ease transition for poorer member states to European economic and monetary union.

## Treaty of Amsterdam

At the meeting of the intergovernmental conference (IGC) at Amsterdam on 16 and 17 June 1997, leaders of the 15 EU member states adopted a new draft Treaty, the Treaty of Amsterdam (TA). Like Maastricht, the Treaty aims to facilitate continued growth and enlargement of the EU, while at the same time introducing changes aimed at increasing the effectiveness of its decision-making procedures. It also attempts to strengthen Community activity in key policy areas such as employment creation and environmental protection. An analysis of the Treaty shows that it is a series of complex amendments to the existing Treaties of Rome and Maastricht. What emerged represents the gradual movement of a Union, responding to external pressures for change. There were strong political reasons for reviewing the workings of the Treaties, partly because public support for further integration was diminishing. The IGC took the lead on three fronts:

- making Europe more relevant to its citizens

- enabling the EU to work better and preparing it for enlargement

- giving the EU greater capacity for external action.

On a more positive note, the election of a Labour government in the UK on 1 May 1997 resulted in the UK agreeing to accept the Social Chapter, thus reopening its re-incorporation into the body of the main Treaty.

The objectives of the Treaty are to:

- enhance the rights of EU citizens, placing further emphasis on the basic principles of the EU

- establish an area of free movement, security and justice

- strengthen EU policy-making in areas such as employment, social policy and the environment

- introduce changes in institutional arrangements and decision-making and simplify the ways in which the EU works, and help prepare it for enlargement

- strengthen the external policy activities of the EU.

The Treaty further develops the fundamental principles of the EU in terms of democracy and individual rights, as well as establishing a procedure to be followed in the event of 'serious and persistent' breaches by member states. The Council of Ministers is provided with powers to take action to combat discrimination based on sex, racial or ethnic origin, religion or belief, disability, age, or sexual orientation. A new chapter of the Treaty of Rome pledges to abolish all restrictions on free movement of people within five years of the adoption of the TA, although a protocol allows the UK and Ireland to retain frontier controls.

Another new chapter is added to the Treaty of Rome on employment, ensuring that promotion of high employment is one of the key objectives of the EU. Member states are expected to develop a co-ordinated strategy for employment, and the Community is given the task of encouraging this. The Council of Ministers, using QMV, may adopt incentives to encourage such co-operation. The Agreement on Social Policy, annexed to the TEU, is repealed, with the contents of that Agreement, now part of the Treaty of Amsterdam, replacing those contained in the earlier Social Chapter. This means that the provisions previously applying to only 14 member states now apply to all 15, so that the UK 'opt out' to the Social Chapter is removed. The objective of achieving sustainable economic and social progress in the EU is emphasised and a new article in the Treaty of Rome states that environmental requirements must be integrated into the definition and implementation of Community policies. When the next enlargement takes place, each member state is to be entitled to just one Commissioner, as long as modification of the weighting of votes in the Council of Ministers has been achieved.

## CITIZENSHIP

Citizenship is a difficult concept to define. According to Marshall's classic definition (1950: 28), it is:

> a status bestowed on all those who are full members of a community. All who possess the status are equal with respect to the rights and duties with which that status is endowed. There is no universal principle that determines what those rights and duties shall be, but societies in which citizenship is a developing institution create an image of an ideal citizenship against which achievement can be directed.

Marshall envisaged citizenship involving three elements: civil, political and social rights. The civil element consists of rights necessary for individual freedom, such as liberty of person, speech, thought and faith and rights to own property, conclude contracts and access justice. The institutions most associated with civil rights are the courts. The political element is the right to participate in exercising political power and is associated with Parliament and the institutions of government, from local to European level. The social element ranges from rights to basic economic welfare and security, where the institutions most closely associated with it are education and social services. For Marshall, civil rights were developed in the eighteenth century, political rights in the nineteenth century and social rights in the twentieth century.

The Commission on Citizenship (1990) sets out a number of rights, duties and obligations related to citizenship. The Commission views rights in the UK as a set of residual, individual entitlements but there is no comprehensive statement of citizenship rights, such as those found in the written constitutions of many countries. Individual freedoms are residual in that Parliament has not enacted restrictions on them, meaning that they are vulnerable to any subsequent enactment. But rights also include social rights. These are rejected by supporters of classical liberalism, because such rights undermine 'the market and the open society within which it is possible for individuals with differing ends and purposes to live together' (Commission on Citizenship 1990: 7). Supporters of social rights, in contrast, argue that these provide a 'floor' below which no one should fall.

By the same token, there is no comprehensive constitutional list of duties. However, citizens in the UK have implicit duties to respect the law, pay taxes, serve on juries and refrain from treasonable activities. Both rights and duties exist in their own ways but the relationship between them is far from simple. Further, citizenship rights or entitlements cannot exist without institutions with responsibility for giving them effect, even if in practice the exercise of citizenship – in its civil, political and social forms – is not wholly contained within that formal structure. Indeed, voluntary contribution of individual citizens to the 'common good', through participation in and the exercise of civic duty, is part of citizenship, as is encouragement of such activities by public and private institutions. Free associations of businesses, trade unions and democratic bodies represent collective rights held in common. Indeed, Pateman (1979) envisages political communities as political bodies incorporating a multiplicity of interests and associations.

If being a citizen involves belonging to a community, then the legally defined national community is the most easily recognised 'society' within which citizenship rights and duties exist. But additional citizenship rights exist for UK citizens within the EU, such as rights to live, work, travel and study within each member state. The UK is also a signatory to the European Convention on Human Rights and other international declarations and conventions. Plainly, the relationship between laws, rules, traditions and conventions is complex and terms such as 'human rights' and 'citizenship rights' overlap. But the concept of citizenship involves the perception and maintenance of agreed frameworks of laws, rules and guiding principles, rather than shared values. As Roche (1987: 376) argues, citizens are not complete strangers, as in the case of people from entirely different places and cultures, 'they are a community of fellow strangers'.

There are a number of impediments to citizenship:

- lack of knowledge about citizenship rights

- confusion over who is or is not a member of a political community, which creates problems of access to civil, political and social rights

- obstacles to participating in political power, arising out of unwillingness or inability to stand for office

- social disadvantage, such as poverty, bad housing, unemployment, sexual, racial and age discrimination, ill health and disability which prevent people from exercising their rights

- administrative complexity resulting in many eligible individuals not getting or claiming their rights.

## POLITICAL PARTIES AND ELECTIONS IN THE UK

Organised political parties seek the support of the electorate in voting for their candidates in local, national and European elections. Table 3.3 summarises the results of general elections 1945–97. It shows that it is two major parties, the

Table 3.3 Number of UK parliamentary seats, by political party, at general elections, 1945–97

Election year

| Party | 1945 | 1950 | 1951 | 1955 | 1959 | 1964 | 1966 | 1970 | Feb 1974 | Oct 1974 | 1979 | 1983 | 1987 | 1992 | 1997 |
|---|---|---|---|---|---|---|---|---|---|---|---|---|---|---|---|
| Conservative | 213 | 298 | 321 | 344 | 365 | 304 | 253 | 330 | 297 | 277 | 339 | 397 | 376 | 336 | 165 |
| Labour | 393 | 315 | 295 | 277 | 258 | 317 | 363 | 287 | 301 | 319 | 269 | 209 | 229 | 271 | 418 |
| Liberal Democrats[1] | 12 | 9 | 6 | 6 | 6 | 9 | 12 | 6 | 14 | 13 | 11 | 23 | 22 | 20 | 46 |
| Plaid Cymru | * | * | * | * | – | – | – | – | 2 | 3 | 2 | 2 | 3 | 4 | 4 |
| Scottish Nationalist | * | * | * | * | – | – | – | 1 | 7 | 11 | 2 | 2 | 3 | 3 | 6 |
| Others (G.B.) | 22 | 3 | 3 | 3 | 1 | – | 2 | 6 | 2 | – | – | – | – | – | – |
| Others (N.I.) | * | * | * | * | * | * | * | * | 12 | 12 | 12 | 17 | 17 | 17 | 18 |
| Total | 640 | 625 | 625 | 630 | 630 | 630 | 630 | 630 | 635 | 635 | 635 | 650 | 650 | 651 | 659 |

[1] Liberal merged with the Social Democrats in 1992

Sources: D. Butler and A. Sloman, *British Political Facts*, Basingstoke, Macmillan, 1980. *Kessing's Archives*, Harlow, Longman, 1983, 1987, 1992, 1997

Conservative Party and Labour Party, that have dominated the elections. Nevertheless, a number of minor parties have won parliamentary seats since the mid-1960s. Political parties have six main functions:

- a representative one, by providing choice of representatives to the electorate and representing it in the legislature

- presenting labels to the electorate and seeking electoral support for their programmes

- as agents of political recruitment

- helping formulate government policy

- mobilising people, raising levels of political awareness and persuading people to vote for them

- a communication and institutional link between government and the people.

**The Conservative Party**

Like most political parties, the Conservatives are a coalition of diverse political and social interests. King (1987: 111) claims that the party has three traditions. The first is 'a pragmatic tradition' rooted in the belief that the Party is not bound rigidly to any particular ideology. The second, by 'supporting certain key values', explains the durability of the Party's electoral success. The third is the mixture of the 'Tory' tradition of belief in a strong state 'as the basis for a durable social order with a "liberal" tradition based on free market principles'. It is arguable that the second tradition overlaps the other two, with the first being strongly associated with pragmatic 'Modern Conservatism' and the third with the ideological 'New Right'.

The ideas associated with one-nation, Modern Conservatism emerged out of the premierships of Stanley Baldwin in the inter-war years, reaching their apotheosis during the Macmillan era of the 1950s and 1960s. The fundamental goal of Modern Conservatism is to support existing political and social institutions, the distribution of power in society, and sustain stability and national unity. Social reform must be controlled and acted upon only in response to specific problems, and as a means of providing practical responses to given political situations. Its thinking is based on the assumption that society is a unity, greater than the sum of its individual parts, reflecting common purpose, national unity and respect for tradition. Modern Conservatives see hierarchy as natural, orderly and desirable, with strong commitment to the monarchy, House of Lords, established Church, and law and order. Modern Conservatism is strongly identified with belief in élite political leadership, patriotism and deference to recognised social and political authority. Modern Conservatives defend thrift, personal initiative and self-help. Individual liberty can be maintained only where the state upholds fundamental human liberties, such as owning property, spending one's income as one chooses and living without undue interference from the state. In upholding these values, the Conservative Party accepts inequality as normal and inevitable, with private property and free enterprise being the necessary conditions for personal liberty and political freedom. )

On economic matters, the Modern Conservative tradition favours market forces rather than government intervention, with private enterprise having the major role in wealth creation. By the 1940s, and until the late 1970s, the Modern Conservative Party accepted, like all other parties, an interventionist role for the state in managing the economy to ensure high levels of employment, consistent with growth and rising living standards. This form of Conservatism came to be associated with the mixed economy, though it was always ambivalent about the role of the unions in the economy. It is a revised version of Modern Conservatism that William Hague appears to be trying to resuscitate in the Party since its enormous electoral defeat in the 1997 General Election, but this is difficult because New Labour, led by Tony Blair, has captured the middle ground in UK politics.

In the 1970s, another set of ideas emerged within the Party, largely from its right wing, emphasising two themes: the primacy of markets in wealth creation and the necessity of reducing the state's role in economic and social affairs. Bell (1985) claims that this 'new Conservatism', or 'neoliberalism' associated with the New Right, is more akin to the ideas associated with the late Enoch Powell than it is to old-style Butler-Macmillan Conservatism. It repudiates Keynesian interventionist policies and it was in the ascendant in Conservative governments during the 1980s and 1990s. Ideas of the New Right developed among Conservatives when the party was in opposition after 1974, out of which distinctive radical policies emerged, with the underlying aims of making the economy competitive, facilitating growth and combating the 'welfare dependency' culture. The major economic policy objective of government was to squeeze inflation out of the economy and change the balance of the mixed economy.

This approach came to the fore when Margaret Thatcher was Prime Minister and has been described as supporting a 'free economy' and a 'strong state'. Gamble (1988) identifies two major strands: a liberal tendency arguing for a freer, more open, and competitive economy, and a social authoritarian tendency more interested in restoring social and political authority throughout society. The liberal tendency embraces the ideas of monetarists, supply-side economists and supporters of privatisation. The economic policies included:

- restricting money supply targets to reduce inflation

- floating exchange rates

- limiting government spending

- reducing income tax to increase economic incentives

- abolishing union immunities to weaken unions and free the labour market

- privatising public industries.

The social authoritarian tendency argues that the state must be strong to: unwind the coils of social democracy; police the market order; make the economy more productive; and uphold political authority. Public spending must be cut, taxes lowered and public assets privatised to restore a free market economy. As Scruton (1980: 45) indicates, the social authoritarian strand is collectivist rather than individualist and emphasises patriotism, nationalism, political allegiance and the concept of family. 'Society exists through authority, and the recognition of this authority requires the allegiance to a bond that is in the manner of the family tie.'

## The Labour Party

The Labour Party, born out of a trade union–working class alliance in 1900, underwent significant changes in its ideas and policies during the 1980s and 1990s. After four successive General Election defeats (in 1979, 1983, 1987 and 1992) the Party and its leadership were forced to review what it stood for and what its policies and strategies should be. Unlike the Conservatives, the Labour Party does not claim to be non-ideological. Webster (1981: 1) argues that there are three sets of ideas in the Party that have influenced its history: ultra-democracy, British Trotskyism and social democracy. He sees the guiding spirit of ultra-democracy being the right of people to make decisions for themselves, 'not only in the area of collective decision-making but also that of private behaviour, so that the decriminalization of homosexuality and abortion are part of the same trend'.

The essence of British Trotskyism, which revived among sections of the Party in the late 1970s and early 1980s, is the doctrine of conflict: struggle and violence are wholeheartedly accepted. This led to Trotskyites supporting a British workers' revolution and pressing for reforms which they did not believe to be attainable, as part of a 'politics of exposure' of capitalism. Revival of Trotskyism in Britain, and growth of Trotskyist entryism into the Party at that time, was traceable to the growth after the 1960s of varieties of western Marxism hostile to orthodox communism in the Soviet bloc, prior to its collapse in 1989.

The third strand of Labour Party ideology – that of social democracy – came to the fore during the late 1980s and 1990s, buttressed by the break-up of orthodox Marxism in eastern Europe. The central idea of social democracy in the late 1980s, sometimes referred to as democratic socialism, was equality. The aim was to create equality of wealth, income and opportunity; equality of esteem, in the sense of the repudiation of class, caste or status; and, crucially, equality of political rights and political power. Social democracy of this sort was also committed to the mixed economy and representative democracy. After its defeat in the 1987 General Election, the Labour Party (1988: 1ff) redefined its democratic socialist aims and values, stating that it wanted a state where the collective contribution of the community was used for the advance of individual freedom, 'real freedom and real chances'.

With a fourth successive General Election defeat in 1992, and the death of its newly elected Leader, John Smith, in 1993, Tony Blair, a 41-year-old barrister and Labour MP since 1983, was elected as Party Leader by an overwhelming majority of constituency Party and trade union members. In his first speech as Leader to the Party's Conference in autumn 1994, he declared, to the surprise of many delegates, his intention of getting the Party to abandon its historic commitment to Clause IV of the Party constitution. Clause IV was pledged to the 'common ownership' of the means of production, distribution and exchange. The revised clause four of 'new' Labour sets out four principles upon which 'Labour seeks the trust of the people to govern' (Labour Party 1995: 5 and 6). The first declares that Labour is a democratic socialist party, seeking to use 'our common endeavour' to create 'a community in which power, wealth and opportunity are in the hands of the many not the few', where 'the rights we enjoy reflect the duties we owe, and where we live together, freely, in a spirit of solidarity, tolerance and respect'.

The second principle of new Labour states that, to these ends, the Party has four aims: 'a dynamic economy', 'a just society', 'an open democracy' and 'a healthy environment'. A dynamic economy is one serving the public interest, where the enterprise of the market joins with the forces of partnership and co-operation to produce the wealth that the nation needs and the opportunity for 'all to work and prosper'. It is also one 'where those undertakings essential to the common good are either owned by the public or accountable to them'. A just society 'provides security against fear' and 'justice at work', promotes 'equality of opportunity' and 'delivers people from the tyranny of poverty, prejudice and the abuse of power'. An open democracy is where the people hold government accountable, communities take key decisions affecting their own interests and human rights are guaranteed. A healthy environment, in turn, is one held in trust for future generations. The third and fourth principles in new Labour's revised constitution state that:

> Labour is committed to the defence and security of the British people, and to co-operating in European institutions, the United Nations, the Commonwealth and other international bodies to secure peace, freedom, democracy, economic security and environmental protection for all.

> Labour will work in pursuit of these aims with trade unions, co-operative societies and other affiliated organisations and also with consumer groups and other representative bodies.

In examining the economy, Labour insists that in the modern world, with its fierce competition for resources and trade, demands made on the environment must be balanced by co-ordinated responses to common problems. To promote economic success and efficiency, investment in research, education and training depend on a positive lead by government. Clear support of the mixed economy is endorsed, incorporating a thriving private sector and high-quality public services, with protection for consumers too. Competition must be fair and the test of the market is to achieve greater freedom of choice for individual consumers.

Labour Party policies were reviewed in the light not only of the new Clause IV and its underpinning principles, but also the findings of the Commission of Social Justice, published in 1994, resulting in what Tony Blair (1998) refers to as the 'third way'. This is what Giddens (1998) describes as an attempt to transcend both old style 'social democracy' and 'neoliberalism'. The Commission set up in 1992 by the then leader of the Labour Party, John Smith, under the chairmanship of Sir John Borrie, inquired into social and economic reform and, in particular, the relationship between social justice and political goals such as national prosperity and economic competitiveness. The propositions running through the Commission's policy proposals were taken up by the Party in its desire to make its political programmes relevant to the needs of people in the twenty-first century. Its four central propositions were (Borrie 1994: 1f):

- the need to transform the welfare state from a safety net in times of trouble to a springboard for economic opportunity

- to improve access to education and training radically, and invest in the talent of people

- to promote real choice across the life-cycle for men and women in the balance of employment, family, education, leisure and retirement

- to reconstruct the social wealth of the country to provide a dependable social environment in which people can lead their lives.

Following Borrie, a number of debates took place within the Party, covering: the economy; industry; transport; health; education; the UK constitution; local government; crime; defence; employment; social security; national heritage; and Europe. The collective outcomes of these debates provided the basis for Labour's manifesto in the 1997 General Election. The debate on economic policy included determining a strategy for growth, macroeconomic policy and relations with the Bank of England. There were also proposals about tackling unemployment, the minimum wage, poverty in old age, competition policy, partnership between the public and private sectors, and training policy. Policy for industry focused on removing tax obstacles to long-term corporate investment and, in transport, developing an integrated transport system. In the health service, the central concerns were decommercialising the NHS, abolishing GP fundholding and making trusts more accountable to the community. Three issues dominated education policy: the under-fives; raising educational standards; and financing higher education.

On constitutional matters, proposals for devolution were reviewed and, in local government, Labour said it would abolish compulsory competitive tendering. To fight crime,

Labour wanted local authority–police partnership schemes. There was a promise of a full defence review by Labour and, on employment issues, Labour said it would legislate for union recognition. Discussion on social security included the future of the basic pension, and taxation of child benefit. The feasibility of creating a self-financing national electronic superhighway, linking hospitals, libraries, citizens' advice bureaux, schools, businesses and homes, was the major task of the National Heritage policy commission. And, on Europe, an intergovernmental conference looked at the powers of the Council of Ministers, the veto, EU defence policy, and expanding the Union.

## The Liberal Democrats

The roots of the old Liberal Party can be traced back to the early nineteenth century and the formation of the Birmingham Liberal Alliance in 1865 that led to the establishment of the National Liberal Federation in 1877. The Liberal Party reached its peak of power in the early twentieth century but was a spent force after 1922, due to the emergence of the Labour Party. The SDP, in contrast, was formed in only 1981, with the initial support of 14 former members of the Parliamentary Labour Party, together with active backing by several members of past Labour governments. Although a formal electoral alliance was forged between the Liberals and SDP at the 1987 general election, it subsequently broke down, largely over the issue of the proposed merger between them.

The Liberal Democrats promptly set out, in a Green Paper published in 1989, to elaborate what they saw as their distinctive political philosophy and values, which have not changed substantially in the intervening period. The paper developed out of the party's constitution and emphasised a fair, free and open society, seeking to balance the values of liberty, equality and community, and in which no one would be enslaved by poverty, ignorance or conformity. The Green Paper drew its inspiration from the traditions of both Liberals and Social Democrats, with their different but parallel political paths. The intellectual and political roots of the Liberal Democrats go back through the great reforming governments of 1945–51 and 1905–14, to the popular radicals of the nineteenth century who fought for the rights of the common people, against privilege and oppression. The Liberal Democrats claim that 'we stand for three basic values – liberty, equality and community' (Social and Liberal Democrats 1989: 17).

Liberal Democrats are concerned with managing change in society, including patterns of production, social and demographic change, cultural and political change and the international economy. They argue that their policies are most likely to realise the full potential of the new order taking shape around us. They abhor the neo-liberalism of the 1980s and 1990s and their impacts on people and society, arguing that the UK needs a different political vision, based on different values. The good society enables all to have freedoms for developing their potential, learning from their mistakes, realising their capabilities and recognising their responsibilities to their communities. Liberal Democrats draw two crucial implications from their view of human nature. One is that there is no simple litmus test for determining policy; the other is that Liberal Democrats are not Utopians. They have three main commitments:

- an open, tolerant, diverse and pluralistic society, with protection for minorities where power is dispersed

- community power, as well as individual power

- equal citizenship.

Liberal Democrats argue that the extremes of left and right concentrate on power to remodel society from top down, in accordance with predetermined ideals. In their view, the foundations of British liberties have always been fragile, while the basic principles of pluralist democracy have never been adequately protected. Accordingly, there is need to secure a new constitutional settlement, embracing explicit protections of basic human rights, including devolution, reform of Parliament, and electoral reform. Linked with this, Liberal Democrats emphasise the importance of community as a buffer between the individual and the state. They condemn short-term economic decision-making in the UK. Free-market theory fails to recognise that the market is effective only when information flows between producers and consumers and, where the market fails, public power must intervene. Three critical areas demanding public intervention are environmental protection, long-term investment, and urban regeneration.

Liberal Democrats would like to facilitate a sustainable economy developing recycling, conservation and pollution control and smaller, energy-efficient products, as well as investing in developing human capital. Quality of life also matters. The three essential tasks for government are: to identify those public goods that the common interest demands, such as education, effective policing and crime prevention; efficient public services; and high standards for the private and voluntary sectors, monitored by government.

Central to Liberal Democrat beliefs is a positive view of freedom, with the state ensuring that all have access to what life offers. The state should make sure that all have a decent level of income, enabling everyone to participate in society and not to feel excluded. The state must also make opportunities widely available for personal development, enabling people to break free of the limiting conditions of their circumstances. They stand for social and economic citizenship, the right to participate in decision-making and holding those in power to account in the workplace, schools and political institutions. Liberal Democrats, therefore, want legislative rights to participation in strategic decisions, profit-sharing and consultation and information in the workplace. Finally, Liberal Democrats are committed to working closely with other countries, with this co-operation finding its closest expression in Europe. They believe that the EU should achieve closer political union with democratic institutions accountable to the EU's citizens.

### Other parties

The other political parties are a heterogeneous group of political interests and ideologies, including nationalist parties, Northern Ireland parties and the Green Party. Scotland and

Wales both have nationalist parties, the Scottish Nationalist Party (SNP) and Plaid Cymru, respectively Compared with the SNP, Plaid Cymru has always been more radical and it lays stress on Welsh cultural and linguistic roots as a basis for Welsh independence. Plaid Cymru has been unsuccessful in raising its share of the vote in Wales and has remained a reservoir of protest votes, drawing on sentiments of Welsh nationalism and local frustration with English domination of the political agenda. However, this may change with the election of the first Welsh Assembly, and Scottish Parliament, in 1999.

Party differentiation in Northern Ireland is based not on class and economic interests, as in the rest of the UK, but on religious and sectarian differences. Even the religious parties are sectarian. Among protestant groupings, there are the Official Unionist Party and the Democratic Unionist Party. Catholic groups include the Social and Democratic Labour Party, Catholic Workers' Party and *Sinn Fein*, which is the political wing of the revolutionary Provisional Irish Republican Army that maintains close links with radical Irish nationalists in the Republic of Ireland. The Irish nationalists' basic aim is political union with the republic, while protestants in Northern Ireland are nationalists wishing to remain within the UK. To what extent the 'Good Friday' agreement of 1998 has reconciled nationalist and loyalist causes remains uncertain.

### Elections
Some individuals join political parties, some participate in them and a few seek public office. Most adults over the age of 18 have the right to vote in local, national, regional and European elections, though participation rates vary. About three-quarters of the electorate turn out at general elections but only about a third in local and European elections. There is no simple explanation of why people vote as they do. Nevertheless, there has always been a relationship between voters' social characteristics, including class, age, gender, occupation, religion and ethnic group, and party choice. Traditionally, there has been a tendency for the middle-class, professional, higher-income groups to vote Conservative and

the working class to support Labour. Most women have tended to vote Conservative, while ethnic minorities generally favour Labour. Votes for the Liberal Democrat and nationalist parties have tended to come from across class, occupational and ethnic divisions but, with the emergence of New Labour as a political force in the mid-1990s, a further realignment of voting appears to be taking place in British politics.

A number of studies suggest that voters have been increasingly reluctant to vote for the two major parties in recent elections and that people's occupational class provides an increasingly poor guide to their party choice when voting. It is generally agreed that between 1945 and 1964 voting preferences had two stable elements. First, people identified with and voted for one of the two major parties. Second, white-collar households tended to vote Conservative, and households headed by manual workers Labour. Since then, it is argued, a dealignment in voting has occurred. One form is 'partisan' dealignment, the other is 'class' dealignment. Partisan dealignment refers to the declining probability that individuals will remain loyal to a single political party in successive elections. Three kinds of evidence are said to illustrate the decline of political partisanship. The first is that since 1970 voters have steadily deserted the two main political parties in general elections. Between 1950 and 1970, over 90 per cent of the electorate chose either the Conservative or Labour Parties. In the following elections, including that of 1997, the two-party share of the poll fell to around 75 per cent. Since 1970, various other parties, such as nationalists in Wales, Scotland and Northern Ireland and the Liberal Democrats have increased their electoral support at the expense of the Conservatives and Labour.

Second, while some of the increased support for third parties could have come from people who might otherwise have abstained, most was taken from the two major parties. But there is little evidence of individuals becoming third-party partisans. For example, although votes for nationalist parties increased proportionally in the mid-1970s, they fell away in the 1980s, rising again in the early 1990s. Similarly, there is little evidence that people became Liberal Democrat partisans or their allies. Liberal supporters appear to be fickle voters, not necessarily supporting the party at consecutive elections. According to Sarlvik and Crewe (1983), during the 1960s and 1970s only 30 per cent of those shifting their votes from a major party to the Liberals at one election voted Liberal at the next election. More recently, increased support for the Liberal Democrats in the 1980s and 1990s meant that a lot of people shifted votes between elections, even if the degree of volatility did not seem to have increased substantially.

A third factor suggesting partisan dealignment is the weakening of party attachment. One explanation is disillusionment with the two main parties because of their failures in government. Another is that voters may be becoming more instrumental politically, choosing between parties on a 'what's in it for me?' basis. Alternatively, it may be that voters are more concerned with political issues appearing to lend themselves to partisan solutions. Sarlvik and Crewe, for example, argued that in the 1980s the Labour Party increasingly offered policies to the electorate of which its own supporters disapproved, implying that Labour was unpopular because of its traditional class politics. These included supporting unions, nationalisation and expanding the welfare state. Such policies, they claimed, had a diminishing appeal to the electorate. New Labour's success, capturing almost 45 per cent of the popular vote, in the 1997 General election, suggests that it has now adopted policies which have a much wider appeal than just that of traditional, working-class and public-sector professional workers.

Class dealignment refers to the declining probability that individuals vote for the party most closely associated with their social class and occupational status. Until the mid-1960s, there were strong correlations between occupational class and voting behaviour. Since then, two developments appear to have occurred. First, between 1964 and 1974, there was an increase in white-collar and professional support for the Labour Party, support which had traditionally gone to the Conservatives, and which was drawn especially from people working in the public sector. Second, since 1974, there has been a steady decline in the number of blue-collar manual workers, especially skilled ones, voting Labour, which benefited the Conservatives and Liberal Democrats.

Some writers deny that class dealignment is happening, while accepting that some degree of partisan dealignment is taking place. They argue that a false impression is given because most studies use inappropriate class categories. Heath and his colleagues (1985: 39) suggested that the class dealignment thesis greatly exaggerated degrees of change in voting behaviour. They argued that it was change in the class structure and political change that were the important factors. Their conclusion was that 'whether for better or worse, Britain is still divided by class'. At the same time, 'the shape of the class structure has changed, with important implications for Labour'. They contended that Labour's decline in the 1980s related to both political and social sources of change. More recent research by Heath and Savage (1994) indicates that although there is a marginal tendency among the professional and managerial groups to identify with the Conservatives, the group is heterogeneous. Indeed, in the period 1983 to 1990 most occupations within this group lacked distinct political leanings. As the middle classes grow in size, this may undermine Heath's earlier thesis.

## PRESSURE GROUPS

In modern society, formal participation in politics, beyond voting in elections, is normally channelled through political groups. Where individuals or organisations become involved politically, they join and participate in organised groups reflecting their political interests and opinions. Organised political groups are of two kinds, political parties and pressure groups, and their memberships can overlap.

### Nature and scope
Parties seek to influence policy decisions directly by getting their leading members into formal positions of political authority in the European Parliament, House of Commons,

devolved assemblies or local government. Parties try to win political control to use political power. What distinguishes pressure groups from parties is that they seek to influence policy decisions, not get their representatives into positions of formal political authority. Some pressure groups, such as Shelter, Age Concern or the Ramblers' Association, are politically independent; others have links with parties or even a single political party and help them fight elections, such as some trade unions and the Trades Union Congress. While it is relatively easy to distinguish between the Conservative Party and the National Union of Teachers (NUT), for example, it is less easy to distinguish between minor parties and pressure groups. In the first case, the Conservatives are a broad-based national political party that fights elections and the NUT is a narrowly based teachers' union which, among its other functions, acts as a pressure group for schoolteachers. The political role of Plaid Cymru, on the other hand, is more akin to that of a pressure group than political party. It is unlikely to win enough parliamentary seats to form a government, thus making it in effect an interest-centred pressure group rather than a full-blown party. It seeks to influence policy rather than determine it.

Both parties and pressure groups are concerned with power, and may themselves be powerful. The power of parties depends on electoral success and support at the ballot box; the power of pressure groups depends on their membership base, resources, appeal and effectiveness. Since parties need to have relatively wide appeal to win votes for their candidates, their political programmes tend to be broadly based. Pressure groups have much narrower political objectives, sometimes based on a single issue, such as the Society for the Protection of the Unborn Child or Abortion Law Reform Society. These lead to differences in organisation between parties and pressure groups. Because parties contest elections, they are organised nationally and locally. Many pressure groups may have branches locally but tend to be more active nationally, except when dealing with local campaigns such as planning and development issues.

Pressure groups may be defined as 'social aggregates with some level of cohesion and shared aims which attempt to influence the political decision-making process' (Ball and Millard 1986: 33). Various typologies include: 'cause' and 'economic' groups; 'promotional' and 'protectional' groups; and 'interest' and 'attitude' groups. Where the interest and attitude group dichotomy is used, the term 'interest group' is commonly applied to organisations created because of their members' common socio-economic goals. Members of employers' organisations such as the Engineering Employers Federation, for example, combine to protect the common interests of federated engineering firms, which may be large or small, multi-plant or single-plant, and geographically concentrated or geographically spread companies. Managers representing them may be young or middle-aged, professionally qualified or not, and religious or agnostic. What brings these enterprises and corporate representatives together is their common commercial interest as organisations, not the organisational characteristics or personal aspirations of their managers. Bodies such as the Confederation of British Industry or the Institute of Directors perform similar functions, but operate largely at central level or through European-wide associations such as the Union of Industrial and Employers' Confederations of Europe.

Attitude groups are based on the commonly held beliefs and values of their members. The motivating force behind joining the Royal Society for the Protection of Birds is not economic self-interest but concern for the protection and well-being of birds. Similarly, members of Age Concern share a compassion for, and commitment to, the elderly. Such groups contain men and women, professional people and non-professionals, atheists and religious people. What draws them together are the attitudes they share as individuals and their wish to organise collectively to protect the rights of the interests they represent.

### Activities and power

In attempting to influence government decisions, pressure groups try to gain access to those taking decisions and, to do so, they lobby key individuals at different levels of power.

They try to influence the prime minister, cabinet, ministers, government, local councillors or the European Parliament. They also seek to influence public opinion. The methods and levels each pressure group uses to communicate its opinions and demands vary widely, according to its power and circumstances. The most powerful pressure groups have almost instant access to the important parts of the political system, but weak ones have to improvise to make their views heard.

Some powerful groups have well-established relations with government, on a permanent or semi-permanent basis, sometimes channelled through advisory or standing committees, staffed by civil servants and pressure-group representatives. The National Farmers Union, for example, has close links with the Ministry of Agriculture and Food and ministers. Relatively few pressure groups have the power to gain access to policy-making machinery but use their representatives to pursue their objectives. If pressure groups cannot influence the main decision makers directly, they are forced to lobby MPs, members in the Lords, or MEPs. If pressure groups cannot influence Parliament, or if parliamentary supporters do not carry enough political weight, they are forced to operate outside Parliament. They may try to influence political parties, for example, by building up support for their policies within them. The Campaign for Nuclear Disarmament (CND) used this approach. For many years its main policy was unilateral nuclear disarmament and CND supporters tried to induce both the Liberal Party and Labour Party to accept non-nuclear defence policies. They were unsuccessful with the Liberals but were eventually successful with the Labour Party. However, Labour moved away from a policy of unilateral nuclear disarmament to a more complex multilateral position, thus requiring CND to adapt its political strategy in response.

Where it is not possible for pressure groups to influence national parties, even outside Parliament, or if they are unsuccessful in doing so, they are forced to use the mass media and influence public opinion. The objective of campaigning at local level is to try to create shifts in public opinion in the hope that those in political power, and with influence, respond to these pressures. Tactics used include rallies, marches, petitions and media campaigns to get the message across. These can lead to media coverage, television documentaries and other in-depth analyses, thus putting pressure on government to modify their policy. An example in recent years has been concern for the environment. Various attitudinal environmental pressure groups, such as Friends of the Earth and Greenpeace, have mounted strong grass-roots campaigns to influence public opinion and government policies on lead-free petrol and organic farming.

Pressure groups vary widely in their power bases, which affects the ways in which they operate. Sometimes the more visible a pressure group the less its influence, and the more likely it is to operate at media and grass-roots levels. The most powerful groups rarely use such tactics. The most important determinant of pressure-group power is its position in the economic system and the sanctions it has to back its demands. These may be positive, such as co-operating with the authorities, or negative, including withdrawal of financial resources or taking punitive actions against those in power. Large employer pressure groups, such as those representing banks, finance and insurance, are crucial to the economy and most governments listen to their views with some degree of deference. Unions had a great deal of power in the 1970s but were rarely consulted or listened to during the 1980s and 1990s, since governments excluded them from the policy process.

Interest groups are generally more powerful than attitude groups, since the latter normally lack effective economic sanctions. Powerful pressure groups have close relations with the machinery of government, including the Association of Chief Police Officers, Police Federations, Law Society, Bar Council and British Medical Association. All these bodies have professional expertise which governments usually need to draw upon. Thus, in general, these and similar pressure groups have good working relations with government rather than antagonistic ones.

The financial resources and leadership of pressure groups are also important determinants of group power and influence, since they affect the types of campaigns and activities that pressure groups pursue. Even the size of the membership is a secondary factor, although representativeness and proportion of potential members in the group are important factors. The National Farmers Union (NFU), for example, represents most farmers, hence government channels all its agricultural communications through that body. If there were several farmers' unions, each would be much weaker than the NFU is collectively. Public support is particularly important for attitude groups, since they have few sanctions to use against the authorities. Powerful groups, with aims generally acceptable to the political system, such as the business community, find it easier to influence policy decisions than those whose views clash with dominant opinion.

## CONCLUSION

Organisations operate in a political environment, whether at local, national or European levels, and all organisations producing goods and services, in either the market place or the public services, are affected by political decisions. Such decisions, whether made by politicians, governments or EU institutions, and the laws underpinning them, impact on the ways in which organisations are managed. The sorts of areas affected include the ways in which organisations produce their goods or services, how they market them, how they deal with their competitors, how they recruit and manage their staff, how they deal with their customers, their health and safety responsibilities and so on. At one level, those responsible for running organisations react to some political initiatives affecting the interests of their organisations on *ad hoc* bases. At another level, they have to be proactive in trying to influence political decisions and public policies before they are taken. This is done through engaging in 'pressure-group' politics and putting pressure on politicians and public bodies locally, in Parliament and the European Parliament, before the political authorities have taken their decisions. The processes used include lobbying, campaigning with other organisations, and joining and participating in organised pressure or interest groups. Business, public and voluntary organisations, unlike citizens, do not vote in local, national or Euro elections. But who has political power, the decisions of politicians, the law and the economic and social policies of governments affect them, directly or indirectly. Organisations need to respond to these accordingly.

# 4 Social structure

**Sylvia Horton**

The social context within which organisations exist, as with economic and political contexts, imposes constraints upon them. It also provides opportunities. How organisations respond to these depend upon their strategic management skills. The social context cannot be separated, in reality, from the other contexts, as they are all inextricably linked, but for analytical purposes a number of components or sub-systems making up the social structure of a society can be identified. At the end of this chapter readers should be able to understand and explain:

- how the external environment impacts on private, public and voluntary organisations
- the changing social structure and its implications for organisations and their stakeholders.

In addition they should be able to:

- report on projected demographic and social changes and their relevance for organisations.

See also the Professional Standards Index (page 345).

## DEMOGRAPHY

Demography is the statistical study of populations. In outline it is concerned with the size, distribution and composition of the population of a country, region, area or world-wide. Data are obtained through census returns, records of births, deaths, marriages, divorces, immigration and emigration. Demography charts changes and trends in population and seeks explanations and causes. The demographic structure of a country clearly has implications for its economy. The size and age structure of the population, for example, affects the actual and potential availability of labour and demand for goods and services. It also affects public policy issues, such as health provision, education, and social services. Governments at both national and local levels need projections of population on which to base their planning.

## The elements of demography

The size of a population is a dynamic social variable as it changes over time. Its composition and distribution also change as people are born, die, move from one area to another, enter or leave the country. Because of the difficulty of keeping track of these changes, the size of a population, at any one point in time, is an approximation. Demographic data are usually historic and based on samples, extrapolated to provide whole population statistics. Because of this, it is estimated that the margin of error is plus or minus 4 per cent. In accounting for population changes, demographers identify the immediate causes as the relationship between births, deaths and immigration or fertility, mortality and migratory patterns. Changes in the total population of a country, therefore, consist of total births minus total deaths, while migratory changes consist of the number of immigrants minus total emigrants. Where both components cause a positive change or one causes a positive change while the other remains stable, total population rises. Where both components cause a negative change or one causes a negative change and the other remains stable, then total population falls. Where natural change in both components remains the same, or a change in one is offset by a change in the other, then total population tends to stabilise.

The composition of a population can be analysed in a number of ways. These include by sex, age, marital status, ethnicity, religion, education, class, occupation and geography. Each of these is related to births and deaths and to those emigrating or immigrating over time. Other things being equal, populations with large numbers of young people in the reproductive years have a high crude birth rate. This measures the number of live births per thousand of the population per year. Conversely, populations with a high percentage of elderly have a high crude death rate. Given similar levels of technology, those societies with large numbers of the population between 16 and 65 have economic advantages in terms of productive human resources or potential working population.

In addition to absolute numbers, demographers use relative numbers. These include demographic ratios, proportions, percentages and rates of statistical change. Relative numbers contribute to understanding demographic facts and changes, because they summarise data, and relationships between data. In the UK, for example, there were 29.9 million females in 1997 and 28.8 million males. The sex ratio is the number of females divided by the number of males. Hence the UK sex ratio in 1997 was 1.4:1 females to males. Similarly, proportions are ratios showing one part of a population relative to the whole of it. Their value always falls between zero and one. In 1997 the proportion of females to males in the UK was 0.51, ie 51 per cent of the population was female and 49 per cent male. Demographic ratios are calculated in the same way as other ratios but they usually express what has happened over a period of time, normally one year. Two of the most commonly used ratios are crude birth rates and crude death rates. With 730,000 live births in 1997 among the 58.8 million population, the crude birth rate was 12.4 per thousand of the population. Similarly, with 639,000 deaths in 1997, the crude death rate was 10.9 per thousand of the population. And with 306,000 male deaths, the ratio was 10.6 per thousand males, while for women with 332,000 deaths the ratio was 11.1 per thousand. The major weakness of crude demographic rates, measuring birth and death rates, is that they do not take into account the age distribution of the population being described (Farnham 1990).

## Population structure and demographic change in the United Kingdom

The population of the UK was 58.8 million in 1996, having grown from 38 million in 1901, as shown in Table 4.1. Although population has increased by more than 50 per cent since 1900, the rate of change has varied. In the first four decades, average growth was 5 per cent every 10 years. Between 1941 and 1951, the increase was 11 per cent, followed by increases averaging 5.5 per cent each decade

*Table 4.1*   Population change – United Kingdom

Average annual change (thousands)

| | Population at start of period | Live births | Deaths | Net natural change | Net migration and other | Overall change |
|---|---|---|---|---|---|---|
| *Census enumerated* | | | | | | |
| 1901–1911 | 38,237 | 1,091 | 624 | 467 | −82 | 385 |
| 1911–1921 | 42,082 | 975 | 689 | 286 | −92 | 194 |
| 1921–1931 | 44,027 | 824 | 555 | 268 | −67 | 201 |
| 1931–1951 | 46,038 | 785 | 598 | 188 | 25 | 213 |
| *Mid-year estimates* | | | | | | |
| 1951–1961 | 50,287 | 839 | 593 | 246 | 6 | 252 |
| 1961–1971 | 52,807 | 963 | 639 | 324 | −12 | 312 |
| 1971–1981 | 55,928 | 736 | 666 | 69 | −27 | 42 |
| 1981–1991 | 56,352 | 757 | 655 | 103 | 43 | 146 |
| 1991–1997 | 57,808 | 754 | 640 | 113 | 87 | 200 |
| *Mid-year projections*[1] | | | | | | |
| 1997–2001 | 59,009 | 719 | 634 | 85 | 69 | 154 |
| 2001–2011 | 59,618 | 690 | 624 | 66 | 65 | 131 |
| 2011–2021 | 60,929 | 694 | 628 | 66 | 65 | 131 |

[1] 1996-based projections
*Source: Social Trends 29,* 1999

between 1951 and 1971. Thereafter, growth rates continued to fall, so much so that an increase equivalent to that of 1941–1951 (ie 11 per cent or so) has only been achieved over the last 35 years. It is projected that population will grow to 62.2 million in 2021 and continue growing until 2030, when deaths will exceed births and the population is expected to fall. Explanations of these trends vary. In the first half of the century, high growth was largely due to a fall in the death rate because of higher standards of living and better health care. In addition to rises in life expectancy, there was also a significant drop in child mortality rates. The high birth rate after the Second World War caused significant growth up to 1951. Large influxes of immigrants between 1951 and 1971, coupled with a second baby boom in the 1960s, as babies born in the 1940s reached child-bearing age, caused the growth between 1951 and 1971. The 1960s, however, heralded widespread use of contraception and the emergence of the feminist

Table 4.2 Population: by age United Kingdom

%

| | Under 16 | 16–24 | 25–34 | 35–44 | 45–54 | 55–64 | 65–74 | 75 and over | All ages (= 100%) (millions) |
|---|---|---|---|---|---|---|---|---|---|
| *Mid-year estimates* | | | | | | | | | |
| 1961 | 25 | 12 | 13 | 14 | 14 | 12 | 8 | 4 | 52.8 |
| 1971 | 25 | 13 | 12 | 12 | 12 | 12 | 9 | 5 | 55.9 |
| 1981 | 22 | 14 | 14 | 12 | 11 | 11 | 9 | 6 | 56.4 |
| 1991 | 20 | 13 | 16 | 14 | 11 | 10 | 9 | 7 | 57.8 |
| 1997 | 21 | 11 | 16 | 14 | 13 | 10 | 8 | 7 | 59.0 |
| *Mid-year projections[1]* | | | | | | | | | |
| 2001 | 20 | 11 | 14 | 15 | 13 | 10 | 8 | 7 | 59.6 |
| 2011 | 18 | 12 | 12 | 14 | 15 | 12 | 9 | 8 | 60.9 |
| 2021 | 18 | 11 | 13 | 12 | 13 | 14 | 11 | 9 | 62.2 |

[1] 1996-based projections
*Source: Social Trends 29,* 1999

movement. Birth rates fell and continued to fall, with the exception of a short upturn in the late 1980s. Finally, the constant rise in life expectancy, due to high standards of living and advances in medical science, and a commensurate decline in the death rate have offset the falling birth rate to explain the small increase in population over the last two decades.

There are variations in the birth rate among ethnic groups, with black minorities tending to have higher fertility rates than the white majority. There is, however, growing convergence, as the total fertility rate of black women has fallen from 3.8 in 1971 to 2.5 in 1991, compared with 1.8 for white women born in the UK. That trend is continuing downwards. Other recent significant trends have been the large percentage of births outside marriage, which increased from 8 per cent in 1971 to over one-third in 1997, and the change in fertility rates among different age groups. While women in the 25 to 29 age group are the most likely to give birth, there have been increases in the fertility rates of women in their 30s and 40s and a decrease in women in their teens and early 20s. The average age of women having their first child was 28 in 1997. There is also an increase in the number of childless women.

The age structure of the population reflects trends in birth and death rates. As Table 4.2 shows, the proportion of the population in the 0 to 16 age group has fallen significantly since 1961, when it represented 25 per cent of the population. Conversely, the over-65 groups have increased from 12 per cent in 1961. In 1996 these proportions were 21 and 16 per cent respectively, and it is estimated that these ratios will be reversed by 2021, when the 0 to 16 age group will fall to 18 per cent and the over-65s rise to 20 per cent. The number of people aged 65 and over is growing both relatively and absolutely. Their number rose by nearly half between 1961 and 1996 to 9.3 million (Social Trends 1998), with the fastest growing group being the over 85s. By 2031, it is estimated that the over-65s will reach 14.5 million or 24 per cent of the population (Social Trends 1993, 1997) and the over 80s will reach 3.4 million, over 60 per cent more than in 1990. These groups tend to make the greatest demands upon health, social services and pensions.

## The working population

The working population (or the labour force) is the economically active population and it is traditionally drawn from the 16 to 64 age groups. The economic activity rate is the percentage of the population in the labour force, and consists of those in work and those looking for work. The working population rose from around 25 million in 1971 to 26 million in 1979, peaking at 28.9 million in 1990. Since then, it has remained fairly stable around 28.5 million, although it is projected to rise to 30 million by 2006. Traditionally, men have constituted the larger part of the labour force, but women now form an ever-increasing proportion as their participation rate increases and men's decreases. In 1971, women accounted for 38 per cent of the labour force but by 1997 that had risen to 45 per cent, when some 72 per cent of women of working age were economically active, compared with 85 per cent of men. Because of the ageing profile of the population in general, the working population profile is also ageing. In 1971, 20.4 per cent of the working population were between 16 and 24 but this had fallen to 15.3 per cent in 1997. Conversely, 20 per cent of the working population were between 45 and 54 in 1971 but this had risen to 22 per cent by 1997.

Reasons for the changes are complex, but one cause is the decline of the manufacturing and extractive industries, which are largely all-male occupations, and growth of the service industries which employ mainly women. In 1978 there were 13.4 million men and 9.4 million women in employment. In 1997, the figures were 11.5 and 11.3 million respectively. Some 90 per cent of the increase in the labour force overall since the late 1970s is accounted for by women entering the labour market, while most jobs lost in declining industries have been by men. Linked to this is the increase in part-time employment. Some 45 per cent of women are in part-time employment in contrast to only 9 per cent of men, although the proportion of men has been steadily growing. Part-time employment enables women with family responsibilities to enter paid employment and combine their dual roles. Further, changes in family structures, the increase in one parent families, and the desire of many women to pursue their own careers have led to more women entering and remaining in the labour market than in the past. Although women with children have lower participation rates than those without, they are taking shorter career breaks and re-entering the labour market in much larger numbers. Another trend has been the increase in self-employment. In 1997, some 3.8 million men and women ran their own businesses and, although the number of businesses failing remains high, at around 60 per cent, there are always new ones being created to maintain and inflate the numbers.

The 'working population' includes those who are unemployed as well as those in paid employment. Over the last 20 years unemployment figures have fluctuated widely because of industrial restructuring and frequent recessions but also because of the way governments have recorded the numbers. Official figures have ranged from 5.6 per cent of the working population in 1976, rising to 12.4 in 1983 and then down to 6.9 in 1990. Figures rose again to 10.1 in

1992, falling slowly to 5.8 per cent in 1997. There are wide variations in the population likely to be unemployed, with the young, black, unskilled manual and the over-50s being the most vulnerable. While gender, race, disability, age and geography are all factors influencing unemployment, in the mid-1990s, the highest rates of unemployment were among young males between 16 and 20, at 20 per cent.

The UK is largely an urban society with almost 60 per cent of its population living in urban areas. The remainder live in rural areas, but most workers commute to urban areas and rely upon urban centres for shopping and recreation. There is an imbalance in the population of the four countries that make up the UK, and variations in their respective trends. England accounts for 83 per cent (49.1 million) of total population, Scotland 9 per cent (5.2 million), Wales 5 per cent (2.9 million) and Northern Ireland 3 per cent (1.6 million). Northern Ireland experienced the greatest percentage increase of 17 per cent growth of population between 1961 and 1997, mainly because of a higher birth rate than in the rest of the country. England's growth was 13 per cent, Wales 11 per cent while Scotland's remained stable, although with some periods of negative growth. Within the UK, there has been a slow migration south throughout the century, with major losses of population in central Scotland, the north east and north west of England and South Wales. The drift was initially to the south-east of England but in recent years the major growth areas have been East Anglia, the south-west and Buckinghamshire. There has also been a drift from major metropolitan areas and inner cities to smaller towns, suburbia and seaside resorts that have had an influx of retired persons. Movement between regions has also been increasing, with over one million people moving over the period of the last census. The UK is becoming an increasingly geographically mobile society.

It is also an increasingly multi-ethnic society. This emanates from the influx of immigrants from Britain's former colonies and commonwealth countries during the 1950s to the 1980s. The first wave were West Indians from the Caribbean and

Indians and Pakistanis from the Indian sub-continent. The second wave was from Bangladesh and East Africa. Today these groups, plus smaller groups from West Africa, the Middle East and South-East Asia make up 6 per cent of the population. The largest group is Indians (30 per cent) followed by West Indians (21 per cent) and Pakistanis (16 per cent). The Arab, African and Bangladeshi communities account for about 5 per cent each. Minority ethnic groups are concentrated in the large conurbations including London, the West Midlands, Merseyside and South Wales. In some areas, such as Hackney and Brixton, they are a majority. In others, such as Leicester and Bradford they make up sizeable minorities. Immigration of black and Asian people has been falling since the 1970s, as successive governments have introduced immigration laws to restrict their numbers. Immigration has remained steady at about 50,000 per annum throughout the 1980s and 1990s but only 35 per cent of these are black or Asian, mainly wives and children of residents. Most immigration now is of white Europeans and Commonwealth citizens.

The demographic profile of minority ethnic groups is different from the white ethnic majority. While 20 per cent of the white population are under 16, 39 per cent of the Pakistan and Bangladesh communities are. Among all minority ethnic groups, there are on average proportionally more children than among the white majority. Conversely while 16 per cent of whites are over 65, only 5 per cent of ethnic minorities are, and only 3 per cent of Pakistanis/ Bangladeshis. Other significant statistics are that minority ethnic groups are more likely to be unemployed and concentrated in lower-income groups. The cultures, languages and religions of the minorities are diverse and have resulted in the UK becoming a multi-cultural society.

## SOCIAL STRATIFICATION

All modern societies are socially stratified and hierarchical, reflecting degrees and forms of inequality including wealth, status and power. Those at the top of the hierarchy tend to have more of all three than those at lower levels. Social divisions within the UK are linked to differing occupations, life opportunities, cultures, lifestyles and patterns of social behaviour. The major divisions are traditionally seen as class, gender and race, although there are also age, national, religious and regional cleavages. This diversity, however, is overlaid and held together by systems of common belief, language, laws and regulations, and identification with national symbols and institutions. Every society consists of elements of heterogeneity and homogeneity, but it is the integration of these elements that produces social stability, while at the same time enabling societies to change. It is widely accepted that the social structure of the UK has changed significantly in the second half of the twentieth century (Halsey 1988, Hamnett et al. 1989, Bradley 1996). New patterns of social stratification have emerged as the UK has been transformed from an industrial to a post-industrial society.

The major differences between industrial and post-industrial societies lie in their economic systems, type of commodities produced, the distribution of the labour force and the dominant technology. Daniel Bell (1973) identified the transition as:

• the change from a goods-producing to a service economy

• the emergence of new professions and technical classes

• the central role of theoretical knowledge as the source of innovation

• the dominance of new information-based technologies.

In the UK today, most people are employed in the service sector (over 70 per cent). White-collar and professional workers have replaced blue-collar workers, and knowledge has become the key resource and root of innovation, change and power. Information and communication technologies have transformed the means of production and structures and locations of organisations. Although the UK is predominantly post-industrial, elements of industrialism remain, including large manufacturing units, factory systems, mass production and low-skilled industrial workforces. These elements of continuity and change are reflected in the class structure.

## Class

The concept of class is a disputed one. One view, the Marxist, is that class refers to a relationship to the means of production and is a purely economic concept. All those selling their labour to survive constitute a working class. In contrast, those owning the means of production constitute a ruling or 'capitalist' class. Other classes consist of the self-employed, professionals and small businesses such as shopkeepers and artisans. The relationship between the two major classes is an inherently exploitative one, as the capitalist extracts part of the value of the social production of the workers as profit and pays wages to the workers, which are less than the value of what they have produced. This exploitation causes class conflict, which is the engine of social change. This crude Marxist view has been refined by neo-Marxists (Poulantzas 1975, Wright 1985). They acknowledge a more complex class structure of lower, middle and upper strata, each with differential economic rewards, which affect lifestyle and give access to other valued resources such as property, wealth, social position and political power. Their more dynamic view of class, however, is still rooted in the relations of production.

An alternative view, associated with Weber, is that class is a complex phenomenon with economic, social, political and cultural aspects linked to occupation, status and power. Weber (1968, 1971) recognised three types of class situation: property classes, commercial classes and social classes. Property classes are determined by property differences and may be positively or negatively privileged. Commercial classes are determined by their ability to sell their skills or goods in the market. Social classes are wider groups than the other two and represent those property and commercial classes within and between which movement by individuals is easy. Such status groups are the working class, intelligentsia, classes privileged through property and education, and small businesses. Weber identified a significant middle class composed of such groups as the self-employed, public or private officials and those in liberal professions. For Weber, classes can be identified in terms of their specific possessions and skills but, unlike Marx, he thought it was status not class that is the root of group solidarity. Status refers to the way that society regards individuals or groups. It is conferred externally and reflects the positive or negative values attached to considerations such as knowledge, skill, circumstances of birth, social position or patterns of behaviour. It has its origins, however, in the ability of groups successfully to claim privileges denied to others. For Weber, conflicts between classes and status groups, and between status groups, cause social change. Finally, Weber introduced the concepts of 'power' and 'party'. Power is the ability to influence decisions, either positively or negatively, and to make things happen, which reflect one's own interest or collective interests. Parties are social groups established to influence or change the *status quo*. Their focus may be broad or narrow, national or local, but they are involved in attempts to effect particular communal outcomes and they may or may not be related to class or status.

Debates about class today revolve around whether class is any longer a meaningful concept that describes 'reality' and whether the meta-narratives of Marx and Weber can accommodate the complexity of modern classes that are increasingly fragmented and relative. There is also debate about how to describe the new systems of social stratification that are emerging and seem to confuse the traditional divisions of working, middle and upper class. Finally, there are debates about how to integrate the structuralist and behaviouralist elements of Marx and Weber into an analysis of class structures in modern societies (Giddens 1973, 1989, Bradley 1996). This debate bears witness to the continued importance of what Bradley (1996: 46) describes as:

> A label applied to a nexus of unequal lived relationships arising from the social organisation of production, distribution, exchange and consumption. These include the allocation of tasks in the division of labour (occupation, employment hierarchies); control and ownership relationships within production; the unequal

distribution of surplus (wealth, income, state benefits); relationships linked to the circulation of money (markets, shareholding and investment); patterns of consumption (lifestyle, living arrangements); and distinctive cultures that arise from all these (behavioural practices and community relations). Class is a much broader concept, then, than occupational structure, though the latter is often taken as a measure of it.

## Changes in the class system

The period between 1945 and the late 1970s was one of relative prosperity, with full employment and a growing working population. New occupations and professions emerged, especially within the continuously expanding welfare state, and wages rose with rising productivity. High levels of consumption led to a general rise in living standards and the high social wage resulted in some narrowing of the inequalities between classes. There was increased social mobility and distinctions and boundaries between classes became blurred as general affluence resulted in converging consumption patterns and lifestyles across old class divisions.

The old class structure was distinguished by a large working class of manual workers, a smaller middle class of white-collar workers, the professions, self-employed and a small upper class. In 1951, about two-thirds of the working population and their families were in manual occupations and identified as working class. Between 1971 and 1981, the proportion of employed people in manual work fell from 62 to 56 per cent for men and from 43 to 36 per cent for women (Halsey 1988). By 1997, less than 30 per cent of the labour force had manual jobs and an increasing proportion of those were women and minority ethnic groups. Explanations of these changes are found, first, in the decline of manufacturing and extractive industries where manual workers were employed, such as in mining, shipbuilding, iron and steel, docks, textiles and transport. Second, jobs have been lost to automation and new technology in industries such as printing and car manufacturing. Third, jobs have been lost as corporations have transferred production to low labour cost countries, and plants have closed. It should be noted that this process of globalisation is creating a new international division of labour and the working class has not declined 'globally'.

In contrast, over the same period the middle class has grown, as white-collar occupations have expanded, new professions have been created and technology has transformed working processes. The middle class has become numerically and socially the most significant social stratum and is predicted to grow between 10 and 14 per cent over the next decade (Social Trends 1997). The middle class, however, is very heterogeneous and has been described by Dahrendorf (1982) as consisting of an upper middle, middle middle and lower middle class. The upper middle class includes the higher professions, senior managers and those holding senior technical posts. The middle middle class consists of the lower professions, middle managers and technical grades, small business owners and farmers. Finally, the lower middle class are those in clerical and supervisory positions, white-collar shop assistants and the para-professionals.

The upper class remains the smallest class, but has also changed. It consists of interconnected families who own a disproportionate amount of property and wealth (probably 5 per cent of wealth holders), control and own large parts of industry, land and commerce and hold top posts in major institutions of the state, commerce and the arts. It includes chief executives and directors of the large national and multinational corporations, those at the top of the major financial institutions in the City including the banks, finance houses and law firms, senior judges, military leaders and some top politicians and civil servants. This class is economically dominant and operates through national and international networks. It is often referred to as 'the Establishment'. Dahrendorf, however, distinguishes between the old and the new upper class. The latter represent 'entryists', and consist of the *nouveaux riches* who are extremely wealthy and have acquired property, but lack the personal attributes of birth and social status. Examples include Richard Branson, Paul McCartney, Alan Sugar, David Sainsbury and Dame Shirley Porter, all of whom appear in the top 200 wealthiest people in the UK along with the Queen and the Duke of Westminster. The *nouveaux riches* themselves are becoming increasingly heterogeneous as the number of multi-millionaires continues to increase (Beresford and Boyd 1999). At the same time, the importance of inherited wealth is declining. A further change is the growing power and control exercised by a transnational capitalist élite which is a crucial feature of the new globalisation.

These changes have led to claims that the class system in the UK is coming to an end and that we live in a classless society or 'we are all middle class now'. Observers point to a new working class, more skilled, educated and affluent than the old working class, with similar lifestyles and consumption patterns to the middle classes. The new working class is more likely to be home owners, have holidays abroad, enjoy eating out and have a wide range of material possessions. In addition, increased social mobility within working class families and the higher status attached to the new occupations are also levelling the distinctions and blurring the boundaries between working and middle classes. An alternative perspective, with its origins in the writings of David Lockwood (1958), is that class is a function not only of market position but also the work situation. While market position is reflected in income, job security and opportunity for upward mobility, work situation is reflected in the degree of autonomy, independence and control an individual has over work. The working class is distinguishable by not only the type of work they do and their market position but also their lack of control or autonomy over the work process. Rather than an 'embourgeoisification' of the working class, Lockwood and others (Braverman 1974, Wood 1982, Crompton and Jones 1989) point to the 'proletarianisation' of the middle classes. Changes in the work process of white-collar and lower professional groups are leading to loss of autonomy, which is blurring the distinction between the classes, with negative effects. Another contributory factor to loss of status and rewards attached to clerical and white-collar jobs is that they have been feminised. Furthermore, movement to more flexible employment patterns, especially for peripheral as opposed to core workers (Atkinson 1984), is reducing job security for manual, white-collar and professional workers. Even the middle classes are being exposed more to risk and insecurity in employment as flexibility crosses the traditional manual/mental divisions.

## Class, income and wealth

Class is a complex concept linked to occupation, market position, lifestyle, education and consumption patterns, which are in turn determined by command over resources giving power and status and freedom of choice. Thus, the class structure reflects the distribution of power within society, differential access to resources and relative life chances. For the majority of people, the only resources they command are reflected in their incomes, although some accumulate or inherit wealth, which is stored resources. Wealth and income have always been unevenly distributed within society, and inequality is an inherent feature of modern capitalist societies (Pond 1989). Between 1945 and 1979, however, mainly due to the redistributive effects of the welfare state, and the status conferred upon citizenship, there was some evidence of a marginal increase in equality. The incomes of the top 10 per cent of the working population fell to around 25 per cent, while incomes of the bottom 50 per cent increased to 25 per cent. This, however, masked the effects of a graduated tax system which resulted in a redistribution of resources in the form of the 'social wage', which included free education, health services, pensions and income maintenance benefits. The distribution of wealth changed significantly, although it was largely a redistribution among the top 50 per cent, which still owned over 90 per cent of disposable wealth in 1979, while the bottom 50 per cent owned less than 10 per cent.

Since 1979 there has been some reversal of these trends, and inequality has actually increased. Townsend (1979) stated that in the late 1970s some 25 per cent of households were in relative poverty. By the late 1990s this had risen to over 30 per cent. The Barclay report on Income and Wealth (1995) stated that since 1977 the proportion of the population with less than half average income had doubled and that income inequality in the UK had grown faster than in any other comparable industrial country. The reasons for this are complex but are linked to the changing economic structure of the UK and the policies of successive Conservative governments from 1979 to 1997. High levels of unemployment throughout the period, and growing economic inactivity, meant that more people lived off income support, which did not keep up with average incomes or the rate of inflation. Also, wages of the lowest paid hardly changed over the period and were lower in real terms than in 1979, while the rewards of the highest-paid rose sharply. There was a growing polarisation of 'work rich' and 'work poor' households. Those below the poverty line included the unemployed, sick and disabled, elderly, one-parent families, and ethnic minorities with lone parents the most over-represented group. Among this burgeoning stratum of poor, a distinction is made between the 'poor' working class and an 'underclass' (Dahrendorf 1987, Field 1996). The underclass is distinguished from the traditional working class, because it is not just poor but economically and politically marginalised and characterised by apathy, non-participation and a dependency culture. Growth in the underclass is attributed to falling demand for manual workers, the dual labour market with low-paid peripheral workers and government policies of reducing social benefits, including pensions. Murray (1996) offers an alternative, more controversial explanation, which he associates with illegitimacy, voluntary unemployment, and a 'dependency' culture. He argues that the welfare state, social acceptance of fatherless families and a growing criminal sub-culture, foster it.

The present class structure is, therefore, less clear than in the past. At every level – upper, middle and lower – it consists of heterogeneous elements. The upper class is becoming more accessible to the *nouveaux riches* who have made their money in the market place, while the traditional aristocracy is being diluted. The UK is moving in the direction of a plutocracy, where money rather than birth is the key to power, and where the national élite is part of a new transnational capitalist class. The enlarged middle classes are the fastest growing and most heterogeneous group. They are expanding as new occupations have status conferred and are able through exclusionary practices to strengthen their market position. The new working class consists of manual, clerical and shop workers who are distinct from both the underclass and middle class. Their lifestyle reflects their relative affluence. They are less class conscious and politically committed than the traditional working class. They also have more private social lives, preferring to spend time with their families and in their own homes. In the work situation, however, they have little control and are the most vulnerable to economic change. Their numbers may actually be increasing as technological change is deskilling lower-level technical and clerical workers and relegating them from the middle to working class. Finally, there is an underclass consisting of groups socially excluded from the mainstream of British society.

## GENDER

Class is not the only basis of inequality in the UK. Gender is a social division cutting across class. Gender, unlike sex, is a social phenomenon and refers to the social attributes, expectations and roles attached to men and women in society. Gender constitutes a powerful form of inequality reflected in the economic, social and political spheres of society. Gender relationships have been changing in recent years, but it is debatable whether there has been a narrowing of the equality gap.

One of the most significant developments in the post-war period has been the feminisation of the labour force. Although women have always been involved in the labour market, they have increased from 29 per cent of the working population in 1901 to around 46 per cent in 1997. There are differences in the economic activity rates of ethnic majority and minority women, with the latter, particularly Bangladeshi and Pakistani women, having the lowest participation rates. In general, ethnic minority women are also less likely to work part time and more likely to be unemployed. This reflects a mix of factors, including cultural traditions, racial discrimination and the economic decline of areas where black communities have settled. Overall, however, there is convergence in the participation rates of men and women, as the latter increase and the former decline. The increase of women in employment can be attributed to changing labour market demands and the increased participation of women with young children. In the past it was marital status that was an indicator of women's economic activity but today it is responsibility for dependent children which is the most significant one. Some 55 per cent of women with children under 5 are now economically active, and this figure rises as the children get older (Social Trends 1998). The major exception to this is lone mothers. Their participation rate has actually fallen over the last decade and is linked to the income support system and poverty trap. Over 70 per cent of lone mothers were receiving income support in the mid-1990s. The New Labour government is in the process of reforming the system to provide incentives for these women to enter or return to work, and to penalise those who do not. It is also increasing the availability of child-care provision, which is still a determining factor in whether a mother works full time, part time or not at all.

The pattern of women's employment has traditionally been different from men's and it is characterised by horizontal and vertical segregation. Most women workers are found in four main areas of employment: clerical and administrative work, the caring professions (teaching, nursing and social work), retailing and catering, and cleaning and hairdressing. Women's opportunities for work have depended on expansion or contraction of these sectors and growth of employment opportunities in new high-tech industries and new professions in the 1990s. Their employment base has been widening in the last decade but horizontal segregation still persists. Women are also found mainly in the lower levels of organisations and men in higher positions. Even in organisations staffed predominantly by women, such as education and nursing, men are found disproportionately in top posts. Although the number of women in management has been increasing, they still hold only one-third of management positions, falling to 5 per cent of managing directors and chief executives. Black women are even more underrepresented at higher levels.

Women are far more likely to be in part-time work. In 1997, over 5.3 million women worked part time as opposed to 6.5 million full time. The comparable figures for men were 1.3 million and 14.7 million respectively. Women also account for some 40 per cent of temporary full-time workers or 8.6 per cent of female employment. This means women are in the least secure jobs and are particularly vulnerable to decisions by employers to reduce their labour forces. Further, women tend to earn on average 25 per cent less than men. This is because they are in lower-paid, lower-status jobs and work fewer hours. This, in turn, has an effect on their career structures and career development.

There are a variety of explanations of women's unequal position in the labour market, revolving around early socialisation into gender roles, personal and social expectations and structures of the family and employment. In addition, black women are discriminated against because of their 'race' and ethnicity. Traditionally, the structure and organisation of work has been based on men as head of the family, working continuously throughout their lives. This continuous working day, week and work life takes no account of childbearing and child-rearing and is difficult to reconcile with the dual role of women. Consequently, women withdraw temporarily from the labour market to raise children. This often results in downward occupational mobility, especially when they return to part-time work. Although the time taken out after childbirth is falling, and more women are returning full time, childbirth still interrupts their careers and limits their opportunities of gaining promotion, experience and rising to the top.

The growing importance of women in the economy, the impact of the EU and pressure from the women's movement since the 1960s, have led governments to pursue policies to maximise the supply of women workers. They have done this by: eliminating unfair discrimination; providing maternity leave, rights to career breaks and other forms of employment protection; introducing equal pay; and improving the skills of women through education and training. Over 50 per cent of graduates are now women. They are entering professions in large numbers and have permeated the male bastions of the city, police, higher civil service and the law (Witz 1992). Women are also the fastest-growing group of self-employed, taking advantage of small business programmes and financial incentives. In the political sphere, women have been successful in gaining greater representation in both local and central government and in the many quangos that have been created since 1979 (Thomas and Wormald 1989). They obtained 116 seats in the House of Commons in the 1997 Election and were given five cabinet posts. A woman Labour MEP, Pauline Green, currently heads the socialist group in the European Parliament.

Inequality persists, however, due to structural, organisational, institutional and attitudinal barriers (Callender 1996, Davidson and Cooper 1992) to gaining employment, better jobs and access to positions of power. Organisations, including the family, remain gendered (Cockburn 1991, Hearn and Parkin 1995). Equal opportunities legislation and the liberal equal opportunities policies of successive governments have proved blunt instruments in attacking the organisational mobilisation of sexual bias (Blakemore and Drake 1996, Cameron 1993, Cockburn 1991). Gender occupational segregation is structurally determined by growth of certain types of jobs, particularly part-time ones. Conversely, lack of part-time opportunities in managerial jobs and many professions, and absence of family-friendly policies within organisations, perpetuates vertical segregation. Furthermore, institutional barriers include lack of access to qualifications and training for different levels. Women, who take time out, work part-time, and especially lone parents, are denied opportunities for training and experience. Women still have a dual role as mothers and housewives, involving many hours of unpaid work. This leaves little time to pursue their careers. Although there is evidence that men now share domestic work, women still perform 75 per cent of it and have major responsibility for children. The introduction of paternity leave may shift that burden in the future, while the introduction of nursery places for all children aged 3 and 4 will make it easier for women to enter or remain in the labour market. However, other government policies (New Deal and Welfare to Work) may actually push women into paid work to reduce the costs to social security.

More significantly, contraction and restructuring of the Welfare State has affected women disproportionately, partly because they constitute the bulk of public employees and are the 'carers'. Changes in social policies such as Community Care translates into care by families and by women. So while there are more opportunities for women to pursue careers, and enlightened employers have taken positive action to promote this, women are still disadvantaged. This is because of their weaker market position, unequal role within the family, lack of skills and experience, and lack of support to enable them to reconcile their domestic and employment roles. Finally, there are the attitudinal barriers of employers, but particularly of women themselves. Employers' gender stereotypes affect their willingness to recruit and promote women, while women's attitudes affect their behaviour in the labour market. There is some evidence that these attitudes are changing as more women are choosing not to have children or to restrict their families to one child.

Women still outnumber men among those living in poverty. They are disproportionately represented in the one-third of families living below the poverty line, including pensioners and lone mothers who may not be in paid work. The abolition of wages councils during the 1980s mainly disadvantaged women, who made up most of the two million workers earning below £3 an hour before the minimum wage was introduced in April 1999. There appears to be a growing polarisation between women in the labour market. There are those being increasingly integrated into higher management levels and the professions with well-paid jobs, and those who are the peripheral workers in low-paid, part-time or temporary jobs and who fall in and out of the labour market. This increasing heterogeneity of women in the labour market is likely to increase over the next decade.

## ETHNICITY

The UK has a rich mixture of peoples with different ethnic identities and cultures. Although waves of immigration since the seventeenth century have resulted in minorities being a traditional feature of the social fabric, these minorities were white, mostly Christian and of European descent (Farnham 1990). Since 1945 waves of immigrants have come from the former colonies of the British Empire and have been distinctive because of their colour, religions and cultures. They came in response to job opportunities, to do work that white residents did not want to do. The first wave of black West Indians, who came in the 1950s and 1960s with their families to resettle in the UK, had British citizenship and also spoke English. Substantial numbers of Indian and Pakistan immigrants also came in the 1950s and 1960s. They had British citizenship, but English was not their native tongue, and most were Hindus, Sikhs or Muslims. They were usually men, who worked to send money back to their families and later many brought their families to settle here. A second wave of immigrants came in the 1970s, mainly from Bangladesh and Pakistan but also from East Africa. The latter group was mostly educated Indians and business people who spoke English and were either Christians or Hindus.

These immigrants were seen as different races. Race is claimed to distinguish people by their biological differences such as colour of skin, physical appearance and hair type (phenotypical characteristics) and underlying genetic differences (genotypical characteristics (Bradley 1996)). In the nineteenth century, a popular taxonomy distinguished Caucasian, Negroid and Mongoloid races. Today, however, most writers reject race as a scientific category and see it as a stigmatised identity linked to colonialism and the ideology of racism. The concept of ethnicity is now used to describe minorities and refers to social groups sharing social characteristics, including language, religion, nationality, culture and common origin. It is these things that bind groups together, differentiating them from other groups. Ethnicity, therefore, is a relational concept that depends on how people see themselves, as well as how others see them.

Minority ethnic groups, as a whole, are generally disadvantaged economically and socially, although there are some important differences between different minorities. They are found in distinct segments of the labour market but are more disadvantaged than white workers in all strata. Ethnic minority workers, male and female, tend to be concentrated in the lowest-paid jobs and the least secure ones. Rates of unemployment are highest among black males under 25 but are also higher than for whites at all ages. This is the consequence of institutional racism that permeates many parts of British society. Racism is a disputed concept but generally describes ideas and attitudes stressing the social significance of biological differences between human populations and is used to legitimise white or black supremicism. In the UK, it is reflected in ethnocentrism, negative attitudes towards ethnic minorities and 'immigrants', who become scapegoats to divert attention away from the social and economic problems facing lower strata of society (Hall et al. 1978). The overall effect is that minority ethnic groups are negatively privileged status groups who are excluded from jobs reserved for whites or from certain areas of social life. Hence, they tend to be distinguished by their concentration in lower-paid jobs and poorer housing, and in certain parts of the country (Mason 1995).

Since the 1950s, there has been talk of race relations problems creating images of differences and conflict between racial minorities and the white majority. Riots in the 1950s and 1960s flamed these views and led liberals to legislate to try to integrate minority ethnic groups into society. In the 1970s, further legislation, modelled on the Sex Discrimination Act 1975, outlawed discrimination on the grounds of race and set up the Commission for Racial Equality to further good race relations. For the first time, in 1991, the Census asked respondents to classify themselves in ethnic terms. Eight ethnic groups were identified:

- White
- Black-Caribbean
- Black-African
- Black-other
- Indian
- Pakistan
- Bangladesh
- Chinese
- Any other ethnic group.

In recent years, more stress has been placed on the differences and diversities found among ethnic groups. Ethnicity is now recognised as a very fluid concept as second and third generation immigrants have become more integrated into the wider society, are more socially mobile and intermarry. Minority ethnic groups are now found in the professions, media, arts and politics and there are more self-employed Asians than in any other group. Whether this social mobility will weaken ethnic identity and ties is not yet clear. One view is that it will not, 'because of the strength of the ties which come from shared experiences of discrimination' (Bradley 1996: 140). Another view is that it will, as multi-cultural communities submerge differences, ethnic groups become more hybrid, new ethnicities emerge and society becomes more ethnically and culturally pluralistic.

Diversity among ethnic groups is reflected in employment and unemployment, educational achievement, housing, health and citizenship (Mason 1995). There are important differences, however, between minority ethnic groups in all these categories. The economic activity rate is far higher among Afro-Caribbean women than Bangladesh and Pakistan women, where it is little more than 25 per cent. The economic and social status of East African Indians is higher than that of Bangladeshis. There are significant differences in educational achievement between the groups and in numbers of young people proceeding to further and higher education

(Social Trends 1998). There are also wide variations in housing tenure, with 80 per cent of Indians being homeowners, compared with only 28 per cent of Black Africans, while less than half of Afro-Caribbeans are homeowners and over one-third are council house tenants.

## EDUCATION, TRAINING AND ECONOMIC PERFORMANCE

Social class and social mobility are closely linked to education. In all societies the functions of education are the same. First, it socialises children into the norms and values of the society, both supplementing and complementing primary socialisation in the home and transmitting culture across generations. Second, it develops personal and interpersonal skills, enabling people to interact socially. Third, schools prepare children for their later roles in life and provide them with knowledge and intellectual skills, so they can continue to learn throughout their lives. In this way the educational system performs the function of providing the economy with the skilled labour force it needs. Fourth, education is a vehicle for self-development and self-fulfilment, by encouraging young people to develop their potential talents to the full. Finally, education provides the opportunity and means for people to move socially and economically. Sociologists differ in their interpretation of schooling and education, ranging from functionalist to Marxist perspectives, but all agree its importance (Haralambos 1995).

Criticisms of the modern education system, created in 1944, began in the 1970s and revolved around different perceptions of the major functions of schools. One view was that schools should be places of instruction, discipline and work; the other that schools should promote individuality, encourage freedom of expression and learning by discovery. Those on the political right argued that schools were failing society and the economy because standards were too low, bright children were being disadvantaged and the system was not developing the skills the economy needed. On the political left, criticisms were that education was perpetuating the existing class structure by promoting academic achievement over practical skills and that élite cultures were being perpetuated (McVicar 1996). In fact, there was little evidence of lowering of standards or achievement and both had risen continuously since 1944. However, numbers of children leaving school with academic qualifications or proceeding to further and higher education were lower in the UK than in many of her competitor countries. There was also a lack of IT skills and shortages of engineers, scientists and other professions.

Conservative governments after 1979 introduced major changes in all levels of compulsory and post-compulsory education. A national curriculum was imposed upon all schools with associated standards of attainment (SATS) expected of children at 7, 11, 14 and 16. Responsibility for running schools was transferred from local authorities to boards of governors and head teachers, and schools were allowed to opt out of local authority control. Schools were given budgets and were expected to manage them efficiently, and regulatory bodies were appointed to monitor their performance – the Audit Commission in 1983 and OFSTED in 1992. Emphasis was placed on the need for more vocationalism, and new syllabuses in business studies, computing and other technical and applied subjects were added to traditional academic programmes. New qualifications were introduced and, in the late 1980s, government sponsored the introduction of a unified system of National Vocational Qualifications (NVQs) designed to provide a standard system for the assessment of work-based learning. General NVQs were introduced into schools and colleges to parallel the more academic A level syllabus. A market for education was created by increasing the diversity of schools available and ensuring that money followed pupils. Schools were encouraged to compete for pupils by raising the reputation of the school and in particular its examination results. Parents were given the right to choose the school they wanted for their children. Poor-performing schools, it was assumed, would not attract pupils, while high-performing schools would (Holloway *et al* 1999).

A similar approach was adopted in further and higher education (FE and HE), although another objective was to increase numbers of students entering these stages. Colleges were transferred from local authority control and set up as independent FE or HE corporations. They are run by boards of governors consisting mainly of local business people, and funded by government funding agencies on a *per capita* basis. They are expected to compete for students and are monitored to assess their performance. There was no national curriculum imposed but government policies encouraged the development of new courses reflecting student demands and business and labour market needs. In 1997 there were over 400 FE colleges and some 100 universities. More than half were 'new' universities created out of the former polytechnics by the Further and Higher Education Act 1992. In 1997–8 there were over 3.9 million students in FE and 1.6 million in HE. This represented a massive expansion and transformed the composition of both sets of institutions. Three-quarters of 16 to 18-year-olds were in FE in 1997 and one-third of 18 to 21-year-olds entered HE, compared to one sixth in the 1970s. This number is projected to rise to 50 per cent by 2000. The largest increase has been among women, who have risen from one-third of students in FE and HE in the 1970s to over 50 per cent in 1997. Women are still very under-represented in the sciences, mathematics and engineering, however, in spite of major recruitment campaigns (Social Trends 1998). Government policy both under Conservatives and New Labour has been to increase access to under-represented groups. The number of mature students entering HE now exceeds those in younger cohort groups.

The move to mass education has resulted in significant changes in the organisation, management and delivery of FE and HE (Holloway *et al* 1999). Students have far more choice about what and when they study, with more students using a part-time mode, especially in FE. Systems of credit accumulation and transfer facilitate mobility between institutions, interrupted study, and accreditation of prior learning. This enables students to obtain qualifications that count learning from experience, so encouraging adults to return to education at any age. Although education and training are difficult to distinguish, in practice the former is associated with developing intellectual skills and knowledge capable of being applied in a range of situations and across time, as well as developing the individual's 'full potential'. Training is the development of more specific skills related to particular jobs, and where the behavioural outputs can be more readily tested. FE and HE have always been involved with both, but training became a high priority for Conservative governments throughout the 1980s and 1990s. Recognising skill shortages and the poor record of training by industry, they sought to raise its profile, stimulate industry to see training as an investment rather than a cost, and provide funding for a massive expansion of training nationally. This was targeted at reducing unemployment, particularly of young people, by giving them job experience and training to increase their employability. It was also designed to assist others, like women entering or re-entering the labour market. Local authorities and businesses, using European Social and Regional funding, have also been training people to alter the skill profile of declining industrial areas.

The New Labour Government, elected in 1997, placed education at the top of its political priorities and set targets for improved literacy and numeracy in schools. It established Education Action Zones in areas with poor educational achievement and enlisted the support of local businesses in tackling the problems. It also set rigorous new targets for entry into FE and HE, and lifetime targets for qualifications. By 2000, 60 per cent of the workforce are to be qualified to NVQ level 3 and 30 per cent of the population are to have a vocational, professional, management or academic qualification to NVQ level 4. This drive for qualifications is causing some concern as employers are using high qualifications as a criterion for selection rather than suitability for jobs. Chasing qualifications also results in many people being overqualified for the jobs that are available, especially as technology is fast de-skilling jobs even within the professions.

The Handy (1987) and Constable and McCormick (1987) reports both demonstrated that Britain's major competitors had more highly skilled and trained workers and spent more on training than did the UK. Finegold and Soskice (1988: 23) claimed that 'Britain's relative failure to educate and train its workforce has contributed to its poor economic record in the post-war period'. They also identified the reasons for the failure to develop a training strategy. Based upon their faith in the market and their belief that business should take responsibility for training the labour force, as they know what skills were needed, the Conservative government set up Training and Education Councils (TECs) in England and Wales, and Local Enterprise Companies (LECs) in Scotland. These are run by employers and assess local training needs, co-ordinate provision of training in the area, help government's technical and vocational initiative, and are assessors for Investors in People (IiP) awards. The latter is a joint government/business initiative promoting training by awarding IiP status to all organisations that reach the national standards, determined by the lead body. The National Advisory Council for Education and Training Targets (NACETTS), established in 1993, sets national targets and assists achieving competitiveness. Training, along with education, is high on the agenda of the New Labour Government, whose commitment is to ensuring that a highly trained labour force has the skills and competencies needed in the labour market.

## SOCIAL CHANGE AND CHANGING SOCIAL ATTITUDES

Social culture consists of the ideas, values, attitudes and beliefs influencing the way that people make sense of and perceive the world and themselves in it. It fashions their behaviour, how they relate to others and how they interpret and understand their experiences. Individuals acquire beliefs and values as a result of their experiences and through reflection. The earliest experiences are within the family and school. It is here that we learn language and the means of communication and have our first experiences of rules and rewards and punishments. And we imitate the behaviour of our parents, siblings and other kin. When we enter school, we learn how to play and relate to others in social settings. We also learn to read and are taught about our history and geography, so we can locate ourselves in the wider world. Socialisation continues throughout our lives and secondary agencies such as university, work place, trade unions, professional associations, peer groups, and increasingly the media, may challenge or reinforce our earlier influences. We also continue to change as a result of our personal experiences and observations of our changing environment.

## Social change

Societies are continually evolving and changing but there is usually a cultural lag because, once acquired, attitudes and perceptions are not easily replaced. People are resistant to change because it threatens their security, understanding of the world and status within it. Change is accompanied by uncertainty, threats and risks, although it may also offer opportunities and benefits. Older people are usually the most resistant to change because they have invested so much in the past and are the least confident in their ability to cope. Younger people find change easier to cope with because they lack the reference points of the older generations, and also reject traditional values to establish their own identity and independence. They also tend to learn more quickly and take on board new ideas.

The UK, along with the rest of the industrial world, has experienced rapid and constantly accelerating change in the last 50 years. This has affected all the major institutions of society, many of which have been transformed. It has also been accompanied by new perceptions of the world, and new values and ideas sometimes referred to as 'post-modernism' or 'post-modernity'. Post-modernism rejects the modernist belief that reason and science can discover the reality of the physical and social world. It rejects objectivism, claiming that there are no facts, only interpretations, and no objective truths, only the constructs of various individuals and groups. In other words, our perception of the world is relative to time and space and experience. This relativism implies that one person's reality is as 'real' as any other and that we should therefore give way to sentimentalism, intuition and the free play of imagination. Post-modernism rejects the Protestant ethic, order and discipline, for nihilism, hedonism and experientialism (Smart 1993, Kumar 1995). Many post-modernists are also environmentalists, who condemn exploitation of the earth by modernism and capitalism, and seek sustainable development through communitarian co-operation.

Change can be seen in all aspects of social life; in the family, marriage, workplace, means of transportation and communication, recreation and the arts, and the role of the state and market. The family is now a rather heterogeneous concept encompassing the nuclear model of two married heterosexuals and their children living in one house, to cohabiting heterosexual or homosexual partners, with or without children, and the large extended families of some ethnic minorities, consisting of several generations living within the same household. Finally, there is the more complex family structure that is the consequence of divorce and remarriage. Serial monogamy has produced complex networks of unconventional extended families at the same time that traditional kinship networks are weakened by social and geographical mobility.

The family began to change as more women, especially married women with children, entered paid work. The size of families declined as contraception enabled women to control their own fertility. Marriage became less permanent as women obtained economic independence, secular values replaced religious ones, and the law changed to make divorce easier. Today, one in two marriages end in divorce and many young people choose to cohabit rather than marry. There are a growing number of one-parent families as a consequence of divorce, and women head most of them. Gender relationships within the family are also changing. Younger women are no longer prepared to take on the whole domestic role, and expect their male partners to share in housework and parenting. Many older men, who are economically inactive due to redundancy or retirement, are also assuming domestic responsibilities. This challenge to traditional gender roles is putting a strain on sexual relationships but there is evidence of changing power relations between men and women. Traditional patterns of authority within the family are undergoing change, and so also are patterns of interaction. Halsey (1988) points to the effects of the 'child-centred family', latch-key children and the socially isolating effects of the television. Halsey also paints a picture of a traditional social culture weakened by these multiple forces of change, where the younger generation are substituting fashionability, hedonism and a desperate individualism for a securely held morality.

The transformation of the economy, driven by globalisation and technology, is leading to changes in occupations, more flexible patterns of work and different expectations among workers. Young people no longer expect to spend their working life in one organisation, or even in one field of work. They have an instrumental orientation towards work and fully expect to be mobile and flexible. They are adjusting to the instability, uncertainty and turbulence with greater ease than many of the older generations. Most people now are used to travelling, or have the world brought to them by satellite, television, video and the Internet. The world is becoming a global village and people are aware of the effects of modernisation, convergence of cultures and lifestyles, but also of gross inequalities within the global village. They know too of the international co-operation and merging of sovereignty through the European Union.

## Social attitudes

Every culture consists of elements of tradition and modernity and is characterised by continuity and change. How far and in what ways the changes that have been taking place in the fabric of society in recent decades have affected social attitudes, beliefs and values is difficult to assess. Since 1983, however, a British Social Attitudes Survey (BSAS) has been monitoring changing attitudes and has provided a moving picture of how people see their world and themselves, indicating how society itself is changing. Eight major topics have been covered to date, with each repeated periodically in order to build up time-series data. During the 1990s, these surveys concentrated on people's attitudes towards the economy, public spending and the role of government, the family and a range of moral issues. In 1998, the survey was on British and European Social Attitudes (Jowell et al. 1998) showing how Britain's culture differs from that of other European member states.

One of the stated aims of the Thatcher governments post-1979 was to change British culture and transform the way that people saw the world, themselves and the role of government in their lives. Government wanted to create an enterprise culture in which people would accept and favour unregulated markets and competition, take responsibility for their own welfare and favour a non-interventionist state. There is very little evidence to suggest this has happened, although Curtice and Jowell (1998) indicate that some people have lower expectations of what governments should be doing. Despite profound changes in government policies and in the economy, however, British attitudes towards the state and its proper role and functions have remained remarkably robust. In fact, there has been an increased willingness to see more state spending on key areas of the welfare state such as health, education and pensions and on law and order. There is little evidence, in spite of 18 years of Conservative governments, that social attitudes among generations are very different. 'Thatcher's children', who came of age during the 1980s, do not have significantly different attitudes and values now to other generations. Although there is some evidence that they are more materialistic, overall differences in attitudes towards work are small. Rather than embracing the enterprise values of Conservative governments, the young appear to be even more disenchanted with Conservative philosophy, less rather than more tolerant of income inequality, and more rather than less suspicious of big business, than are older generations. They are equally supportive of the welfare state, although there are 'real generational differences in support for the monarchy, attitudes towards Europe and the principle of freedom of expression' (Heath and Park 1997: 19).

Changes in the economy over the last 20 years have clearly

had a general impact on people's perceptions of work. There is now near unanimity that the gap between high and low incomes is 'too large', with 87 per cent holding this view in 1995 compared to 72 per cent in 1983 (Bryson and McKay 1997). Although perceptions of job insecurity are higher when unemployment is high, there is also a long-term trend towards greater feelings of insecurity. Finally, there is clear evidence of deteriorating attitudes towards management in spite of the record fall in industrial disputes since 1979. Overall, workers feel they have too little say in the work situation and this is reflected in a more instrumental attitude towards work and low levels of motivation. A comparative study on the rewards of work (Russell 1998) further indicates that in Britain there has been a decline in work commitment over time, linked to perceived job insecurity and use of non-permanent employment contracts.

People's attitudes towards the welfare state have not changed significantly in spite of the sustained attack on it throughout the period since 1979 and there is still widespread support for it. In the 1980s, 98 per cent of BSAS respondents supported government provision of health and 97 per cent a decent standard of living for the elderly. These figures have been sustained throughout the 1990s, with 75 per cent supporting increased state pensions, only 20 per cent supporting a selective health service and 60 per cent actually prepared to deny the choice to others of buying themselves out of the NHS, in 1997. Attitudes towards the unemployed and welfare recipients are more divided. There is less consensus on support for single parents and the unemployed. The working class is more likely to regard 'the provision of jobs, unemployment benefits and housing for the poorer groups as essential government responsibilities, to name social security as a priority for social spending and to criticise unemployment benefit as being too low' (Jowell et al. 1992: 32). In contrast, middle classes tend to favour increased government expenditure on health and education and are prepared to pay more taxes to support those universal services but are more critical of welfare payments. Over the last decade, public support for welfare has fluctuated and there has been a trend towards viewing those dependent on benefits as 'undeserving', although the majority still support the system. Only 30 per cent supported the view that the welfare state made people less willing to look after themselves (Bryson 1997).

The areas where there is evidence of cultural change are in relation to family and gender roles. Attitudes towards extra-marital relations, cohabitation and birth outside marriage are quite different from the past. Two-thirds of respondents in the BSAS 1998 supported cohabitation. Only 57 per cent thought that people wanting children should get married, and only 17 per cent thought that the main purpose of marriage was to have children. Attitudes towards children have certainly become less 'pro-child'; with only 18 per cent of respondents thinking that people without children lead empty lives, a fall from 23 per cent in 1988. Divorce is also now widely accepted as the best solution when relationships fail (53 per cent) with only 18 per cent thinking people should stay married. Attitudes towards women and work have also changed. Two-thirds of respondents think that working mothers can still have good relationships with their children, although 50 per cent think that family life suffers. This indicates some of the tensions that are felt between individual freedom and family ties. The British tend to be most liberal in their attitudes towards gender roles but they have not abandoned traditional views about the effect of working mothers on pre-school children. In this area, attitudinal change has been quite slow (Scott *et al* 1998).

Throughout the 1980s and 1990s there has been a clear loss of trust in politics and politicians, and in the system of governing Britain. In 1973 a Royal Commission on the Constitution (Kilbrandon 1973) indicated that more than 50 per cent of the population were satisfied with the system of government. This had fallen to 24 per cent by 1996 (Curtice and Jowell 1998), when 75 per cent indicated they 'almost never' trusted politicians. Paradoxically, support for constitutional change is only weakly tied to levels of trust in the political system. There is now widespread support for devolution, reform of the House of Lords and freedom of information, although there is less support for electoral reform, with 66 per cent favouring the *status quo*. It was evident in the surveys conducted in 1996 that the constitutional reforms advocated by the Labour Party reflected public opinion.

Attitudes towards Europe have wavered since 1983. They became more favourable throughout the 1980s as the percentage favouring withdrawal declined to a low of 16 per cent in 1991, when 77 per cent favoured continuation. However, throughout the 1990s, greater Euro-scepticism emerged and, in 1997, only 55 per cent favoured continuation, 8 per cent withdrawal and 17 per cent were unsure (Evans 1998). Decline in support for European integration reflects a number of factors. One was the ERM fiasco in 1992, followed by the BSE crisis in 1996, but more significantly perhaps the rise and fall of the Referendum Party, splits within the Conservative Party and the anti-European stance of the tabloid press. Much opposition to Europe is linked to ideas of national identity. The public are very loath to give up national control over a range of policies such as taxes, farm production and immigration, although there is a greater willingness to concede control of drug trafficking and pollution. It is difficult to assess to what extent knowledge about Europe is an important influencing factor. People's attitudes about Europe are closely linked to their perceptions of the impact of Europe on British interests. Those opposed to the Euro and EMU think it will cause unemployment, while those opposed to removal of passport controls think this will lead to massive immigration. What is interesting in the surveys is that fear of losing national and cultural identity seems to be less important than economic fears and concerns in explaining attitudes towards Europe. The UK is not alone in its growing Euro-scepticism, as public attitudes in other European countries first became more supportive of European integration up to 1991 and then began to decline, with no subsequent recovery (ibid).

There is a great degree of consensus on social attitudes and beliefs, which cuts across class, gender and ethnicity in the UK. This consensus has changed slowly over the years, with large elements of the post-war consensus merging with a new consensus on the role of the state and the market, inequality and the welfare state. The consensus does not extend to support for unmarried mothers or censorship, and there are widespread disagreements about drugs, extra-marital relationships and cohabitation, which tend to be generational rather than class based. Class no longer seems to be the major division within British society, nor as significant in defining social attitudes, determining social status or political views and affiliations, as it did in the past.

## CONCLUSION

British society has changed over the last 50 years. The population is growing slowly, but is ageing and becoming more multi-ethnic. Minority ethnic groups, because of their higher birth rates, will grow as a proportion of the population over the next 30 years. They will therefore become an important source of labour, make demands upon social services, be important consumers of goods and services, and be significant citizens. The working population is being feminised, as more women are entering the labour market and new patterns of employment are reflecting the transition from an industrial to post-industrial society. These changes are reflected in the system of stratification, as social mobility increases and differences between classes and statuses are becoming blurred. Inequality, however, is still a major characteristic of the UK and there is evidence that it has increased since 1979. Social culture is adapting to this changed environment, although there are time lags. There are generational, class, gender and ethnic differences in values, attitudes and beliefs, but the UK remains a fairly integrated and homogeneous culture, with the exception of Northern Ireland. The social system today is highly dynamic and is being influenced and shaped by economic, technological and political forces that are increasingly international and global. All organisations need to understand the structural and attitudinal changes that are occurring, as they are a source of both opportunities and constraints for their strategic decision-makers.

# 5  Legal framework

The law is that body of rules, formally enacted or customary, which the state recognises as binding on its citizens. It has also been described by Kahn-Freund (1977: 3) as 'a technique for the regulation of social power', where power is the ability to direct and affect the behaviour of others, ultimately by sanctions. Sanctions that are positive reward people; negative ones threaten them. In any liberal society, naked power to determine rules and decisions and enforce them, by individuals, organisations or government, is insufficient to maintain social stability and social order. The power to act needs to be accepted as legitimate by those affected by such decisions, whether property owners, employers, workers, consumers or citizens. To be acceptable in democratic societies, the right of those with power to take decisions has to be recognised by those without positional or resource power, irrespective of any sanctions the powerful may possess. In an ordered society, ultimate power and the right to enforce it rest with those controlling the machinery and agencies of the state – ie in the legislative, executive and judicial organs of government.

Three major functions of government are law-making, applying the law, and adjudicating it. In liberal democratic states, the concept of the 'rule of law' is a fundamental one. First, it reflects the preference of citizens for 'law and order' rather than anarchy or civil strife. It implies that conflicts and disputes between parties should be settled by peaceful and constitutional means rather than by use of armed force, terrorism or physical coercion. If the state is identified with force and coercive might, the rule of law lacks any moral authority or legitimacy. Second, the rule of law can also be interpreted as meaning that government itself must be conducted in accordance with the law and that the machinery of government must always operate through the law. Thus, the law acts as a buttress of democratic principles, since new governmental powers can be conferred on the executive and administrative authorities only by the law-making assembly, ie Parliament in the UK. Third, as law develops, it should result in the rule of law reflecting changing social values, because the legal system exists in a wider social and economic context.

By the end of this chapter, readers should be able to understand and explain:

- how the external legal environment impacts on private, public and voluntary organisations

- the nature, sources and administration of law, especially the elements of contract, employment, consumer and competition law.

In addition, readers should be able to:

- advise management on the possible effects of legislation and European directives on organisations and their activities.

See also the Professional Standards Index (page 345).

## SOCIETY, LAW AND THE LEGAL SYSTEM

Harris (1993) argues that an understanding of the law cannot be acquired unless the subject matter is examined in close relationship to the social, economic and political contexts in which it is created, maintained and implemented. Law, far from being a social glue holding us all inside a boundary of legality, is part of the overall social structure, having links and dependencies with other social elements and forces. These social elements include:

- political institutions, such as Parliament, political parties and pressure groups

- economic institutions, including employing organisations, trade associations and unions

- cultural institutions such as literature, the arts, the press and television.

Some of these institutions and social groups are more important than others, some have more power than others, and some enjoy considerable prestige.

### The social contexts of law

Law plays an important part in defining and regulating all kinds of social relationships, including relations between individuals, organisations, individuals and organisations, and citizens and the state. Laws are made, interpreted and applied but there are differing viewpoints about the nature of the law and the legal system in which the law operates. The social ambiguities inherent in creating and applying the law are summed up in the view that (Harris and Buckle 1967: 6):

> Law may be regarded as a benign facilitating mechanism, making transactions possible between men [sic] and solving awkward problems as they arise; it may, alternatively, be seen as a mechanism of social control, regulating activities and interests in the name of either the community, a ruling class or the state. The state itself may be defined as either 'neutral arbiter' or 'interested party' in the solution of disputes and the balancing of interests. Again, law may be seen as an institution for the furtherance and protection of the welfare of everyone, or it may be seen, crudely, as an instrument of repression wielded by the dominant groups in society.

Put simply, competing viewpoints about the relationship between law and society are essentially dichotomous. On the one side, society and the legal system are seen as reflections of a prevailing social consensus. On the other, they are seen as reflecting fundamental social conflict between competing interest groups. The former perceives the law to be protecting social values to which all subscribe, while the latter holds that the law is less than neutral, protecting some values and interests at the expense of others.

Developments in the law also reflect the historical, political and social contexts in which society evolves and changes. The emergence of a free labour market, for example, was a product of the industrial revolution. With the breakdown of the feudal agrarian system, by the mid-eighteenth century landless labourers moved to the expanding towns to become wage workers in the developing factory system. The growth of market capitalism and *laissez-faire* individualism led to the relationship between 'master' and 'servant' being based on a legal contract, despite the vast disparity in bargaining power between them. The contract of service was viewed as a legally binding agreement between the two parties in the employment relationship, containing agreed rights and obligations for each of them. Any breach of these legal rules entitled the aggrieved party, normally the master, to seek a legal remedy by bringing a civil action against the other for breach of contract.

The doctrine of *laissez-faire* assumed that all members of society, including masters and servants, were free and equal parties before the law, able to regulate and arrange their affairs with one another without constraints being placed upon them by third parties or the law. It assumed that individuals were equal in terms of their bargaining position and that, if people were left free to make their own decisions, competitive trade and industry would flourish and the national economy thrive. In practice, of course, there were fundamental inequalities in terms of bargaining power, social position and wealth between most masters and servants. None the less, the employment contract, supposedly freely made between what later came to be known as employer and employee, was deemed legally to be made between consenting parties of equal standing.

Given the early predominance of these ideas about freedom and equality of contract, it took many years before the state began to intervene to provide basic legal protections for individual employees in their contractual relations with employers. It was the infinite variability of the terms of employment contracts, together with the fact that in many cases employees could neither negotiate their terms nor readily ascertain the terms dictated by the employer that led, over the years, to growing state intervention in regulating the employment relationship. This was done through a series of statutes. A number of social and political factors led to this development, including:

- changed philosophies about the role of the state in society
- the reforming zeal of some politicians and social reformers
- absorption of working people into the democratic process
- the growth of union power and influence.

All these factors led slowly to the furthering of legislative intervention in employment matters, so that laws now provide protections for employees regarding: information about the terms of their contracts; their job rights; health and safety at work; and union membership rights.

It is not only in the field of employment and employment relations that the nineteenth-century emphasis on *laissez-faire* has given way to state and legal intervention, although there was a partial revival of *laissez-faire* ideas during the 1980s and early 1990s. Slowly, *laissez-faire*, with its emphasis on state abstention or 'voluntarism', gave way to the view that government through legislative and other measures should participate in economic affairs in an active and direct way. Yet, prior to the Second World War, economic ideas were dominated by the notions of free trade and freedom of competition, with the corollary that the economy was best left to regulate itself, unimpeded by any form of state intervention. This was accompanied by an assumption that the state should support that sort of economy by creating, through the law, an economic environment conducive to trade, industry and business interests, as demonstrated by various measures protecting the economic interests of the business community in preference to other interests. State support for the growth and consolidation of the industrial and commercial economy came from a number of sources. One was an imperialist foreign policy. Another was the judiciary, which constructed a legal framework within which business affairs could operate smoothly and predictably. The legal notion of 'contract' was, and remains, the essence of the legal relationship between buyers and sellers in product, capital and labour markets.

The basic legal rules governing contract stem almost wholly from cases determined by superior courts in the nineteenth century. The insistence of nineteenth-century judges on deciding cases, and creating legal contractual rules, using the juristic equivalent of *laissez-faire* economics – notions of freedom and equality of contract – eventually led to legislative intervention in the twentieth century, especially in the areas of employee and consumer protection. The nineteenth century also saw the development of legal rules relating to the form that business enterprises might take and of the legal protections that particular types of enterprise enjoyed. The most common forms of business enterprise were, and still are, the limited company and, to a lesser degree, partnership. In the case of the limited company, for exmaple, its most striking legal feature is its 'corporate personality'. Once created, the company is regarded in law as if it were a person, a legal entity in its own right, separate from the people owning and running it, with various legal rights and duties including owning and transferring property, entering into contracts and suing or being sued. By treating the company as a legal person, having ownership of corporate assets, the law not only allows the relatively free use of those assets in the running and expansion of the business but also provides significant legal protections for individual shareholders.

The legal systems of capitalist market economies, therefore, inevitably exhibit comprehensive sets of legal rules and rights concerning private property, because private property is of such fundamental importance to these societies. Yet the law does not treat property as a homogeneous category. Because it has taken different forms and values at different times, each type of property has particular legal rules attached to it. The legal rules dealing with land, for instance, can be traced back to feudalism, while those relating to material objects such as manufactured goods, plant and machinery emerged during the development of early capitalism. Since capitalist market economies, such as those in Europe, depend upon the creation and acquisition of private personal wealth, legal systems concern themselves, to a large extent, with protection of that wealth, how it can be invested and consolidated, and how it can be transferred. Yet while the law purports to afford equality of treatment to everyone in society, regardless of social class, wealth or position, in practice it is used primarily for protecting and transferring property by only a small proportion of the total population.

The law is one of the most powerful carriers of dominant definitions of acceptable and unacceptable social behaviour, as well as being the most significant institution for settling disputes, so it is important to understand the social background of lawyer practitioners. The law embodies dominant social norms and values, and lawyers in their daily work engage in maintaining these values through their function of applying the law. Given these circumstances, it should not be surprising that, like all professional groups, the legal profession remains middle-class in its origins and outlook. Research shows the predominance of professional and managerial backgrounds among lawyers, as indicated by fathers' occupations. It is the peculiarities of recruitment into the legal profession, and its unique position in the social structure, that tend to favour middle-class aspiring lawyers. Further, the high cost of legal education, especially postgraduate training, is prohibitive for many potential recruits, though the female:male ratio has changed dramatically since the 1970s in favour of females entering the profession.

Senior judges, however, are still appointed largely from the ranks of experienced and established barristers, 'it may be fairly said that members of the higher levels of the judiciary represent a distillation of those social-class currents within the legal system' (Harris 1993: 327). The uniform social and educational background of senior judges, largely from an independent school and Oxbridge backgrounds, raises questions about the general social and political outlook of the judiciary as a whole. In analysing cases with political elements coming before judges, Griffith (second edition, 1981: 34 and 320) writes that:

> we find a remarkable consistency of approach in these cases concentrated in a fairly narrow part of the spectrum of political

opinion. It spreads from that part of the centre which is shared by right-wing Labour, Liberal and 'progressive' Conservative opinion to that part of the right which is associated with traditional Toryism – but not beyond the reaches of the far right.

Griffith concludes that UK judges cannot be politically neutral 'because they are placed in positions where they are required to make political choices which are sometimes presented to them'. Lord Devlin (1978: 510), in replying to this analysis, declares that too much is made by Griffith of the 'politics of the judiciary'. Their politics, he argues, 'are hardly more significant than those of the army, the navy, and the air force; they are as predictable as those of any institution where maturity is in command'.

It would seem, then, that at the apex of the legal system there is still a body of judges whose social class and educational background is likely to persuade them towards a conservative perhaps even reactionary outlook on the social world. On the other hand, there is the rest of society, comprising groups and individuals with very heterogeneous beliefs, values and attitudes. In Harris's (1993) view, it is no answer for the judiciary to argue that changes in society and the law are the business of Parliament, not of the judges. The problems which critics of the judiciary raise are not merely legal problems. They are at the heart of the political structure and any far-reaching reforms will inevitably arise through pressure brought to bear on legal and political institutions in modern Britain.

## Sources of English law

Because of its history and origins, the English legal system differs from that of Scotland and western Europe. English law is a common law system, as are those in Ireland and the Anglo-Saxon states of the US, Canada, Australia and New Zealand. European legal systems are based on civil law (or codified Roman law) as in France, Italy, Germany, Spain, the Netherlands and Portugal. The laws of Scotland, and South Africa, Quebec, Louisiana and Israel, embody elements of both (David and Brierley 1978). There are various ways of classifying English law, and its rules are derived from a variety of legal sources. English law is divided into two great branches, the criminal and the civil; of these the civil is the greater. The distinction between a crime and a civil wrong does not rest on the nature of the wrongful act itself but on the legal consequences that may follow it. Normally, criminal and civil proceedings are easily distinguishable, brought in different courts, with different procedures, different outcomes and different legal terminology. Crimes are divided into 'indictable' and 'summary offences', with indictable offences the more serious crimes and tried by judge and jury in higher courts, and summary offences tried, often before magistrates, in lower courts.

There are three main types of civil wrong:

• breach of contract

• torts

• breach of trust.

A breach of contract occurs where one party breaks the terms of a legally enforceable contract with the other party. Torts include wrongs such as assault, battery, trespass, false imprisonment, defamation of character, negligence or nuisance. Thus a tort is a civil wrong independent of contract. It gives rise to an action for damages irrespective of any agreement not to do the act complained of. A trust is an obligation enforced by the courts and occurs when a person, technically called a settlor, transfers property to another person, called a trustee, on trust for someone else, called a beneficiary. If a trust is breached the courts can enforce it. More generally in civil cases, where proceedings result in judgement for the plaintiff, the court may order the defendant to:

• pay the plaintiff money

• do, or not do, something through an injunction

• perform a contract

• transfer property to the plaintiff.

Another branch of civil law concerns government of the state and its relationship to individual citizens. This is called constitutional and administrative law. Constitutional law is largely concerned with the organs of government, explaining where these bodies have come from and how they derive their constitutional power. It deals with: royal prerogative; functions of the executive, legislature and judiciary; the role of cabinet government and that of the prime minister; and the position of the courts and judiciary in the constitution. Administrative law is that branch of the law focusing on administrative agencies of the state, such as public corporations, delegated legislation and administrative tribunals. The essential difference between these branches of the law is that constitutional law studies the organs of the state, while administrative law studies them in operation.

Alternative classifications of law include:

• private law and public law

• substantive law and procedural law

• civil law and common law

• statute law and common law

• common law and equity.

Private law incorporates all the branches of law concerning cases where one party is making a claim against another. It takes in contract, tort and family law. Public law concerns cases where the state is involved and the public has a direct interest in the outcome. It includes criminal, constitutional and administrative law, and law affecting welfare services and local government. Substantive law focuses on the legal principles established by the courts in particular branches of the law, while procedural law is concerned with how law is used in those courts. Civil law and common law distinguish between those legal systems, as on the continent of Europe, based on codes of law – civil law systems – and those, such as in England and Anglo-Saxon countries, based on legal precedents and interpretation of statute law – common law systems.

The main sources of English law are:

• legislation

• common law

• equity

• custom

• books of authority.

Until the nineteenth century Parliament was primarily a deliberative body, and in practice parliamentary legislation, or statute law, was not a very productive source of law. With the rapid changes in society following industrialisation and growth of modern government, it is legislation that is the most important source in English legal theory. Sources of policy come from the party in power, departments of state and public opinion, represented by pressure groups and the mass media. Normally, the legislative process represents a continuous interaction between these forces. There is also the Law Commission, which acts as a major source of ideas for legal reform and plays an advisory role to Parliament on less controversial matters.

Parliament, or more exactly the monarch in Parliament, is defined as the supreme law-maker in the UK. Though judges make law, but in an increasingly limited way, legislation overrides the law that judges make in the courts. Before becoming an act, a bill is initiated in Parliament and proceeds through various stages of enactment. Public bills deal with matters affecting the public generally, and private bills deal with matters of limited or sectional interest. Ministers or MPs introduce public bills; in the latter case they are called 'private members' bills'. Government bills originate from:

• government's election manifesto

• national emergencies

• government investigations

• recommendations of the Law Commission.

Private members' bills are normally the result of MPs being approached to support proposals put forward by pressure groups operating outside Parliament. In practice, the amount of time allocated private members' bills is strictly limited and the majority of such bills fail to reach the statute book. For government bills, the parliamentary process falls into three phases: a period of consultation before a bill is introduced; a debate and examination of the bill in the Commons and Lords; and implementation as an act after the bill has received the royal assent.

Since the UK's admission to the European Economic Community, under the European Communities Act 1972, legal provisions contained in the relevant treaties have become part of UK law, thus challenging the legislative sovereignty of Parliament. There is also provision for European legislation to be incorporated into UK law. In addition to the various treaties themselves, the most important legal devices are 'regulations' and 'directives'. EU *regulations* automatically become legally binding on all member States, while *directives* normally need to be specifically implemented. Member states have no powers to question European legislation, except through the European Court of Justice, and since it is implemented in the UK by subordinate legislation, or administrative circulars, such laws are not debated in Parliament in the same way as public or private bills. There is, however, a special joint committee of the two Houses of Parliament that reviews European legislation and draws the attention of the Commons to matters of importance.

The 'common law' originally meant law that was not local, ie law that was 'common' to the whole of England. This may still be its meaning in particular contexts but is not the usual meaning of the term. More usually the term signifies law that is not the result of legislation, that is, the law created by the custom of the people and decisions of the judges. Within narrow limits, popular custom creates law, as do the decisions of the courts, which are called precedents. The term 'common law' may also mean law that is not equity, ie law which was developed by the old courts of common law as distinct from the system technically called 'equity', developed by the old Court of Chancery. In this sense, common law may even include statutory modifications of the common law. The precise meaning of the phrase 'the common law' therefore depends upon the particular context in which it is used. A third meaning sometimes attributed to the term is law that is not foreign law. Used in this context, it contrasts English law, and that of other countries like the US that have adopted it, with the continental legal tradition based on Roman law.

Judge-made common law, then, as developed through the doctrine of binding precedent, is one of the oldest and most fundamental features of the English legal system. The doctrine of precedent states that a decision made by a court in one case is binding on other courts in later cases involving similar facts. Precedent is the basis of the common law, and its essence is both its certainty and flexibility. On the one hand, judicial decisions can be determined in accordance with previous cases. On the other, the possibility always exists for judicial pronouncements to be modified if the decision proves unjust, inadequate or out of date. Moreover, one of the peculiarities of common law is its ambiguity. For every precedent cited by one counsel in support of a client's case, another proffers precedents supporting the case of his or her client. Judicial discretion does, then, make a difference. As Twining and Miers (1982: 291) argue:

> The exercise of discretion in choosing one particular formulation of the [rule of law] of a prior case involves basically the search for the most persuasive or cogent argument in its favour. While it is difficult to classify these reasons according to their acceptability or to the weight and priority that is attached to them, the status, acceptability, and permanence of decisions is in this country to a large degree controlled by judicial recognition of and adherence to a great number of constraints that operate on interpreters of precedent cases.

Judges, in other words, select creatively from the mass of precedents cited and, by virtue of their different interpretations of precedent, their decisions can oscillate between the certainty and flexibility of the common law.

Judges also interpret statute law, since the doctrine of precedent also applies to statutory interpretation. The courts define their role in interpreting statutory provisions as applying the statute to the facts before them and giving effect to the intentions of Parliament, as expressed in that statute. The courts have various techniques of interpretation. These are important, given the complex nature of modern statutes and that they are sometimes poorly drafted. The three common-law techniques used are the 'literal rule', 'golden rule' and 'mischief rule'. The literal rule requires that words in statute are given their ordinary meaning. The golden rule aims, in interpreting words literally, that the courts ensure that no absurdity or inconsistency results. The mischief rule is the principle whereby courts ask themselves what the 'mischief' is that the statute seeks to remedy. According to Harris (1993: 160), there are two basic issues in statutory interpretation: 'what were the intentions of Parliament in passing a particular statute? And do the facts in the present case before the court fall within the ambit of the provisions of the statute in question?'

Equity came into being in the Middle Ages, when the courts of common law failed to give redress to individuals in certain cases. A rule of equity means that it has to be read in the light of the whole complex of rules developed by the Lord Chancellor, and these rules do not necessarily apply if the rule in question is a rule of the common law. In other words, to claim that a particular right is an equitable right means that all subsidiary rules of equity apply to it. On the other hand, saying that a particular right is a common-law right is shorthand for saying that it is to be interpreted in a common-law atmosphere, leaving out of account such equitable rules as apply only to equitable rights. There is always the possibility that those relying on an equitable rule may find themselves outside its limits.

There are three generally accepted meanings of the term 'custom' in English law: general custom, mercantile custom, and local custom. General custom is common law built up on the basis of existing customs of the various regions of what was Anglo-Saxon England. It is now accepted that general custom is no longer a creative source of law, since it has been absorbed into legislation or case law. Internationally accepted legal customs are known as mercantile customs where they are accepted into the English legal system as part of commercial law. As these customs develop, the law takes notice of the changes and they become formalised as laws. Local custom is the term used where people claim by virtue of a local custom, such as a right of way or use of common land, that they have a legal claim that can be adjudicated by the courts. When the courts accept the claim, local custom is treated as local law.

The last sources of English law are the books of authority, largely books of antiquity. Certain ancient textbooks fall into this category and are treated by the judges and the legal profession as universally accepted, in each branch of law to which they apply. Whether a book is accepted as authoritative depends on its professional reputation. There is no way of knowing this other than by a study of professional legal practice.

## THE COURTS IN ENGLAND AND WALES

The courts are the most obvious official means of resolving conflicts between disputing parties in the modern world. In practice, relatively few disputes end up in court since there are several factors militating against court hearings, including the costs of litigation, the time it takes to get issues to court and alternative methods of settling conflicts out of court. The court system is nevertheless a central feature of the legal system. Decisions of higher courts have great significance for the substance of law itself, with courts of law being the ultimate arenas where disputes which cannot be settled any other means, may be taken. The courts in England and Wales are structured according to three sets of criteria (Scotland and Northern Ireland have different arrangements):

• whether the court deals with civil or criminal matters

• the court's jurisdiction

• whether the court is one of first instance or appeal.

The division between civil and criminal matters is central to English law. Civil law comprises all legal rules not part of the criminal code and criminal law covers offences such as murder, theft, crimes against public order and many traffic offences. Private individuals or public bodies may be party to civil proceedings, whereas the Crown Prosecution Service brings the vast majority of criminal cases, although there is no legal reason why private individuals may not initiate criminal prosecutions. In most instances, distinctions are made between the aims and remedies associated with civil law and those of criminal law. Civil law is concerned primarily with restitution or compensation; criminal law is aimed at apprehending and punishing wrongdoers. These distinctions are firmly embedded in the court structure.

In terms of civil jurisdiction, county courts, at the lowest rung of the civil court ladder, are limited in their powers of determining actions in contract and tort and other matters. In terms of hierarchy, county courts are courts of first instance, with both the Court of Appeal (Civil Division) and House of Lords acting as appellate courts only. The three divisions of the High Court of Justice – Chancery, Queen's Bench, and Family – deal in the main with first-instance trials. Chancery Division hears disputes over property, trusts, wills, revenue and company matters. Queen's Bench Division is concerned with contract and tort cases that cannot be dealt with in county courts, while the Family Division hears divorce cases and other matrimonial matters. It is through its appeal channels that the court structure is designed to ensure that justice is done in virtually all types of cases. In theory the doctrine of precedent requires that decisions of higher courts are binding on all courts below them. In practice, judges use interpretative devices to modify precedent. In this way the doctrine of precedent ensures that the law is kept up to date. Jurist and legal writers claim that the formal functions of the courts are:

- dispensing justice to solve disputes

- maintaining stability in the law through precedent

- keeping the law in touch with the needs of a changing society.

The structure of the civil courts in England and Wales is outlined in Figure 5.1.

*Figure 5.1* The structure of the civil courts in England and Wales

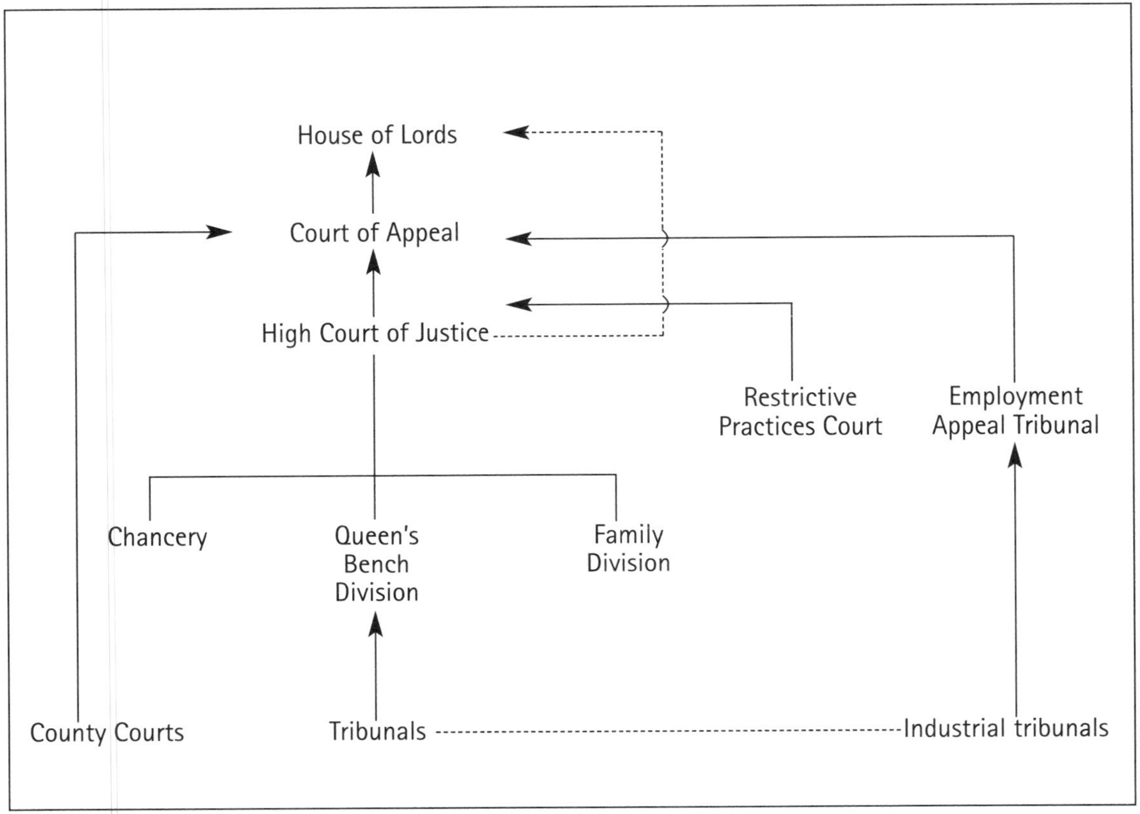

House of Lords

Court of Appeal

High Court of Justice

Restrictive
Practices Court

Employment
Appeal Tribunal

Chancery

Queen's
Bench
Division

Family
Division

County Courts

Tribunals

Industrial tribunals

The jurisdiction of county courts includes relatively small claims, covering:

• actions founded on contract and in tort

• actions concerning land

• equity matters

• probate disputes

• winding up of small companies

• bankruptcy matters

• undefended divorce petitions

• consumer credit

• a special scheme for pursuing small claims.

In contrast, the overwhelming majority of cases heard in magistrates' courts are criminal, but they have limited jurisdiction in certain family proceedings, recovery of some debts and licensing matters.

As outlined above, the High Court of Justice is divided into three divisions: the Chancery Division, Queen's Bench Division (QBD) and Family Division. The headquarters of the High Court is in London but there are a number of district registries in larger cities. Each division of the court is presided over by a senior judge, with the Lord Chief Justice heading the QBD and Lord Chancellor nominal president of the Chancery Division, assisted by a number of high court judges. Queen's Bench is the largest division and its jurisdiction is civil and criminal, original and appellate. In terms of its civil jurisdiction, QBD covers all cases in contract and tort, whatever the value of the claim, though in practice it considers only claims above county court limits. One branch within QBD is the Commercial Court, which hears cases of a commercial nature, including insurance, banking and interpretation of mercantile documents. QBD also incorporates a separate Admiralty Court, with its own judge. Additionally, five High Court judges are appointed to hear cases in the Restrictive Practices Court, which examines agreements restricting prices or conditions for the supply of goods. Similar arrangements apply to the Employment

Appeal Tribunal, which hears appeals from employment tribunals and the Certification Office. In its role as an appellate body, the Queen's Bench Divisional Court exercises supervisory jurisdiction of the High Court over inferior courts and tribunals.

Chancery Division of the High Court, as the direct descendant of the Lord Chancellor's equity jurisdiction, is substantially concerned with matters formerly belonging to the old Court of Chancery. Statute has also allocated responsibility to it for such important matters as the winding up of companies and revenue cases. Its jurisdiction includes:

- execution of trusts and wills
- redemption and foreclosure of mortgages
- partnership actions
- specific performance of contracts
- conveyancing and land matters
- patent and copyright actions
- revenue and taxation matters
- company matters.

Many of the cases coming before the Chancery Division are not disputes but proposed courses of action calling for judicial approval. One example is when arrangements need to be legally approved for altering a company's structure. Chancery Divisional Court hears certain income tax appeals and appeals from county courts in bankruptcy and land registration matters.

The Family Division retains jurisdiction in matrimonial cases formerly vested in the Probate, Divorce and Admiralty Division. It has jurisdiction of wardship proceedings and other matters concerning minors. Its legal responsibilities include:

- the granting of legal title
- complex divorce and matrimonial cases
- applications relating to adoption, custody of minors and presumption of death

• appeals on family law matters.

Appeals from any of the three divisions of the High Court normally go to the Court of Appeal (Civil Division), though in a limited number of cases it is possible to leapfrog the Court of Appeal and go direct to the House of Lords. The present jurisdiction of the Court covers appeals from the High Court, including divisional courts, county courts, Employment Appeal Tribunal and Transport Tribunal. The Master of the Rolls is in practice the senior judge of the Court of Appeal, although the Lord Chancellor, ex-Lord Chancellors, Lord Chief Justice, Vice-Chancellor, President of the Family Division and Lords of Appeal in Ordinary are all members of the Court.

The House of Lords in its judicial capacity is the final court of appeal in civil and criminal matters from all courts in England, Wales and Northern Ireland and in civil matters from courts in Scotland. In addition to the Lord Chancellor there are a number of Lords of Appeal in Ordinary to try such appeals. The Court, for which a quorum is three, normally has five judges to hear appeals. The cases always raise a point of law of general importance and this is the sole ground for obtaining leave to appeal. Judgements of the House of Lords are always reported, because each one adds some new principle to the law or clarifies an existing principle. As the supreme court, decisions of the House of Lords are binding on all lower courts, thus forming an important element as a source of law through the doctrine of judicial precedent.

In addition to the courts, there is an extensive tribunal system. Tribunals are quasi-legal bodies for deciding or adjudicating in disputes, normally after a decision has given rise to a disagreement. During the twentieth century, tribunals have proliferated on a piecemeal basis, being established when and as necessary. Tribunals, which dispose of over 250,000 cases per year, have two main functions. One is resolving disputes between private individuals or between individuals and corporate bodies. The main areas here are employment and land and property. Employment tribunals, for example, determine issues between employers and employees in matters such as unfair dismissal, redundancy payments and discrimination, while rent tribunals and rent assessment committees arbitrate between landlords and tenants. The second function of tribunals is to resolve disputes between public bodies and private citizens such as social security appeal tribunals and income tax appeals. The claimed advantages of tribunals are their specialisation, accessibility, informality, flexibility, speed and low cost. On the other hand, there has been a tendency in recent years for tribunals, such as employment tribunals, to become more like formal courts. This is partly because of an increase in use of legally qualified chairpersons and legal representation by the parties. One result is a loss of some of their claimed advantages such as informality, flexibility and cheapness. Access to tribunals is seriously impaired by non-availability of legal aid for most tribunal hearings. Delay is also a problem because of overloading and resource deficiencies in some tribunals.

From April 1999, a series of legal reforms were instituted, aiming to make the civil courts in England and Wales more accessible and efficient. The main purpose of the so-called 'Woolf reforms' is to curb lengthy litigation by introducing new rules encouraging mediation and giving judges more power to control cases. This transformation of the legal system, it is hoped, will change it, over the years, from one in a 'state of crisis' to one that is fairer, simpler, faster and cheaper to use. The reforms, based on the recommendations of Lord Woolf, Master of the Rolls, are designed to transform the legal culture and overturn the expensive and adversarial nature of the system, in which highly-paid lawyers fight cases to a bitter end. In its place, government wants an environment favouring mediation over litigation, and one curbing the costs and delays of those cases going to trial. The changes, complemented by the spread of 'no-win, no-fee' arrangements following the access to justice bill, are designed to open the courts to 'middle' England. The Woolf reforms are aimed at being more evolutionary than revolutionary. Under Woolf, cases are to be assigned to three tracks, depending on their value and complexity, with strict deadlines fixed for lower value claims. These mechanical changes are underpinned by a more central, interventionist role for judges. They are responsible for managing cases and given extensive powers, including cost sanctions, to punish troublesome litigants. Judges also have the power to use financial penalties to encourage mediation. A new concept of proportionality means courts are unlikely to award costs to big companies fighting small claims against financially weaker opponents. Lawyers will have to seek earlier resolutions to disputes and be more transparent about charges to clients.

## ELEMENTS OF CONTRACT LAW

A contract is, in essence, an exchange of promises. Sometimes the agreement refers to a promise to be fulfilled by one party in the future, which is called an 'executory' contract. More usually, in everyday contracts, exchange is instantaneous and the contract completed straight away, as in the case of purchases in shops: these are called 'executed' contracts. The law of contract, as developed by the judges, paralleled the development of social and economic *laissez-faire* in the nineteenth century, which held that the affairs of business, manufacturing, trade and employment were best left to the individuals concerned, with minimum state intervention or parliamentary legislation. Legal counterparts to this individualist philosophy were the twin assumptions of freedom and equality of contract. In a free market economy, competition is crucial and the attitude of judges and legislators was that it was up to the individuals concerned to strike the best bargains that they could negotiate. It was certainly not up to the courts or Parliament to repair bad bargains. Within the legal framework, it is contract that remains the legal cornerstone in business, consumer and employment transactions. Contract is the legal device facilitating exchange of goods or services between individuals and organisations in liberal democratic societies. It is a legally binding agreement between two parties, whereby each party undertakes specific obligations, or enjoys specific rights, conferred by that agreement. The expression 'breach of contract' (ie breach of a term of the contract) underlines the fact that, if one party fails to honour part of the bargain, the other can sue and obtain a remedy through the courts.

The essential elements in a valid contract are:

• offer and unconditional acceptance

• intention to create legal relations

• capacity of the parties

• consideration

• genuine agreement between the parties

• the contract must not be contrary to public policy

• the requirement of written formalities in some cases.

An offer must state all the terms of the offer, be communicated to the offeree and distinguished from an invitation to treat. It must not be vague and can be terminated before it is accepted by revocation, lapse of time, rejection or death. Acceptance must be unconditional or else it is regarded as a counter-offer. Acceptance, in turn, must be communicated to the offeror, though it can be implied from the party's conduct and it has to be made within a reasonable or stipulated time.

In determining a valid contract, there must be genuine agreement and consent between the parties and a number of factors affect this. Misrepresentation, for example, may be either fraudulent or innocent. Where fraudulent misrepresentation occurs, the aggrieved party may avoid the contract with or without seeking damages. Alternatively the aggrieved party can affirm the contract and seek damages. With innocent misrepresentation, the main remedy is to avoid the contract, though damages may be awarded even after performance has taken place. Similarly, fraud, if proved, allows the injured party to avoid the contract, with or without seeking damages. Mistake involves the subject matter of the contract, or the identity of the parties, and if the mistake is fundamental the contract is normally rendered void in law. Duress and undue influence also affect the genuineness of consent. Duress is actual or threatened violence against, or imprisonment of, the party concerned, and, at common law, any contract induced by duress is void. Undue influence is where a party is coerced and precluded from the exercise of free judgement. Contracts induced by undue influence are voidable at the court's discretion.

There are two presumptions regarding intention to create legal relations. In social or domestic agreements the courts hold that there is normally no intention to create legal relations. In business agreements, by contrast, the courts presume that there is such an intention. This presumption is rebutted, however, if there is express provision to that effect between the parties.

It is essential that the parties to a contract have proper capacity to make one. The contractual capacity of contracting parties is affected by a number of factors. For their own protection, for example, minors have limited contractual capacity. As a general rule, minors can enforce contracts against other people but cannot, with certain exceptions, have contracts enforced against them. The main exceptions are contracts for 'necessaries', contracts for minors' benefit and voidable contracts. Thus, if goods are deemed necessaries, minors are obliged to pay a reasonable price for them, not necessarily the contract price. Contracts for minors' benefit include educational, service or apprenticeship contracts, provided it can be shown that the fundamental purpose of such contracts is to the minor's ultimate benefit. By statute, certain contracts are void and cannot be enforced against a minor, including contracts for repaying money debts or money loans and contracts for goods supplied or to be supplied, other than necessaries.

Contracts with persons of unsound mind are generally valid but there are a number of exceptions. First, if the contracting party is aware of the other party's mental disability the contract is voidable at the discretion of the mentally unsound person. The onus of proof lies with any persons claiming insanity. They must prove that their disabilities prevented them from understanding the consequences of the transaction and that the other party knew this. Second, where the property of the mentally ill person has been placed under the courts' control, any contract involving disposal of the property does not bind the patient. Contracts are also voidable if individuals who were drunk at the time of making a contract can prove that they were incapacitated owing to intoxication and that the other party was aware of it. Although bankrupts are not devoid of contractual capacity, certain limitations are placed upon them. It is an offence for undischarged bankrupts, for example, to obtain credit beyond a limited amount without disclosing their position.

Another feature of contract law is that, at the time of its formation, the contract should be capable of being performed. Where it is reasonable to do so, future difficulties should be anticipated and provided for. A contract that is illegal at its formation is devoid of legal effect. Where a contract is legal when made, and subsequently becomes illegal, because of a change in the law, such a contract will normally be discharged on the ground of frustration. Contracts may be illegal because statute or common law forbids them. Examples of contracts, which are contrary to common law, include contracts for immoral purposes, interfering with the course of justice, in restraint of trade, or defrauding the Inland Revenue.

The general rule in English law is that unless something of value is given in exchange for a promise or undertaking, the promise cannot be enforced against the promisor. Consideration or form, therefore, may be regarded as the element of the bargain in a contract and, at its simplest, involves a *quid pro quo* between the parties. There are a number of legal rules relating to consideration, though there are many exceptions arising from case-law decisions. The main ones are:

- every simple contract has to be supported by a consideration, which must be legal

- consideration must move from the person making the promise to the person to whom the promise is made. This rule is connected with the legal doctrine of privity of contract, which means that only those who are parties to the contract acquire rights and obligations under it

- consideration must be something beyond the promisor's existing obligations to the promisee

- consideration must not be in the past. This means that a promise made in return for some past benefit or service is normally unenforceable at law. Where it can be shown that services were rendered at the express or implied request of the promisor, however, the courts take the view that this is sufficient consideration to support a subsequent promise to pay

- consideration must be real, though it need not be adequate, since it is up to the parties to make their own bargain.

The following remedies are available for breach of contract:

- an action for damages

- a claim for *quantum meruit*

- an application for a decree of specific performance

- an application for an injunction.

An award of damages by the courts is intended to be compensatory, not punitive. If a legal right has been infringed, but no actual loss has resulted, the courts normally award nominal damages only. Further, injured parties are expected to take all reasonable steps to mitigate the extent of any damage and are unable to claim compensation for losses due to their own failure to act in a reasonable way after the breach occurred. A distinction is drawn between 'liquidated' and 'unliquidated' damages. The former is damages agreed upon by the parties at the time of entering into the contract and the latter is damages agreed upon after the contract has been entered upon. Only the fact that a breach has occurred needs to be proved; no proof of loss is required. To be enforceable by the courts, liquidated damages must be shown to be a genuine pre-estimate of loss and not a penalty inserted as a threat of punishment in the event of breach of contract. Where the courts conclude that the prearranged sum is in fact a penalty, it will not be awarded.

A number of legal rules are applied by the courts to determine whether a penalty is involved, including where:

• the words used by the parties are not conclusive

• a single sum is payable as damages for any one of several breaches, varying in gravity

• the sum involved is extravagant.

The essence of a penalty is a payment to frighten defaulters into carrying out their side of the bargain, while the essence of liquidated damages is a genuine pre-estimate of the likely loss in case of default.

*Quantum meruit* is a claim based on reasonable remuneration and is distinct from a claim for compensation for loss based on action for damages. The following are circumstances where a claim based on *quantum meruit* is appropriate:

• work has been carried out under a contract which subsequently turns out to be void and damages cannot be awarded for the breach of a void contract

• substantial performance of the contract has been carried out

• there was an express or implied contract to render services, with no agreement to remuneration

• the original contract has been replaced by a new implied contract.

A claim for *quantum meruit*, in short, offers an alternative course of action to plaintiffs who might otherwise seek damages.

Awards for specific performance were formerly available only in courts of equity but are now available in any court. However, courts exercise discretion according to the following principles:

• action must commence within a reasonable time, since delay defeats equity

• the plaintiff's conduct is also taken into account by the

courts, with those going to equity needing to have 'clean hands'

- specific performance is never granted in the following circumstances: where damages are an adequate and appropriate remedy; where the contract is one for personal services; where the courts are not able to supervise the contract; where a promise is not supported by consideration; where undue hardship would be caused to the defendant; or where the contract is not binding on both parties.

Injunctions are another equitable remedy that the courts may award in cases where damages are neither an adequate nor an appropriate remedy. At their simplest, injunctions are court orders restraining an actual or contemplated breach of contract. There are several forms of injunction, such as 'interlocutory', 'prohibitory', 'perpetual' and 'mandatory'.

## LEGAL PROTECTION FOR EMPLOYEES

The relationship between employers and employees, covering terms and conditions of employment, execution of work and collective bargaining between them, is complex and of vital significance to both parties and society generally. It is important to the community that employer–employee relations are relatively harmonious and mutual, and social considerations demand that employees should not be exploited by being underpaid or exposed to unnecessary dangers in carrying out their tasks. The legal relationship between the two parties has evolved over the centuries by the application of common law rules on contract, tort and crime in various employment situations. Since the complex and special needs of employers and employees are not always adequately met by the application of broad common law principles, statutory provisions have been created to establish a detailed framework of legal rules affecting them. These are aimed at regulating and controlling the conflicting demands of employers, employees in the labour market and the place of work. Basically, employment or labour law covers three main areas:

- individual employment relations, especially the law focusing on the contract of employment and job protection rights of employees

- collective employment relations, especially the law affecting trade unions, collective bargaining and industrial conflict

- health and safety at work, such as the Factory Acts and law of industrial injuries.

Given the wide scope of labour law, this section concentrates solely on the nature of the contract of employment and the employment protection rights of individual employees.

## The contract of employment

In law, employees are individuals working under a 'contract of service' for an employer, in return for wages or a salary. This contrasts with the self-employed, who work under 'contracts for services' for fees, commission or similar payments. Since the nineteenth century the working relationship between employers and employees has been legally embodied in the contract of employment, which is an arrangement whereby an employee agrees to work for an employer, who agrees, in turn, to pay for the work done, thus resulting in a 'pay–work' bargain. Formation of the contract is according to the general law of contract. Apart from merchant seafarers and apprentices, who are covered by special provisions, the contract may be oral, or in writing, or both. Until recently, it was usual to find only a few terms of the contract specified, such as rates of pay and hours of work. Today, as can be seen in Figure 5.2, the employment contract derives from a variety of sources that have developed from the law, collective bargaining, managerial rules and custom and practice over the years.

The express terms of the contract are those that are spelled out, either in writing or orally, and can include the following:

- the identity of the parties

- the date of starting work

- the terms of payment

- hours

- holiday entitlements

- holiday pay

- sickness pay

- grievance and disciplinary procedures

- pension arrangements, and so on.

Some of these terms may be expressly incorporated in the contract of employment by reference to documents such as collective agreements, works rules or employee handbooks. Express terms take precedence over all other sources of the contract, apart from statutorily implied terms. Under the Employment Rights Act 1996, employers are required to provide their employees, including part-timers, with a written statement of the main terms and conditions of their contract within two months of commencing work. This contractual statement is not the contract of employment itself but is normally the best evidence of its express terms.

*Figure 5.2*  Sources of the contract of employment

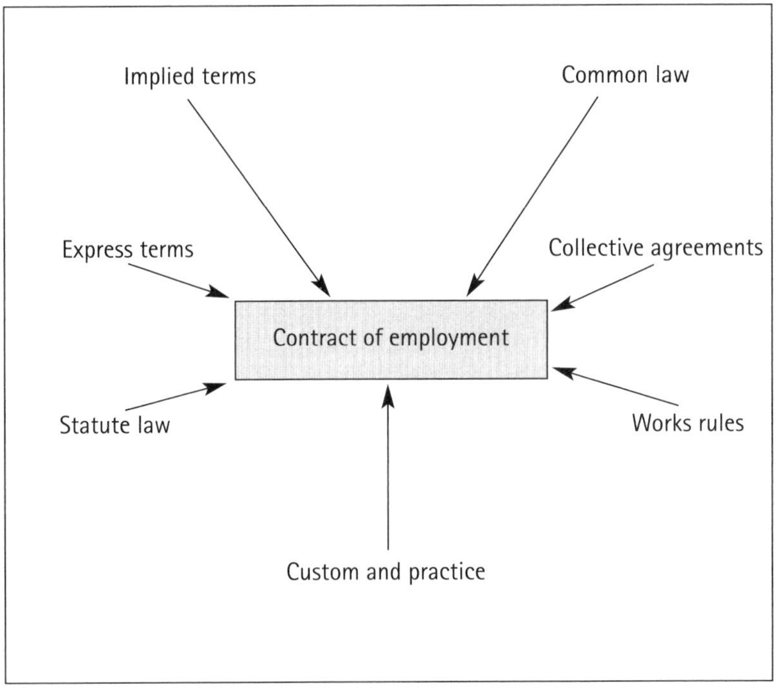

The implied terms of the contract are those inferred by the courts. Both employers and employees have certain common-law duties which are implied in the contract of employment. In the case of the employer, there is the duty to provide agreed pay, take reasonable care of the employee's safety, maintain the trust and confidence of the employee, and not to expose the employee to grave danger of health or person. On the employee's part, there is the duty to give honest and faithful service, use reasonable skill and care when working, and obey all lawful and reasonable instructions given by the employer or its agents. The latter is sometimes known as the duty of co-operation and provides the basis of the employer's common-law powers of discipline.

A collective agreement, or particular terms of it, may be incorporated into individual contracts of employment, either by express words or by implication. It is quite common in the individual contract to find words stating that the employee's pay and hours of work are to be determined in accordance with the relevant collective agreement. Even where no express words are used, and the normal practice is to pay wages and provide conditions negotiated with union representatives, there is no difficulty in implying a term that pay and conditions are to be provided in accordance with the collective agreement. This normally applies to union members and to non-unionists working for the same employer.

Works rules, or those incorporated in an employee handbook, may also become terms of the contract of employment. Like collective agreements, these employment rules may be incorporated into the contract, either expressly or by implication. Where employees sign a document saying that such rules form part of their contract, they become express terms and the signatories are bound by them. Works rules and those in employee handbooks may also become part of the contract by being displayed prominently in the workplace or where they are proved to be local custom in the establishment. Works rules offer an advantage to employers because they are determined unilaterally by the employer.

A custom or practice may be implied as a term of the contract of employment if it is 'reasonable, certain and notorious'. To be reasonable, judges must approve it. To be certain, it must be precisely defined. And to be notorious, it must be well known. Not every custom and practice, therefore, can be considered as part of the contract of employment. But 'with workers increasingly getting written statements of terms which cover most of their workplace rights and duties this incorporation is becoming less relevant' (Painter *et al* 1998: 50).

### Statutory employment rights

Since the 1960s, employees have been provided with a series of statutory employment rights, which effectively supersede and extend their rights at common law within the contract of employment. Some of the main statutory employment rights of individuals are outlined below. Generally, enforcement of statutory rights is kept separate from enforcement of common law rights. Cases determining whether the statutory rights of employees have been infringed can be referred to employment tribunals. Cases determining infringement of common-law rights, such as breach of contract, have traditionally been heard in the civil courts. The legislation currently providing employment and job protection rights for employees is largely incorporated in the:

- Equal Pay Act 1970

- Sex Discrimination Act 1975

- Race Relations Act 1976

- Transfer of Undertakings Protection of Employment Regulations 1981

- Trade Union and Labour Relations (Consolidation) Act 1992

- Disability Discrimination Act 1995

- Employment Rights Act (ERA) 1996

- National Minimum Wage Act 1998.

### *Right to a written statement of the main terms and conditions of employment*

Within two months of starting work, employees are entitled to a written statement from their employer setting out the main terms and conditions of their employment. This right applies both to full-time and part-time employees. The written information provided should include details of:

- names of the employer and employee

- place of work or, where the employee is required or permitted to work at various places, an indication of this and the address of the employer

- date on which employment/continuous employment began

- where the employment is not expected to be permanent, the period for which it is expected to continue or, if it is for a fixed term, the date when it is to end

- scale and method of remuneration and intervals at which it is to be paid

- any collective agreements which directly affect the terms and conditions of employment including, where the employer is not a party, the persons by whom they were made

- terms and conditions relating to hours of work, including normal working hours and contractual overtime

- entitlements to holidays, including public holidays and holiday pay, and any entitlement to accrued holiday pay on termination of employment, to be precisely calculated

- terms relating to sickness, notification of sickness and pay for sickness

- pension arrangements, including a statement as to whether or not a contracting-out certificate is in force

- length of notice that an employee is entitled to receive and the amount to be given if he or she wishes to terminate his or her employment

- title of the job that the person is employed to do

- disciplinary rules, or an indication of where the person can go to find out about the rules

- name of the person to whom a grievance should be taken and the steps and stages of the appeals procedure

- if the employee has to work outside the UK for a period of one month or more, details of the periods, any additional remuneration or benefits entitlements while abroad, and any terms and conditions relating to his or her return to the UK.

The ERA 1996 requires employers to put certain of these terms and conditions into a single document known as 'the principal statement', such as:

- names of employer/employee

- date of employment/continuous employment

- rate of pay and interval of payment

- hours of work

- holiday entitlement

- place of work.

Employees may be referred to other documents for details of sickness/sick pay arrangements, pension rights, collective agreements and disciplinary and grievance procedures. However, if employees are referred elsewhere, especially to read collective agreements applying to them, these must be readily accessible in working hours.

### Right to a minimum wage

Workers aged over 21, other than the self-employed, are entitled to a national single-hourly pay rate. This is determined by the Secretary of State after considering advice from the Low Pay Commission. Certain groups, such as share fishermen and voluntary workers, are excluded from these provisions.

### Right to an itemised pay statement

Employees are entitled to receive an itemised pay statement

at regular intervals from their employers, setting out their gross pay, net pay and amounts and reasons for any deductions.

### Right to a guarantee payment

After one month's service, employees are entitled to receive a fixed payment for up to five days in any three-months period in which they would normally work but do not do so because their employer is unable to provide work for them. The amount guaranteed is reviewed annually by the Secretary of State for Education and Employment.

### Right to medical suspension payments

Employees with at least one month's service are entitled to receive a week's pay for each week of suspension from work on medical grounds. This provision is subject to a maximum of 26 weeks' pay.

### Right to equal pay

When employed by the same or an associated employer, men and women have the right to equal treatment in respect of their terms and conditions of employment. The legislation works by inserting equality clauses in contracts of employment. This means that there should be equality of treatment where a man and woman are employed on 'like work', 'work rated as equivalent' or work that is of equal value. After the European Court of Justice had decided that the British Equal Pay Act was deficient in meeting the requirements of European Community standards in 1982, an amending statutory instrument was issued in 1983. This means that equal pay can be claimed even when the jobs are different, provided that the demands made, such as effort, skill or decision-making, are of equal value. Moreover, the whole remuneration package has to be considered, not just pay. The Act does not apply solely to pay but extends to other terms, and applies both to men and women. The comparator has to be in the same employment as the claimant.

### Right to payments in the event of employer insolvency

Where an employer becomes insolvent, employees have the

right to certain payments as preferential debts, including any unpaid items such as wages and salaries, guarantee payments, medical suspension pay, accrued holiday pay and statutory sick pay. Certain other debts may be claimed, including notice pay, unfair dismissal awards and statutory redundancy pay.

### Right to restrictions on deductions from pay

Deductions from workers' pay by employers may not be made unless authorised by statute, by the worker's contract or the workers themselves, in advance, and in writing. Nor can contractual changes be used to authorise changes retrospectively. Payments from which deductions cannot be made include wages, salaries, holiday pay, bonuses and statutory payments. Benefits in kind, pensions and redundancy payments are specifically excluded. Deductions from workers' pay in the retail trade for cash shortages or stock deficiencies are limited to 10 per cent of gross wages on any pay-day, though there is no limit on termination of employment. Further, repeal of the Truck Acts means that manual workers no longer have a statutory right to be paid in cash, and this is subject to employment contracts and employer-union negotiations.

### Rights of expectant mothers

A pregnant employee has the right to paid time off work for antenatal care, maternity leave, maternity pay, to return to employment after the birth of her child and not to be dismissed because of pregnancy. No service qualification is required for an employee claiming paid antenatal care during working hours, provided she has an appointment on the advice of a registered medical practitioner, midwife or health visitor. Further, the EU Pregnant Workers Directive makes provision for the health and safety of pregnant workers. All employers of women of child-bearing age are required to carry out a risk assessment on an employee's role and reduce or remove the health risks to any pregnant worker.

Expectant mothers also have rights to basic maternity leave, extended maternity leave and statutory maternity pay. Basic maternity leave consists of 18 weeks' leave beginning any time from 11 weeks before the expected week of childbirth. There is no service requirement for this. The pregnant employee has to give 21 days' notice in writing before beginning her leave, stating that she is pregnant, the date she intends to start her leave and the expected week of childbirth. Because her contract continues to subsist during her period of maternity leave, an expectant mother has the right to return to work at the end of her 14 weeks' leave. No notification of her return is needed, unless the employee intends returning earlier than the end of 14 weeks, in which case seven days' notice is required. The employee has the right to return to the same job on the same terms and conditions, though not necessarily the same position or job title. Where an employer refuses to allow a woman to return after maternity leave, this is normally regarded as unfair dismissal and the woman is entitled to make a claim to an employment tribunal.

Where a female employee has had two years' continuous service by the eleventh week before her estimated week of childbirth, she has a right to extended maternity leave. This means that she has the right to maternity leave from 11 weeks from the beginning of the week in which childbirth occurs. She must give 21 days' notice in writing before the leave that she is pregnant, the date she intends starting leave and that she intends to exercise her right to return to work. She has the statutory right to return to work any time up to 29 weeks from the beginning of the week in which the birth occurs. To qualify, she must give written notice at least 21 days before the day on which she intends to return. Her employer may ask, no earlier than 21 days before the end of the initial 14 weeks' leave, if she intends to return to work.

To qualify for statutory maternity pay (SMP), a pregnant employee must have at least 26 weeks' service ending with the qualifying week, 15 weeks before her estimated week of childbirth. She is entitled to 18 weeks' SMP, six weeks at 90 per cent of normal weekly earnings and 12 weeks at the standard rate of statutory sick pay. She must give 21 days' notice in writing before her leave begins that she is pregnant, the date she intends to start the leave and her estimated week of childbirth.

### Right not to be dismissed or have action taken short of dismissal because of union membership or activities

Employers may not dismiss, or take action short of dismissal, against employees who are members of independent trade unions or who take part in union activities. Nor are employers allowed to take action against their employees to compel them to join a union, whether it is independent or not.

### Right not to be discriminated against on the grounds of sex, marital status, race or disability

It is unlawful for employers to discriminate against individuals on the grounds of their sex, marital status, colour, race, nationality, ethnic origin or disability. Discrimination can be direct, indirect (not in the case of disability) or by victimisation. Direct discrimination is where one person is treated less favourably than another on one of the prohibited grounds. Indirect discrimination is applying a 'requirement or condition' to one group which is or would be applied equally to another but is such that the proportion of one group complying with it is considerably smaller than the proportion outside that group which can comply. Victimisation is treating persons less favourably because they have used the anti-discrimination legislation, or are suspected of having used it, or have properly alleged breaches of it. However, both the Sex Discrimination and Race Relations Acts permit discrimination, where it is a 'genuine occupational qualification'.

### Right to a minimum period of notice

Employees with at least one month's service are entitled to at least one week's notice of termination of their contract of employment. The period increases to two weeks' notice after two years' service and then goes up by one week for each additional completed year of service, subject to a maximum of 12 weeks. The minimum notice to be given by an employee to an employer is one week and does not increase with length of employment.

### Right to time off without pay for public duties

Employees holding certain public offices, such as justices of the peace and local councillors, are entitled to reasonable time off without pay, irrespective of their length of service.

### Right to transfer employment with a change of ownership

The Transfer of Undertakings Protection of Employment Regulations 1981 reverses the common law position that a change in ownership of an enterprise automatically results in termination of contracts of employment, since these regulations expressly state that the contract of employment continues after a business has been transferred. Although these regulations apply where there are legal changes of owner, they do not include changes in control arising from changes in share ownership alone.

### Right to a redundancy payment and time off work in redundancy situations

Employees dismissed by reason of redundancy may be entitled to statutory redundancy payments. They must have been employed by the employer, or an associated employer, for at least two years continuously and be under 65 in the case of men and under 60 if women. The amount of payment depends on the employee's age, length of service and weekly pay. Employees lose any right to a redundancy payment where the employer offers suitable alternative employment and employees unreasonably refuse it. Employees declared redundant are entitled to time off with pay to look for work and make arrangements for training for future employment.

### Right not to be unfairly dismissed

After the passing of the Employment Relations Bill, employees who have been employed for at least one year continuously have the right not to be unfairly dismissed by an employer, though where the dismissal is by reason of race, sex or union membership that right does not require any continuous employment. To justify dismissing an employee lawfully, the employer has to have a fair reason and act reasonably in carrying it out. Where employees think they have been dismissed unfairly they have the right to take their claim to an employment tribunal. If a claim is upheld, the tribunal has power to recommend re-engagement or reinstatement or award compensation. Compensation, which is awarded against the employer, can consist of a basic award plus a compensatory award, based on the applicant's net loss as a result of the dismissal. Dismissal is always unfair unless it is on account of:

- employee misconduct

- capability or qualifications of the employee

- employee redundancy

- contravention of a statutory duty

- some other substantial reason.

Further, dismissal is always automatically unfair where it is on the grounds of:

- proposed or actual union membership or activity

- proposed or actual non-membership of a union

- complaining about working in unsafe working conditions

- refusing to work on Sundays

- employees acting as trustees of occupational pension schemes

- employees acting as employee representatives

- asserting a statutory right

- unfair selection for redundancy

- pregnancy

- transfer of an undertaking.

In addition to having a fair reason for dismissing an employee, employers must be able to demonstrate that they have carried out the dismissal in a reasonable way, if they are to avoid claims for unfair dismissal at an employment tribunal. A main test of reasonableness is whether the dismissal was carried out in accordance with the code of practice on disciplinary procedure, issued by the Advisory, Conciliation and Arbitration Service and relevant case law.

This means, in practice, that any disciplinary action is expected to:

- follow proper procedure, including a reasonable investigation of the circumstances

- be consistent in the application of disciplinary measures

- be appropriate for the situation

- take account of any mitigating circumstances.

*Right to a written statement of the reasons for dismissal*
Employees with a minimum of six months' service are entitled, on request, to receive a written statement from their employer giving reasons for their dismissal.

## COMPETITION LAW AND RESTRICTIVE TRADE PRACTICES

Business enterprises now have to deal with a spectrum of law covering fair trading and fair competition. This branch of the law has grown piecemeal, especially in the post-war period. Legislation against restrictions on trade arose from changing government attitudes to business arrangements after the Second World War. Prior to this, trading monopolies and restrictive practices were generally tolerated and even encouraged as means of protecting industry and employment. A different philosophy developed subsequently, supporting the view that the economy is better stimulated by competition than by protectionism. Hence, over the years, Parliament has passed legislation aimed at prohibiting a wide range of restrictive or collusive practices and at controlling monopolies and mergers. Legislation to limit restrictive practices and monopolies was first passed in the 1940s and 1950s. These Acts were limited in their scope and effectiveness. Some of the legislation covering these areas is:

- Fair Trading Act 1973

- Restrictive Trade Practices Act 1976

- Competition Act 1998

- Resale Prices Act 1976.

The Fair Trading Act 1973 extends restrictive trade practices legislation to restrictive agreements covering services, as well as to goods, and to information agreements. It also transfers the functions of the Registrar of Restrictive Trading Agreements to the Director General of Fair Trading (DGFT). The Act repeals and replaces the provisions of earlier legislation on monopolies and mergers, renaming the Monopolies and Restrictive Practices Commission the Monopolies and Mergers Commission (MMC). In addition, DGFT is given certain responsibilities for administering the law on monopolies and mergers.

The Restrictive Trade Practices Act 1976 covers restrictive agreements on goods, services and information. A restrictive agreement is one between two or more persons on:

• prices charged or to be charged

• terms of supply or purchase

• recommended prices

• quantities and descriptions of goods

• manufacturing processes

• persons or areas to be supplied.

For an agreement to be deemed 'restrictive' there must be acceptance of a negative obligation restricting a right which would otherwise exist. Such negative obligations must be accepted by at least two parties. Certain defined terms and conditions are disregarded by the Act and certain types of agreement are exempt from its provisions. Where an agreement is caught by the Act, the DGFT normally refers it to the Restrictive Practices Court. In these circumstances there is a statutory presumption that the agreement is contrary to the public interest and, unless the court is persuaded otherwise, the agreement will be declared void in respect of its restrictive provisions.

In order to justify an agreement before the court, the parties must show, first, that it is within one of the eight 'gateways' provided in the Act for satisfying the court that the agreement is permitted. The gateways are:

- protecting the public from injury

- specific and substantial benefit to the public

- the necessity to counteract competitive activity

- necessity in dealing with a third party enjoying a monopoly position

- protecting employment

- benefiting export earnings

- necessity of another restriction, already found in the public interest

- no material adverse effect on competition.

Second, the parties must satisfy a further provision that the agreement is not unreasonable, having regard to the 'balance' between the circumstances pleaded before the court and any detriment to the public. This double test – that of the gateway and of balancing provisions – is a difficult one to pass in practice.

The Competition Act 1998 gives the Office of Fair Trading (OFT), and industry regulators, powers to combat anti-competitive practices, as well as the abuse of a dominant position in the market place by firms. The OFT has powers to enter premises and demand production of documents and order termination of an offending agreement or conduct. It can also impose financial penalties of up to 10 per cent of UK turnover and take action against companies failing to co-operate in an investigation.

The Resale Prices Act 1976 consolidates earlier legislation by prohibiting resale price maintenance, in the sense of enforcing minimum retail prices, unless their enforcement is justified before the court. Terms of contracts requiring minimum resale prices are rendered void in contracts for the sale or supply of goods between suppliers and dealers. The Act also prohibits the withholding of supplies as a means of coercing dealers to maintain minimum resale prices. The only means of exempting specific goods from the Act are on application to the Restrictive Practices Court. The grounds for exemption are that:

- quality of the goods would otherwise be reduced

- the number of retail outlets would otherwise be reduced

- prices in the long term would generally rise

- goods would be retailed in circumstances likely to cause a danger to health through misuse

- any necessary services would cease to be provided or would be substantially curtailed to the detriment of the public.

The law relating to monopolies and mergers is principally consolidated in the Fair Trading Act 1973. Both the Secretary of State for Trade and Industry and DGFT have powers to refer matters to the MMC. These matters fall into four categories:

- monopolies in supply of goods or services or export of goods

- mergers where the merger creates a group adding considerable market share to such an existing monopoly

- references on restrictive labour practices

- general references.

The MMC may be charged with simply preparing a factual report or be asked to make recommendations for action. The latter may be persuasive, but power to adopt remedies rests solely with the Secretary of State.

Enforcement of legislation against restrictive trade practices lies mainly in the hands of the Secretary of State, the DGFT, the MMC, the Restrictive Practices Court and the European Commission. The Secretary of State, for example, has powers under the Restrictive Trade Practices Act 1976 to apply legislation to certain agreements, exempt other agreements and instruct the DGFT not to take proceedings against certain registered agreements. The Secretary of State can also institute inquiries by the MMC and make orders following a report. The DGFT has a number of roles: acting as registrar of restrictive agreements and information agreements; making monopoly references to the MMC;

investigating anti-competitive practices; and acting as the competent authority in the UK regarding the European Commission. The MMC reports on references made to it requiring factual reports or requests for recommendations. The Restrictive Practices Court, which has both lay and judicial members, decides on questions of fact by majority, with no appeal. The court's judicial members decide questions of law, with appeals going to the Court of Appeal.

## LEGAL PROTECTIONS FOR CONSUMERS

Intrusion of public law into private sales and marketing, which was once the preserve of commercial law, is one of the striking legal developments of the twentieth century. Today its main aim is to protect the consumer. This change of object is related to legal, political and economic factors. The largest single influence has been an increase in social awareness in the twentieth century, resulting in a corresponding concern for regulating consumer markets by legislation. Another factor is the inadequacy of civil law as a remedy, especially given its cost and the relative ignorance of consumers regarding their legal rights.

One of the most potentially valuable forms of protection to the consumer was introduced by the Fair Trading Act 1973. The legal protection provided to consumers under the Act is threefold:

- it creates a watchdog or Ombudsman for consumer affairs, the DGFT

- it creates a mechanism for facilitating consumer protection, whereby the Secretary of State is able to define new offences operating against the interests of consumers

- part of the Act provides particular protection against the abuses of 'pyramid selling'.

The DGFT has five functions. The first is protecting the economic interests of consumers by keeping under review, and collecting information on, commercial activities in the UK, especially those relating to supply of goods or services to consumers. The second function is receiving and collating evidence of those commercial activities that appear to affect the general interests of consumers adversely. Third, the DGFT has the duty of advising the Secretary of State on matters concerning the above, and making recommendations of action to be taken to protect consumer interests. Fourth, the DGFT can seek orders from the Restrictive Practices Court against persons persistently maintaining courses of conduct detrimental to the interests of consumers or regarded as unfair to them, where such conduct contravenes criminal law or a civil obligation. This enables the DGFT to deal with suppliers of goods and services who persistently contravene consumer protection legislation. Fifth, if the matter proceeds to the Court, any judgement given in civil proceedings, which includes a breach of contract or breach of duty, is sufficient evidence of proceedings.

Machinery for consumer protection established under the Act involves several stages. These are:

- reference by the DGFT to the advisory committee provided by the Act

- recommendation of the DGFT to the Secretary of State

- consideration by, and report of, the advisory committee

- an order by the Secretary of State in furthering the advisory committee's report.

In determining whether to refer a consumer trade practice to the advisory committee, the DGFT includes any practice in connection with the supply of goods or services relating to:

- terms or conditions of sale or supply

- the manner in which those terms are communicated to customers

- promotion of goods or services

- methods of selling in dealing with customers

- methods of packing or supplying goods

• methods of demanding or securing payment for goods or services.

All these matters are scrutinised by the DGFT in determining whether to proceed with the matter on the grounds that it affects the economic interests of consumers adversely.

The Act has a number of advantages for consumers. First, it provides experienced, centralised machinery for combating unfair trading practices. Second, abuses are dealt with as they arise by the flexibility of statutory instruments, without recourse to new or amending legislation. Third, the existence of the Act provides a statutory deterrent against unfair trading practices. Fourth, local enforcement of the Act is delegated to local authority Departments of Weights and Measures or consumer protection units, which have detailed experience of enforcing the Trade Description Acts, as well as the Weights and Measures Act. Fifth, consumers have the knowledge that, although they may be reluctant to sue, the state can prosecute on their behalf and the courts can award compensation where it is applicable.

The Trade Descriptions Act 1968 provides that any manufacturers or traders who, in the course of business, apply false trade descriptions to goods, or supply goods to which a false trade description has been applied, commit an offence. For all practical purposes, goods can be regarded as having a false trade description applied to them when they are described in terms that lead people to consider buying them, or making a purchase, when they would not have done so had the terms been different and more accurate. The Act also contains provisions about statements of price by sellers of goods and about inaccurate descriptions of any services offered. There are also provisions applying to false trade descriptions used in selling business services, and covering the wording of competitions and promotions that are used to boost the sale of goods. Part of the Act is amended by the Consumer Protection Act 1987, which introduces provisions prohibiting misleading indications on prices. These apply to most businesses, including services, and are designed to protect consumers from inaccurate statements about prices. A code of practice for traders is linked with the 1987 Act and gives detailed guidelines about what is and what is not allowed. Any infringement of the code of practice is strong evidence that there has been a breach of the Consumer Protection Act. Legislation also makes it an offence to sell goods or services by relying on the inertia of selected customers. With goods, this normally means supplying them so that the customer has the choice of sending them back or keeping them and paying for them. With services, it normally means providing the customer with a note indicating that payment should be made for an offered service and that the service will be provided unless the receiver of the note takes action to reject the offer.

The main civil law statute setting out the basic terms and conditions that any buyers, businesses or consumers are entitled to expect from business sellers of goods is the Sale of Goods Act 1979, as amended in 1994 and 1995. This incorporates revisions made by the Supply of Goods (Implied Terms) Act 1973 and Unfair Contract Terms Act 1977. The Supply of Goods and Services Act codifies existing common law rights regarding contracts for the supply of a service, and gives statutory authority to the rights of consumers by implying certain terms into every contract for the supply of a service. These are that:

- the service will be carried out with reasonable care and skill

- the service will be carried out at a reasonable price, unless a price has already been agreed

- the service will be carried out within a reasonable time, unless the time has already been agreed by the parties.

Since the passing of this Act, the law relating to the supply of goods and services has been placed on a similar footing to the law affecting the sale of goods.

The Unfair Contract Terms Act 1977 made far-reaching changes in the law of contract and tort. Virtually all types of contract are affected by it, including sale of goods, hire purchase, services and manufacturers' guarantees. The Act applies between businesses and consumers, and between businesses and businesses, and deals with exemption clauses and any clause where a party seeks to limit or avoid liability for non-performance. The Act also protects consumers from unscrupulous indemnity clauses, where traders require consumers to indemnify them against loss or permit them to substitute manifestly different goods or services from those for which they had bargained.

Consumer credit is largely regulated by the Consumer Credit Act 1974. Its purpose is to provide a comprehensive legal code governing consumer credit, consumer hire purchase, and effective means of securing its enforcement. The Act provides general terms covering different types of financial transaction, with the object of classifying various forms of such transactions and making it easier to apply uniform rules to them. The Act is a valuable instrument for protecting consumers. The range of techniques goes far beyond most other forms of consumer legislation. Its two most striking features are, first, creation of a central enforcement mechanism based on a licensing system controlled by the DGFT. The second is the remarkable power conferred on the courts to intervene in the agreement between the debtor and the creditor. Debtors are given the right to cancel the agreement, or terminate it, despite the fact that they are unable to prove misrepresentation or illegality. Debtors may also apply to the courts to reopen the agreement if it is deemed to be extortionate for the debtor and, under this power, the courts may alter the terms of the agreement or indeed cancel it altogether.

## CONCLUSION

The modern English legal system has evolved over many centuries and embodies the dominant social values of the time, as well as being associated with contemporary moral values. The law thus reflects moral values, and moral values affect the law. Changes in the law are expected to reflect changing social values and standards of morality, whether through legislation or case law, although in practice there is often a time lag between *de facto* new moral standards and what the law legitimises *de jure* subsequently. For businesses, and even public organisations, this morality is rooted essentially in market values. These market values are broadly reflected in the laws of the land as they affect relations between firms and their competitors, shareholders, suppliers, creditors, workers and customers.

It is clear that the legal contexts in which organisations, whether private, public or voluntary, conduct their business affairs is complex and ever-increasing, in terms of both British and European legal developments. Managers need not only a basic understanding of the law, its principles and major legislation, but also to ensure that their subordinates are aware of their legal duties and responsibilities, so that they do not break basic legal rules. Larger organisations are likely to employ their own legal specialists but medium-size and smaller organisations are more likely to need legal advice on an *ad hoc* basis. Keeping up to date with legal changes is an incredibly demanding task, but is vital if an organisation's legal rights are to be protected and its legal responsibilities fulfilled.

# 6 Technology

**David Preece**

Technology and technological change and their impact upon people, organisations and society have long been a key interest of organisational researchers and management theorists. It is only in recent years, however, that an interest has been taken in the converse relationship – that is, the impact of people, organisations and society on technology.

The upshot has been that a perspective which sees given social effects flowing directly and simply from a given form of technology would be regarded, at best, as a partial view, and at worst as misguided if not downright wrong. As a minimum, then, the 'technology-people, organisations and society' relationship should be seen as one that flows in both directions. Thus, to understand what is happening, one needs not only to take a view or perspective upon organisations, people and society, but also a perspective upon the nature of technology and how technology 'connects with' organisations, people and society.

Whatever perspective is taken upon the nature of technology and its relationship with and implications for people, whether in organisations or society in general, it is very difficult to decide where to begin an overview of the area. The somewhat arbitrary decision has been taken here to begin the narrative during the later 1980s. Here the focus is upon certain technological developments which have a significant importance for the nature of work in contemporary organisations, that is information technology (IT), or as it is sometimes alternatively referred to, information and communication technology (ICT). Why focus upon ICTs? Quite simply, it is because in the 1990s ICTs, in the form of the Internet, company intranets and other forms of ICTs, have, as McLoughlin (1999: 1) has observed, 'emerged as perhaps one of the key technological developments of the 20th century'. Why is this so? 'Ideas such as flexibility, team-based and telework . . . and network, distributed and virtual organisations all point to what appears to be radically new ways of working and organising based on new technological possibilities.'

Jones (1997) talks about the 'automation of automation', or 'cybernation', whereby 'taken together . . . the totality of an organisation's automated operations are electronically integrated and linked together' (McLoughlin 1999: 1). We can begin to understand what has been occurring at the organisational and work levels when we locate these technological changes in recent developments in 'local' and international business and organisational contexts. The distinction between these two levels is made because people can be undertaking remunerative work outside an organisation, where they have no contract of employment, and yet could well be using IT, either in a 'stand-alone' mode, or with electronic links to organisations. Teleworking is perhaps the best-known contemporary example, but it should be noted that this too can take a variety of forms (Jackson and van der Wielen 1998).

At the end of this chapter, readers should be able to understand and explain:

• how the external technological environment impacts on private, public and voluntary organisations

• new technologies, their applications and implications for organisation stakeholders.

In addition, they should be able to:

• identify current technological developments and consider their significance for organisational stakeholders.

See also the Professional Standards Index (p 345).

## INFORMATION TECHNOLOGY AND CHANGING ORGANISATIONAL CONTEXTS

Throughout the 1990s, ICTs were adopted by organisations at an accelerating rate, to the extent that it has become commonplace to find that 'ICT is now an intrinsic part of the way organizations work and can achieve substantial and uncontested efficiency gains. Investment in ICT is therefore no longer generally seen as problematic. Instead, attention has turned to achieving cost reductions through major organizational restructuring that takes full advantage of the opportunities presented by ICTs' (Coombs and Hull 1996: 160). One result of this is that many managers have come to focus more upon concerns with horizontal, customer-oriented operational processes than vertical, functionally-oriented management controls. As part of this change, 'ICT infrastructures have become more embedded in organizational processes than was the case in earlier periods when "islands" of ICT capabilities existed in different parts of a company to meet the needs of local management' (ibid: 170). What is more, in contrast to the 'technically-determinist' way (see below) in which technology was often deployed until the late 1980s, the orientation that emerged during the 1990s involves a more enlightened appreciation:

> of the relationships between ICTs and firm-specific organizational arrangements. This new awareness becomes increasingly valuable as the artefacts and techniques of ICT become extremely diverse and widely diffused throughout all aspects of organizational and everyday life. This makes it ever more urgent to develop better understandings of the specific ways in which particular capabilities emerge, are used, and change within each organizational arrangement (ibid: 173–4).

In 1991 a group of academics from the MIT Sloan School of Management published their findings from a programme of research begun in 1984 entitled 'The Management in the 1990s Research Program' ('MIT 1990s' hereafter) (Scott Morton 1991). The primary data were collected from 12 organisations, many of which are internationally known multinational companies. The primary objectives of the project were to study the impact that IT was having upon organisations and how this was affecting – and was projected to affect during the1990s and beyond – their competitive performance in the increasingly turbulent environments in which such organisations found themselves. Four key elements of context were identified: social, political, economic and technical. In this chapter, the latter and its impact upon and relevance to people and work is explored in some detail. The main findings of this project help us to locate technological change in its changing contexts. The study focuses upon technology as IT/ICT, as, indeed, does much of the present chapter, but this is only one, albeit very important, form of new technology. The other main restriction is that our interest is primarily in technologies used in and by formal organisations and their connections to the 'people' dimension of work and employment. A key premiss of the MIT 1990s project was that (Scott Morton 1991: 4):

> Information technology now consists of a powerful collection of elements that are undergoing change and have wide and significant applicability. These elements go well beyond what has been available during the last thirty years... In the 1990s we expect organizations to experience the effects of the integration and evolution of a set of elements collectively termed information technology.

IT was defined as consisting of hardware, software, telecommunications networks, workstations, robotics, and 'smart chips'. The central thesis of the project was that when environmental turbulence and major technological change are combined, the result is a need for significant organisational change in order to survive. What is more (Scott Morton 1991: 5):

> IT offers the opportunity for organizations to react constructively ... there is no reason why organizations will necessarily continue in their present form. These challenges suggest that it will not be possible to survive as a company just by working harder within existing organizational structures and using conventional practices and tools. Given what IT now allows an alert organization to do, an organization that merely works faster and harder will become uncompetitive in the global marketplace of the 1990s and beyond.

MIT 1990s identified six main findings from the research programme:

## IT is enabling fundamental changes in the way work is done

Work will be increasingly affected by IT according to the extent to which jobs use information to inform: what to make and/or what service to offer; the provision of services and/or production of products; when to perform the work; and who else to involve in the process. It is argued that IT has the potential radically to change cost structures and the nature of jobs, but that this will be achieved only if appropriate organisational changes occur at the same time. Three major IT-enabled changes to work forms were identified:

- Production work. Here, robotics, process control instrumentation and the use of intelligent sensors in production processes were highlighted. Data processing computers, for tasks such as billing and accounts payable, were identified with respect to production information, and 'knowledge production' was found to be affected by such technologies as computer-assisted design/drafting and computer-assisted manufacturing (CAD/CAM) and workstations. The observation is made that 'these forms of change are readily understood in the case of physical products and standard information processing but do not seem to be as easily grasped and exploited when it comes to knowledge work' (Scott Morton 1991: 12).

- Co-ordinative work. This is associated with developments in communication networks, through diffusion of ICTs at local, intra- and inter-organisational (at both the national and international) levels. 'The new IT is permitting a change in the economics and functionality of the coordination process', such that 'distance can be shrunk toward zero, becoming increasingly irrelevant as far as information flow is concerned. Thus, the location of work can be reexamined, as can potential partners' (ibid). Likewise, the distancing of work by time has also reduced, or changed to different time zones, for example, where organisations co-operate through using common data bases as a way of shifting time. The compound effect is that IT is enabling organisations to share work and skills, for example, through team working, where the co-ordinative elements of distance, time and memory are combined.

- Management work. This has two main aspects: 'direction' and 'control'. The former is defined as being about detection of changes in the organisation's external context and understanding of changes in employees' views. Both are key inputs into the objectives and vision-setting process. The latter relates to the measurement and analysis of organisational performance and resultant actions.

**IT is enabling the integration of business functions at all levels within and between organisations**

As a result of developments in ICT networks, 'boundaries of organizations are becoming more permeable; where work gets done, when, and with whom is changing' (Scott Morton 1991: 13). The MIT researchers perceive a new, 'deeper' level of organisational integration emerging, in four main forms:

- Within the 'value chain', as exemplified in Xerox linking up design, engineering and manufacturing staff through a local area network (LAN), with teams focusing upon products.

- 'End-to-end' links of value chains between organisations. An illustration here is ICT links between customers and suppliers.

- Value chain substitution via subcontracting or alliances. To illustrate: a task or stage in the value chain is subcontracted to another supplier organisation, and the second-level supplier's designers are linked electronically via CAD/CAM technology to the first-level supplier, thus allowing the necessary data interchange to achieve a collaborative design. The MIT researchers argue that 'these collaborations are enabled by IT and would not be feasible without it. They lead to the host organization being able to take advantage of the economies of scale and unique skills of its partner. To be of lasting value, of course, there must be reciprocal benefits' (Scott Morton 1991: 14).

- Electronic markets. Here, co-ordination is achieved through an open market. For example, travel agents can link direct into, and reserve aircraft seats from, the main carriers. As IT costs continue to fall, so transaction costs are reduced to a point where such electronic markets become more and more economically attractive.

### IT is causing shifts in the competitive climate in many industries

IT is being employed to create both intensified competition and collaboration between companies. It is possible to gain sustained competitive advantage through being an early IT and HR/organisational innovator. Environmental scanning is especially important so that companies can respond proactively in these 'turbulent times'.

### IT presents new strategic opportunities for organisations that reassess their missions and operations

The MIT 1990s project found that the majority of the organisations they studied were passing through three main technology-related stages in responding to their changing contexts:

- The 'automate' stage. This is focused upon reducing costs, typically by reducing headcount through IT.

- The 'informate' stage. This term is borrowed from Zuboff (1988: 188). She defines it as: 'An informating technology textualizes the objects, events and processes that constitute an organization's work ... engenders new possibilities for the production and distribution of knowledge, and ... challenges a system of managerial authority that has depended on exclusive control of the organization's knowledge base' (Zuboff 1988: 319). Jackson (1997: 188) captures the essence of the concept: ' "Informate" refers to the way IT can be employed to convert material practices into information which can then be recorded and displayed on video screens or computer print-outs.'

- The 'transformation' stage. This is seen as an obligatory technological path. All successful organisations in the 1990s 'will have to pass through this stage, characterised by leadership, vision, and a sustained process of organization empowerment so basic as to be exceptionally hard to accomplish' (Scott Morton 1991: 17). This turns out to mean going beyond Total Quality Management by adding a strategic orientation to it, which is facilitated by IT.

### Successful application of IT will require changes in management and organisational structure

The findings here are that, due to the enabling role of IT, unit costs of co-ordination have reduced significantly and economies of scale have changed, as for example flexible manufacturing systems allow smaller companies, as well as larger ones, to be low-cost producers (Scott Morton 1991: 18). 'Thus IT is enabling a breakup . . . of traditional organizational forms. For example, multiple skills can be brought together at an arbitrary point in time and location . . . IT's ability to affect coordination by shrinking time and distance permits an organization to respond more quickly and accurately to the marketplace.' Significant social and work organisation implications flow, of course, from the management of interdependence in the turbulent business environment of the 1990s and beyond, including the need for new management systems and processes and new forms of work monitoring, rewards, incentives and skills.

### A major challenge for management will be to lead their organisations through the transformation necessary to prosper in the globally competitive environment

Given the number of very upbeat comments about IT made up to this point, one can perhaps be forgiven for being somewhat taken aback by the stark business reality of this section: 'A very few firms are better off, and there is a larger group of isolated examples of successful exploitation in particular individual functions or business units. However, on average the expected benefits . . . [of IT] . . . are not yet visible' (Scott Morton 1991: 23). Why is this so? In essence, the MIT 1990s team argues that it is organisational culture that is responsible; that is, a reluctance to give up accustomed ways of doing things for the brave, new, empowered, IT-enabled world envisaged from the 1990s.

Thus, the need for understanding and the effective managing of organisational culture takes centre stage, implying innovative human resource management policies and practices aimed at providing all employees with a sense of empowerment. 'They need to feel that they can make a difference, that their efforts directly affect the organization's performance, and that they are able to take on as much responsibility and commensurate reward as they are willing to work for' (Scott Morton 1991: 21).

The sorts of technological changes referred to above have been seen by some authors as the key cause of a transformation in organisations. In the manufacturing sector, this has typically been discussed in terms of the decline of Fordist production systems and the emergence of new 'Post-Fordist' paradigms such as 'Lean Production' (Womack et al 1990) and 'Flexible Specialization' (Piore and Sabel 1984) and the emergence of what is called a 'Second Industrial Divide'. Business Process Reengineering (Hammer and Champy 1993) and the so-called 'virtual organisation' (Barnatt 1995) are the latest manifestations of this genre.

There are a number of problems with the sort of analysis provided by writers taking the unitarist and managerialist line exemplified in the MIT 1990s programme. The overview later in the chapter of the variety of ways in which technology has been theorised illustrates some of the problems associated with such a position (Grint and Woolgar 1997). A central problem is the implicit assumption that technological change is inevitably of benefit to everyone. People 'problems' occur only because the change process is poorly managed or because of an inability to appreciate the need for change. Thus, a 'human relations' or 'human resources management' response and managerial style is perceived as providing the answer. However, if instead one does not assume a commonality of interests in the workplace, then it is not surprising to find disagreement, differing interpretations and conflict associated with technological change, and there may be no easy solution. As McLoughlin and Harris (1997: 7) observe:

> If new technologies are designed and used to serve particular interests, and if organizations are seen, not as arenas of consensus, but rather the locus of conflict, then disagreement over particular technical changes may be seen as an inevitable and legitimate feature of organizational life, and not as the aberrant consequence of bad communications, poor management or 'Luddite' unions.

There is a long line of research and writing on technological change which explicitly recognises its inherently political nature, as in the labour process discussed below.

A second major objection is that technological change should not be seen as emanating 'naturally' or inevitably out of an 'inner economic or technical logic' which projects it forward. Rather, it should be viewed as a product of social and political factors, including those arising from the interests of the state and employers and managers. Third, and similarly, rather than managers acting as unreflective conduits of the organisation's technological and commercial context, critics argue that: 'managers should be seen as "creative mediators" whose decisions and choices critically influence the ways in which particular technological and market options are selected for development' (McLoughlin and Harris 1997: 7). Important policy implications, at state and organisational levels, flow from a recognition of the above reservations and critiques. Dutton (1996: 12), in his overview of a volume reporting the findings of a number of UK Research Council-funded research projects, has noted that:

> ICTs do not represent a quick fix to deep and historically rooted problems ... The economic payoffs of ICTs are not automatic ... managers, users and politicians need to make informed policy choices – backed by the vision and will to see through a successful implementation of the strategy. Moreover ... many social and economic objectives can be at odds, necessitating wise trade-offs between competing values and interests.

## THEORISING TECHNOLOGY AND TECHNOLOGICAL CHANGE IN ORGANISATIONS

A key requirement for an effective 'intervention' in the 'technology-organisation' dimension of organisations would appear to be that one has an understanding of what the technology is, what it consists of. The fact is, however, that both 'everyday' and academic conceptions and definitions differ widely, and there is no consensus around the nature of organisational technology. As Winner (1977) observed, definitions of technology have changed through time and place. The word derives from the original Greek word *techne*, meaning art or skill. During the twentieth century, the term came to encapsulate tools, the process of work and work organisation. Winner has provided an influential definition of technology. He makes a distinction between: 'apparatus', that is physical, inanimate devices, such as machines and tools; 'technique', that is activities involving human action such as the application of skills, following of procedures; 'organisation', that is social arrangements integrating apparatus and technique; and 'networks', that is organisations linking technique and apparatus across space.

In Grint and Woolgar's view (1997: 9–10), what a technology is and is not, and what it can and cannot do are all socially constructed. 'In other words, there is no boundary between the technical (non-human) and the social (human) other than that which is socially defined' (McLoughlin 1999: 6). While Grint and Woolgar argue against drawing any meaningful boundary between technology and the social, other researchers wish to preserve a distinction on the argument that technology does make a difference to organisational processes and outcomes. However, this presents some serious challenges to researchers with respect for example to where the boundary is to be drawn.

Orlikowski (1992) has moved some way towards resolving this problem. He distinguishes between the *scope* of the definition of technology (that is, what is defined as technology) and the *role* ascribed to a particular form of technology (that is, the nature of the interaction which is seen as occurring between technology and people/organisational factors). Scope definitions range from the restrictive, where technology is equated essentially with hardware, through to those that embrace 'social technologies', that is the tasks, techniques and knowledge required to use the technology. Role definitions range from those that suggest technology has a strong determining influence on organisational and people variables, through to those that suggest a 'soft determinism', that is they see technology as a 'reference point' whose effects are mediated by people.

It follows that in order to understand the relationship between technology and organisation, the question must be addressed: 'what, if any, influence does technology have in shaping organisational behaviour?' The key concerns preoccupying researchers in the area over the years have been to avoid and, indeed, counter:

• 'technological determinist' analyses of the capabilities of technology and its impact on work, organisations and society

• the view that effective responses to organisational problems are either wholly or mainly to be found in technological solutions.

In recent years, such concerns have perhaps become even more pressing 'as the pace of technological innovation has increased and determinist images of technology and their supposed transformative effects on organisation have remained dominant in some academic, and much practitioner and popular thinking' (McLoughlin 1999: 5). The problem is that theorisation of the technology-organisation relationship has been at best ambiguous and conflicting (Orlikowski 1992) and prone to the 'technicism' which it commonly claims to avoid (Grint and Woolgar 1997). Alternatively, technological determinism has often been replaced by 'social and/or economic determinism'.

## Technological determinism
A 'technological determinist' approach to understanding

technology and its significance in business organisations has often been employed by organisational analysts and management consultants. A form of technological determinism can be detected, for example, in the MIT 1990s work referred to above. Here it is implied, as McLoughlin and Harris (1997: 6) have put it: 'firms are primarily driven by technological and competitive imperatives to innovate and have little choice in the matter if they wish to survive.' Williams and Edge (1996) have argued that there are two main forms of technological determinist argument. The first is where the nature of technology and the direction of change are seen as unproblematic or predetermined by factors such as an 'inner technical logic' or 'economic imperative'. The second is where technology is seen as having inevitable and identifiable 'impacts' upon work, economic behaviour, and/or society.

It is argued by Grint and Woolgar (1997: 11) that technological determinism is a myth. It makes technology appear 'to advance spontaneously and inevitably, in a manner resembling Darwinian survival, in so far as only the most "appropriate" innovations survive and only those who adapt to such innovations prosper'. One of the questions which should be posed to people taking a technological determinist line is *why* it appears to them that technology has a life of its own.

## Socio-technical systems approaches

Socio-technical approaches have the overriding objective to identify the 'best fit' between the 'social' elements, such as employees' 'psychological needs', and 'technical' elements, such as machinery and its physical location. Trist and his colleagues (1963) have been influential in this area. According to Buchanan and Huczynski (1997: 568), the essence of the argument put forward by Trist and his co-researchers is that:

> an effective socio-technical system design could never fully satisfy the needs of either sub-system ... Clearly a system designed with an emphasis on social needs and ignoring technical system needs could quickly run into technical problems. Conversely, a

system designed according only to the demands of technology could be expected to generate social and organizational difficulties. What is required is a design approach aimed at 'joint optimization' of the social and technical components and their requirements.

What is more, the design that is selected is arrived at as a result, primarily, of organisational choice, rather than technological imperative, as it would be according to technological determinists.

Notwithstanding this attempt to emphasise the importance of social concerns and objectives, the socio-technical approach has a strong 'technicist' orientation, seeing technology as having a direct influence on matters of work organisation, quality of working life, and so on. But this approach 'tended to carry the implicit assumption that the nature and capacity of technology remained beyond the remit of sociological analysis; in effect, the nature and capacity of technology was treated as given, objective and unproblematic' (Grint and Woolgar 1997: 15). Thus 'what starts out as a radical assault upon traditional conceptions of technology actually reproduces the very same conventions which regard the capacity of technology as inherently unproblematic'. Newer forms of technology such as ICTs, including internets, the world wide web and telecommuting, present particular challenges to the socio-technical approach, as the boundaries between different forms of technology, and between the technical and social-organisational, are increasingly ambiguous.

## Processual approaches

In this perspective, as McLoughlin and Clark (1994: 56) observe, the focus of research and writing is upon 'the assumption that the outcomes of technological change, rather than being determined by the logic of capitalist development, or external technical and product market imperatives, are in fact socially chosen and negotiated within organizations by organizational actors'. Pettigrew (1973), for example, in an early processual study, examined the organisational politics and decision-making behaviour associated with the development and structuring of computer applications. He showed how the head of a management services department was able to influence the computerisation process through taking up a 'gatekeeper' role allowing him to 'shape' the information reaching key management decision-makers. A later influential study by Wilkinson (1983) adopted a processual perspective in examining industrial relations and work organisation issues associated with technical change in a sample of manufacturing companies. Focusing upon skill and control, he showed that a range of choices presented themselves and that the outcomes of technological change were primarily a result of the mediation of lower managers, such as shop floor supervisors, and the responses of the affected workers and their unions. Of course, mediation and negotiation does not begin from scratch each time some form of technological change takes place. Rather it occurs in social and economic contexts where working practices and remuneration arrangements have already been formulated, and possibly contested, and are part of 'custom and practice'; but a 'custom and practice' that is often subject to continual creation and 're-negotiation'.

Buchanan and Boddy's (1983; 1986) writing on technical change was also located within the processual perspective. It was typified by their argument that 'the capabilities of technology are enabling, rather than determining', and that it is 'decisions or choices concerning how the technology will be used', and not the technology itself, that leads to organisational outcomes (1983: 255). From this position, then, technical change is viewed as a phenomenon occurring at a level more or less unique to a given organisation. It therefore makes little sense to predict uniform outcomes before the changes take place or without knowledge of change processes and the organisational context. There is sometimes a lack of attention to the influence of external organisational contexts and the role of the technology itself is under-theorised.

### Radical/Marxist perspectives

Here, the organisational search for profitability is accorded a central place in the analysis 'and is seen as influencing or determining much else that goes on in organizations, including events related to the introduction of new technology' (Preece 1995: 41). The point of departure for much research and writing in this tradition since the mid-1970s has been a labour process perspective inspired by Braverman's *Labor and Monopoly Capital* (1974: 193), where it was argued that:

> Machinery comes into the world not as the servant of 'humanity', but as the instrument of those to whom the accumulation of capital gives the *ownership* of the machines ... Thus, in addition to its technical function of increasing the productivity of labor ... machinery also has in the capitalist system the function of divesting the mass of workers of their control over their own labor.

Technological change, and its associated organisational and social changes, can be understood, then, only through their contextualisation within capitalist society. At the level of the organisation, this means technology will be used by managers to intensify their control over labour, through deskilling and degrading work. Use of IT for monitoring and surveillance of employees in JIT ('Just-in-Time') and TQC ('Total Quality Control') regimes in Sewell and Wilkinson's (1992) electronic consumer goods manufacturer provides an example of this. Here, an 'Electronic Panopticon' is used 'to bring its disciplinary gaze to bear at the very heart of the labour process' and discipline is achieved through electronic tagging (1992: 283). For Braverman, Scientific Management, or 'Taylorism', was the means by which management deskilled work, thereby further extending its control over employees in the era of monopoly capitalism.

According to this perspective, it is not the technology *per se* which deskills jobs, as strict technological determinists would argue, but rather the necessity for capitalists and managers (McLoughlin and Clark: 44–5) to:

> control the labour process in order to increase profits. Under a different social system, advanced technology would open up the possibility of different forms of job design and work organization

which would benefit the workforce. This would involve workgroups possessing the engineering knowledge required to operate and maintain the technology, and a rotation of tasks to make sure everyone had opportunities to work on both highly complex and routine jobs.

It is important to add that labour process theory itself – as with all theories and perspectives – has changed and developed over the years since Braverman's highly influential reformulation. It is impossible to do justice to this critique and reformulation here. But commenting upon the ways in which the nature of work and work organisations have changed over the years, from the 'vantage point' of 1994/5, Thompson and McHugh (1995: 190–1) observe that:

> Though workers' knowledge continues to be appropriated by management, the move away from narrow specialisation and devolved responsibilities, however limited, marks a significant break from those parts of Taylorism based on a clear separation of conception and execution ... changes in the commercial vehicle industry illustrate the point. Many of the *individual* tasks continue to be further deskilled under the impact of standardised procedures and uses of new technology ... But, the *collective* labour of the group involves expanded cognitive abilities and extra-functional skills (emphasis in original).

## The social shaping of technology

In essence, the social shaping of technology (SST) argument is that technology is shaped by the economic, technical, political, gender and social circumstances in which it is designed, developed and utilised (MacKenzie and Wacjman 1985). These factors are embodied in the emergent technology, and thus technology *per se* does not have an 'impact' on work or organisations. The SST perspective has been informed from the beginning by a wish to democratise technological decision-making or, at least, subject it to modes of social accountability and control (Winner 1977, 1985).

The conceptualisation of science and technology as arenas of social and organisational activity, and thus subject to social shaping and amenable to social analysis, has sought to overturn the view that science and technology hold a privileged 'neutral' standing, 'outside' of society. As Williams and Edge (1996: 59) have observed:

> The shaping process begins at the earliest stages of research and development ... SST researchers have explored how technologies develop within the specific local contexts of industrial and academic laboratories. They have also examined how innovations must later be transformed as they move to commercial production and widespread use. This contrasts with conventional ideas about technological diffusion, which treat technical products largely as fixed entities.

An illustration of the social shaping of technology within adopting organisations is provided from Computer Integrated Manufacturing (CIM), where there can be found 'systems [which] cover a diverse range of activities that can rarely be supported in the form of standard solutions. Instead, firms must customize solutions to fit their particular organizational structure, working methods, and functional requirements' (ibid: 62). Fleck (1993) uses the label 'configurational technology' to refer to that technology which is highly specific to the organisations in which it is adopted and implemented. Here, 'local' organisational knowledge is just as important as knowledge about the technology itself. He has also coined the term 'innofusion' to refer to innovatory activity that occurs during the diffusion of a product or process. What occurs here has much less to do with the 'inherent' properties of the technology and much more to do with how organisations assimilate technology and tap into its capabilities. This is especially true of configurational as compared to generic technologies. The latter is that form of technology where user requirements and information about possible use are largely anticipated in the design of the system before its first adoption. There may be some fine-tuning, post-adoption, but this is seen as not altering the essential character of the technology-organisation design. It follows that with configurational technology, the attention of the researcher turns to what occurs within adopting organisations, and especially how the technology is used.

Two influential variants of SST draw upon Marxian and gender analyses, arguing that capitalism and patriarchy are primary contexts that influence the development and use of technologies. 'That is, the emergence of new technologies in some way responds to the expression of class and gender interests – whether through the industrial military, the domination of scientific and technological spheres of activity by men or through the activities of particular organizations in the economy' (Knights and Murray 1994: 8).

## The social construction of technology (SCT)

SCT has much affinity with the SST perspective discussed above but is distinct from it in that the focus is more upon the *construction*, design and development of the technology, wherever this may occur. Rather than seeing technology emerging from a rational-linear process of invention, design, development and innovation, SCT draws upon the sociology of scientific knowledge to examine the unfolding of technological change over time in its social and economic contexts. A key objective of SCT is to demonstrate that technology is created through a multi-actor/multi-directional process (Pinch and Bjiker 1987; Bjiker and Law 1992). SCT theorists argue that there is always a range of technological options, which a variety of people, such as suppliers, designers, IT specialists, engineers, seek to promote or challenge. These people's concerns are partly technical but also social, moral, and economic. Technical change occurs where either consensus emerges for a particular design option, or a powerful actor or group imposes it. Search activity and debate is then closed and the technology is 'stabilised' in a particular configuration. From this point it is justifiable to see the technology as having 'impacts' or 'effects' upon the organisation, working practices, skill requirements, job design, and so on, but, as with SST, these effects are not purely of a 'technical' nature.

## Actor-Network analysis (ANA)

ANA is associated historically with the work of Latour (1987, 1988) and Callon (1986). They argue that actors define one another and their relationships through intermediaries such as literary inscriptions (such as books and magazines), technical artefacts (such as computers and machines), skills (such as the knowledge possessed by people) and money. From the ANA perspective, technology has a certain robustness or 'facticity', making a difference in and of itself to organisational processes and 'outcomes'. As Coombs *et al* (1992: 17) have noted, 'the fact that technology is not infinitely plastic, to be shaped in any way whatsoever by social forces, any more than technology is driven solely by its own internal logic, independently of society'.

ANA theorists tend not to attach any major significance in their theories to pre-existing macro-social structures such as social classes and markets. They have been criticised for 'ceding too much power and autonomy to individual actors and eschewing existing social theory, leaving them poorly equipped to explain particular developments and beset by a tendency to offer mainly descriptions and *post hoc* explanations' (Williams and Edge 1996: 65).

## Technology as text and metaphor (TTM)

In a sense, we have now reached the opposite end of the spectrum to the technological determinist argument, in that with TTM not only is technology argued to have no independent effects upon people and organisations, but it is seen as having no impact whatsoever other than that which is attributed to it by people. Hence, TTM is also distinct from other 'intermediate' perspectives such as SCT and SST, where technology is viewed as 'stabilising' in terms of having a facticity, capability, and 'effects' at certain points in time. Grint and Woolgar (1997: 10), for example, as TTM theorists, argue that 'Technologies...are not transparent; their character is not given;...instead, capabilities...are attributed to the machine by humans. Our knowledge of technology is in this sense essentially social; it is a construction rather than a reflection of the machine's capabilities.' Grint and Woolgar (1997: 11) go on to argue that the above view does not mean or imply that any construction is possible, for, indeed, some technological constructions are more influential than others. Why is this so? If technical capacity is not a reflection of inherent properties of the technology, why are some accounts of technology accepted rather than others? Perhaps some accounts are so convincing 'that we end up treating them as a direct reflection of the "actual capacity" of technology'. The theorising of technology as *text* is probably counter-intuitive for a lot of people and requires some further explanation. Drawing upon Woolgar (1996: 93, 98) to help us: 'The technology-as-text approach indicates an irremediable ambiguity about what the technology is and can do, which is overlaid by sets of preferences for its interpretation and use.' As McLoughlin (1999: 9) has observed, from the TTM perspective 'what a technology is and is not and what it can and cannot do are all socially constructed.' The nature of technology, what it can and cannot do, what social and organisational impacts it has, is viewed as *always* a socially negotiated phenomenon. A given technology is understood – or 'read' – only in the particular social contexts in which it is found. It follows that different representations of the nature of technology/organisation can be created using different metaphors or 'readings'. Hence, the focus of interest turns not to what a particular technology can or cannot do but rather how such accounts of what it can do are derived (Jackson 1997). Thus, TTM takes a strong relativistic position. And, as McLoughlin and Harris (1997: 17) have argued, its key problem is that 'the influence of broader social structure and distributions of power, even organizational structure and the roles of competing stakeholder interests are viewed as superfluous to the analysis of technology and technological change' (see also McLoughlin 1997).

## CONCLUSION

Two key objectives have been set for this chapter. One is to 'identify current technological developments and consider their significance for organisational stakeholders'. This was addressed through focusing at a number of points in the text upon ICTs and the ways in which they are being deployed in contemporary organisations. The other objective is to consider the nature of new technologies and their impacts on people, organisations and society. A number of illustrations of this have been provided at various points, but especially in the first main section which examined IT and changing organisational contexts. However, throughout the chapter, but particularly in the second main section, it has been emphasised that what these 'impacts' are seen to be depends very much upon how the nature of technology and the nature of organisations is understood. And it has also been emphasised that it is equally interesting and important to ask the reverse question, 'what is the impact of people, organisations and society upon technology?'

What is required is a perspective that recognises the simultaneous social construction and shaping of both technology *and* change within organisations (Preece *et al* 1999). Although technology is hardly unalterable and fixed forever once it has been introduced into an organisation, the primary characteristics either cannot be changed, or can be changed only through expenditure of time, effort and expertise. This involves costs, seen by organisational decision-makers as unnecessary and/or prohibitive. Knights and Murray (1994: 91), in their study of the politics of systems development in a UK insurance company, have observed that:

> the use of any technology is the result of complex decision-making processes which do not simply flow from the given state of markets and technologies. Rather, those decision-making processes are crucially dependent on habituated practices and relations of power between diverse specialisms in organisations.

Technology, then, is socially created and socially shaped by the ideas, interests and objectives of, and interactions between, designers, technologists, engineers, managers, users and other actors. This occurs from the earliest stages of the creation and design of the technology in the design laboratory or software engineering department (MacKenzie and Wajcman 1985, Grint and Woolgar 1992). There continue to be opportunities for the technology to be shaped or 'configured' during the period when it is being implemented into an adopting organisation and during everyday utilisation (Fleck 1993). Certain actors and groups may well have more opportunity than others to shape the technology-organisation configuration during implementation and deployment. This is one reason why it is important to know, if one is trying to understand what is going on, who has those opportunities, and their objectives for and orientations towards work, the organisation, people, technology and themselves. It is these factors that are likely to influence the technology shaping and operational processes (Preece 1995). It might be added that the later that actors enter the technology creation/design-implementation/configuration-utilisation process, the less opportunity they normally have to exert influence over it and, if they are not 'present', then their chances of influence are negligible or non-existent. This fact alone goes some way to explain the low level of involvement and influence of personnel specialists in shaping technical-organisational change (Legge 1993).

# 7 International factors

National economies in the developed world have become increasingly deregulated and opened up to international competition from other countries, including those of the developing world, in both their manufacturing and service sectors over the past two decades. As a result, global markets are playing a steadily significant part in today's business relationships. Some UK businesses, for example, are competing not only with one another in the European Union (EU) but also with their mainland European counterparts, which are sometimes parts of the same multinational corporations (MNCs), in both the EU and other international markets. Globalisation, or the internationalisation of economic activity, has implications for many organisations in the private, public and voluntary sectors. It also impacts on those managing them, their workers and other corporate stakeholders, such as customers, suppliers and local communities. Globalisation impacts, in turn, on governments, state agencies and regional supra-national bodies such as the EU. The essence of contemporary economic globalisation is its links with the international spread of production and new information and communications technologies (ICTs), which are promoted by the mobility of finance capital and changing patterns of international trade in what some have controversially called the 'borderless world' (Ohmae 1995). The key features of contemporary globalisation are: expansion of cross-border trade; exponential growth of ICT systems; internationalisation of finance and production; and the downsizing of governments and the public sector. It is a phenomenon described by the French as *mondialisation*, by Germans as *Globalisierung* and the Spanish as *globalizacion*.

By the end of this chapter, readers should be able to understand and explain:

• globalisation and competing theories of economic change.

In addition, readers should be able to:

• identify and comment on indicative international factors affecting organisations.

See also the Professional Standards Index (page 345).

## GLOBALISATION AND PATTERNS OF INTERNATIONAL TRADE

Globalisation is a complex and controversial phenomenon. Petrella (1996) says that a new competitive era has emerged in the last 20 years, especially in connection with the globalisation of economic processes. In his view, competition no longer describes a particular type of market configuration but 'has acquired the status of a universal credo, an ideology'. For industrialists, bankers and financiers, competitiveness has become the short-term primary goal of businesses, with profitability remaining their long-term *raison d'être*. In the UK, for example, Hutton (1995: 13 and 170ff) argues that the financial system, already biased to thinking only in the short term, has been further deregulated and this has intensified its greed for high, quick returns. In his view, 'the more market-based the financial system, the less effectively it mobilises resources for investment'. The reduced powers of the trade unions and abolition of wages councils, in turn, have contributed to deregulation of the UK labour market, thus making it more flexible. These changes have allowed employers to bid down wages and working conditions for the unskilled and poorly organised, with the impact particularly marked in the high-labour-content domestic services industries like hotels, catering and cleaning. For governments, too, national competitiveness is a major concern, because they want to attract and retain capital within their own territories 'in order to secure a maximum level of employment, access of local capital to global technology, and revenue needed to maintain a minimum of social peace' (Petrella 1996: 62ff).

The process of economic globalisation is associated with

international trading between business corporations operating in relatively free, unregulated markets, uninhibited by tariff barriers and protectionist, national economic policies. Polanyi (1944: 69) describes the idea of the 'free market' as follows:

> Nothing must be allowed to inhibit the formation of markets ... Neither must there be any interference with the adjustment of prices to changed market conditions – whether the prices are those of goods, labour, land, or money. Hence there must not only be markets for all elements of industry, but no measure or policy must be countenanced that would influence the action of these markets. Neither price, nor supply, nor demand must be fixed or regulated; only such policies and measures are in order which help to ensure the self-regulation of the market by creating conditions which make the market the only organizing power in the economic sphere.

Seldon (1990: 1ff) identifies the free market with an 'imperfect capitalism', rather than an 'imperfect socialism'. For him, the market is a capitalist instrument that rewards the risks and penalties of individual ownership and judgement. It is 'not a socialist instrument subject to the irresponsible mercurial collective decisions of "public" men or women who control other people's resources, but are ultimately compelled, like the rest of fallible mankind, to put their personal interests first'.

One implication of the emergent global free market is that sovereign national states are set against one another in geo-political struggles for dwindling natural resources. What makes the 'new globalisation' different is that ICTs throw the economic and social division of labour into turmoil, as traditional Keynesian full employment policies become unworkable and unsustainable within independent nation states.

Gray (1998: 6f) defines economic globalisation as the world-wide spread of industrial production 'promoted by unrestricted mobility of capital and unfettered freedom of trade', while Giddens (1990: 64) sees it as the displacement of local activities by networks of relationships whose reach is worldwide. He defines globalisation as the intensification of world-wide social relations 'which link distant realities in such a way that local happenings are shaped by events occurring many miles away and vice versa'. For Ruigrok and van Tualder (1995), globalisation encompasses a more complex set of features:

• globalisation of financial markets

• internationalisation of corporate strategies, in particular their commitment to competition as a source of wealth creation

• diffusion of technology and related research and development and knowledge on a worldwide basis

• transformation of consumption patterns into cultural products with worldwide consumer markets

• internationalisation of the regulatory capabilities of national societies into a global political economic system

• the diminished role of national governments in designing the rules for global governance.

The essence of the globalisation phenomenon, then, is that national economies become networked with other economies around the world, through international trading, ICTs – especially e-mail, electronic commerce and the Internet – and a common consumerism. This consumerism is fuelled by sophisticated marketing techniques, a continual search for new products and services and large-scale MNCs claiming to be 'customer-centred', 'quality-focused' enterprises.

Some writers view globalisation as a new phenomenon; others see it as something that has been around, in one form or another, ever since the discovery of the 'new worlds' by European explorers in the sixteenth century. Those supporting the novelty of current global markets argue that the 'new' globalisation has rendered the nation state irrelevant and that it is powerless countries and homeless big business corporations that now inhabit the 'global economy' and 'global market place'. For Ohmae (1995: 20), 'in a borderless economy, the nation-focused maps we typically use to make sense of economic activity are woefully misleading'. In his view, people must 'face up at last to the awkward and uncomfortable truth: the old cartography no longer works. It has become no more than an illusion.' Others, such as Negroponte (1995: 1), write: 'Like a mothball, which goes from solid to gas directly, I expect the nation-state to evaporate … Without question, the role of the nation-state will change dramatically and there will be no more room for nationalism than there is for smallpox.' For 'new globalisers', global markets are the unique creations of late twentieth-century, ascendant capitalism. Such markets are seen as orderly and stable institutions, operating under conditions of near perfect or perfect competition, where the nation state is perceived as an increasingly anachronistic and redundant entity.

Those who claim that globalisation is not new argue that prior to 1914 the world already resembled a global market. Their view is that from about 1880 till 1914, money, goods and people flowed freely, and an international financial system based on the gold standard came into existence, which effectively limited the economic autonomy of national governments. Hirst and Thompson (1996: 6 and 31) argue, for example, that present-day globalisation 'is a myth for a world without illusions', where it is held that Western social democracy and socialism of the Soviet block are finished. 'One can only call the political impact of "globalization" the pathology of overdiminished expectations.' In their view, international trade and capital flows were much more important relative to GDP before 1914 than they are today, both among the industrialising economies themselves and between these and their colonial territories. 'Thus the present period is by no means unprecedented.'

Boyer and Drache (1996: 13), while accepting that globalisation is an important contemporary phenomenon, argue that it is neither totally new nor completely overwhelming. According to their analysis, quantitative evidence demonstrates that globalisation is not novel when measured by national indicators such as share of exports as a percentage of GDP or share of foreign investment in total investment flows. In their estimation, the internationalisation of economic activity has not changed dramatically from the time when Great Britain was the leading global power, and many features of the contemporary world were present then. They claim that the internationalisation of trade, production and finance has fluctuated widely over time, collapsing at the end of the 1930s and recovering only in the 1950s. Nevertheless, they see today's globalisation as quantitatively and qualitatively different from that of previous periods. 'State activity has been internationalized to an unprecedented degree in all industrialized countries.'

Even countries such as France, Japan and Sweden, which were not initially advocates of economic *laissez-faire*, have accepted the need to open up their national markets to international competition. Furthermore, with recurrent financial crises and a slowdown in economic growth, governments have not changed their basic policy frameworks. They continue to support the orthodoxy that external markets must be kept open, unlike state policy in the 1930s, when protectionism was in the ascendant. Boyer and Drache suggest, therefore, that it would 'be erroneous to conclude that capitalism has become global, since production methods, industrial relations, taxation and economic policy styles remain very specific to each national state'. They reject the contention that the nation state is *passé* or an accident of history.

Apologists of globalisation and the free market, such as the international financier and speculator George Soros (1995: 194), argue that 'the collapse of the global marketplace would be a traumatic event with unimaginable consequences'. Support for globalisation, and the transformation of social markets into free markets, is the overriding objective of transnational organisations such as the World Trade Organisation, International Monetary Fund and Organisation for Economic Co-operation and Development. In advancing this project, they are following the lead of the US, where progress today is seen as another step towards a universal civilisation – one based on a global free market. This model of a single worldwide civilisation, supported by the 'Washington consensus', Gray (1998: 105, 108) argues, expects 'democratic capitalism' to be accepted throughout a world in which a global free market becomes a final reality. He attributes this to the 'neo-conservative ascendancy' in the US, where free markets are seen not only as a way of organising a market economy but also 'as a dictate of human freedom everywhere'.

Supporters of economic globalisation view it as being commercially and socially benevolent, adding to the total sum of human happiness, while its critics see it as potentially challenging, with several harmful effects. Thus, for the World Trade Organisation (http://www.wto.org – 25/03/99), the economic case for an open, international trading system, based on multilaterally agreed rules, 'rests largely on common sense', since economic 'protectionism leads to bloated inefficient companies', business closures and job losses. Writers such as Fukuyama (1992), with his vision of the 'end of history', claim that the inevitability of 'democratic capitalism' constitutes 'the final form of human government' and its global reach is 'the triumph of the Western idea'. Those arguing for a global free market, then, see its growth as a period inaugurating a universal civilisation, replicating Western societies throughout the world.

For critics like Hirst and Thompson (1996: 10), in contrast, today's world economy shows many features bringing it closer to a disorderly global market, rather than an orderly one. According to them, the international system becomes socially disembedded as markets become truly global. 'Domestic policies, whether of private corporations or public regulators, now have routinely to take account of the predominantly international determinants of their sphere of operations.' Other critics, such as Gray (1998) argue that this is an Americo-centric perspective, purveying a view of the world that is unrecognisable to most Europeans and Asians. By this view, indigenous varieties of capitalism emerging in eastern Europe and the Far East cannot be contained within a single framework designed to reproduce the 'American dream' with its 'ideal type' of corporate, shareholder capitalism.

For other observers, such as Held *et al* (1997: 257ff), globalisation is not a singular condition, 'a linear process or a final end-point of social change.' This means, first, that globalisation is not an end state towards which all economies are converging, since different countries are developing along different pathways to the market economy. Second, globalisation does not mean that world markets affect all aspects of economic life. Some economic activity, such as local, labour-intensive services or local public services, continues to be largely unaffected by world markets. Third, globalisation is not a homogenous phenomenon, since global markets, where capital and production systems move freely across national frontiers, depend on differences among localities, regions and nation states to operate effectively. Fourth, growth of global markets does not mean that north American business culture is being copied throughout the world, since the spread of globalisation and ICTs does not result in convergence of national cultures. In fact, globalisation retains cultural differences among national economies. Fifth, globalisation does not lead irrevocably to the withering away of the nation state, which remains the decisive mediating structure that MNCs compete to control, whether in Europe, north America or Asia-Pacific.

Hampden-Turner and Trompenaars (1993: 6–10) examine seven cultures of capitalism, focusing on the US, UK, Sweden, France, Japan, the Netherlands and Germany. They identify 'seven fundamental valuing processes' without which wealth-creating organisations could not exist, though each value has a tension within it. These are:

- making rules and discovering exceptions: here the integrity of enterprises depends upon how well 'universalism' or rules of wide generality are reconciled with 'particularism' or special exceptions to rules

- constructing and deconstructing: here the mental and physical processes of 'analysing' and 'integrating' keep enterprises in a constant state of renewal or refinement

- managing communities of individuals: here the integrity of enterprises depends on how well the 'individualism' of employees, shareholders and customers is reconciled with the 'communitarianism' of the larger system

- internalising the outside world: here enterprises have to reconcile their 'inner-directions' and 'outer-directions' so that they can internalise the outer world to act decisively and competently

- synchronising fast processes: here the task is reconciling 'sequential time' with 'synchronised time' (ie how time is organised)

- choosing among achievers: here the capacity to create wealth depends upon balancing 'achieved status' with 'ascribed status'

- sponsoring equal opportunities: here the integrity of enterprises depends on how to balance the need for 'equality' of inputs with that for 'hierarchy' in judging the merits of inputs.

Tensions arise, Hampden-Turner and Trompenaars argue, because values are contrasts or differences, but any nation or organisation creating wealth must manage all seven valuing processes. Each culture in their study, however, starts in a different place, with the US, for example, scoring highly on 'individualism' and Japan scoring highly on 'communitarianism'.

Despite the claims of free market utopians, a universal model of contemporary market capitalism does not exist. It is precisely the combination of unfettered market competition, weakened social institutions (such as trade unions) and the torrent of technological innovation that produce the

*Figure 7.1*  Types of market economy

| System | Market | Regulation | Accountability | Labour market | Value system |
|---|---|---|---|---|---|
| Anglo-Saxon | free | contract | share-holder | de-regulated | individualist |
| Central European | social | public law | stakeholders | regulated | social cohesion |
| Russian | anarchic | power | managers-workers | local | mutual-aid |
| Japanese | managed | trust | networks of firms | internal | collectivist |
| Chinese | interpersonal | trust | families | parochial | paternalist |

contemporary but diverse global economy. Figure 7.1 suggests that there are at least five types of market economy around the world; each varying according to how its markets are regulated, the accountability of the market, the nature of the labour market and its underpinning value system. Using this typology (though there are others), Anglo-Saxon systems, such as those found in the English-speaking world in the UK, US, Canada and Australasia, are typified by free markets, the centrality of contract law, dominance of shareholder interests, de-regulated labour markets and an individualistic value system. In contrast, central European economic systems are typified by social markets, public law, stakeholder interests, regulated labour markets and social cohesion.

In the Far East, two types of market system stand out – the Japanese and Chinese. In the Japanese system, businesses work within a framework of managed markets; market regulation is based on trust and market accountability is through networks of firms working together. Japanese businesses favour internal labour markets and a collectivist value system. In the Chinese case, including Hong Kong, Taiwan and other parts of the world with Chinese businesses, markets are largely interpersonal and, as in Japan, are based on trust, with market accountability being centred on family networks. Labour markets are parochial, since employers often rely on the recruitment and employment of ethnic Chinese workers, in a system incorporating strongly paternalist values. In the emergent economy of the Russian Federation, markets are anarchic, they are regulated by naked power, and market accountability is to managers and workers. Russia has largely local labour markets and a 'mutual aid' value system based on extended families.

Globalisation impacts not only on businesses but also on public services, governments, customers, suppliers, employees, and all organisational stakeholders. In some respects, it is the impact of globalisation on governments in market economies that is one of its most distinctive features. The main implications of globalisation for governments are:

• the redistribution dimensions of the welfare state are weakened, since market solutions to resolving economic and social welfare problems become the preferred approach to making resource decisions

- governments emphasise the importance of flexible labour, product and capital markets
- government's regulatory role is no longer a managerial one but a steering one
- governments recognise and accept the central role of the private sector in creating wealth
- a culture of 'low taxation' emerges, where personal and corporate taxpayers have expectations of tax reductions
- a more limited concept of citizenship emerges, with the boundaries of the public domain becoming narrower and more circumscribed
- the financing of public goods becomes harder to achieve.

The principal reactions of private-sector businesses to globalisation include:

- responding to competitive pressures in the market place
- seeking to retain and expand their market share of products or services, domestically and internationally
- searching for new markets, products and methods of providing them
- investing in information and communication technologies
- taking over and merging with other businesses
- investing and relocating operations overseas in transnational groupings
- responding to pressures on productivity, quality and performance
- improving profits and profitability.

Public services react to globalisation by:

- emphasising 'good' management and the effective managing of their limited resources

- responding to governmental demands for more efficiency, greater effectiveness and better value for money

- splitting into 'purchaser' and 'provider' units through the creation of internal markets

- redrawing the boundaries between the public and private sectors, through subcontracting, market testing and creation of public agencies

- using private-sector benchmarks to guide best management practices

- responding more directly to client needs.

Some of the consequences of globalisation for the people employed in private businesses and the public services include:

- less job security

- widening pay differentials

- more job flexibility

- changing job structures

- higher unemployment in flexible labour markets.

It is also argued that globalisation provides greater consumer choice and benefits to customers in the market place.

To conclude, two main interpretations of contemporary economic globalisation have been presented here: the 'Utopian' scenario and the 'sceptical' one. Utopians argue that globalisation is associated with the establishment of a single global market, which will benefit all interests concerned – suppliers, consumers, workers and societies. The aim is to establish a global free market – free from politics – where the manifold economic cultures and economic systems that the world has always contained will die out and become redundant. Most international agencies and many MNCs support this agenda, because they want to impose free markets on to societies throughout the world. The ultimate objective is to incorporate the world's diverse economies into a universal, global market, benefiting the corporate sector. It is MNCs overseeing the world economy that are the vehicles of this post-Keynesian orthodoxy. With the demise of Communist regimes in eastern Europe, and the former Union of Socialist Soviet Republics, Utopians believe that the advance of a singular, universal type of Western capitalism – the American free market model, in which government is a bystander – will eventually emerge triumphant throughout the world. As Ohmae (1995: 7 and 15ff) argues:

> with the ending of the Cold War, the long familiar pattern of alliances and oppositions among industrialized nations has fractured beyond repair. Less visibly, but arguably far more important, the modern nation-state itself – that artifact of the eighteenth and nineteenth centuries – has begun to crumble ... For more than a decade, some of us have been talking about the progressive globalization of markets for consumer goods, like Levi jeans, Nike athletic shoes and Hermes scarves ... Today, however, the process of convergence goes faster and deeper. It reaches well beyond taste to much more fundamental dimensions of worldview, mind-set, and even thought-process.

Sceptics, on the other hand, explore what is different about globalisation during a period of increased capital mobility, internationalisation of production and introduction of ICTs into business processes. They argue that if Keynes, Beveridge and Fordist employment relations structures were once the pillars of state policy, they no longer are. The emergence of a 'lean and mean' state dedicated to providing lower levels of public services is symptomatic of the new economic order. For many countries grappling with new competitive pressures, home markets remain where the best jobs are, where investment needs to occur and where indigenous firms make the difference. Petrella (1996) argues that globalisation is partial and unstable and creates cleavages between social classes in advanced countries and between developed and developing countries. Sceptics also view markets as complex social institutions that are not self-organising and do not respond to universal laws of supply and demand. To be efficient, markets have to be embedded in national institutions, including money, labour and the environment. Writers such as Cohen (1996), in turn, address the way in which the nation state is being challenged and changed by new international trade agreements, such as the Canada–US Free Trade Agreement and North American Free Trade Agreement. She concludes that free trade agreements adversely affect equality-seeking groups, by disenfranchising and excluding them from power. Such analyses lead Bienefeld (1996) and others to conclude that the nation state remains a necessary and feasible response to the pressures driven by increasing global disorder. In his view, the nation state is the only entity capable of restoring some congruence between the economic, social and political dimensions of modern life.

In Gray's analysis (1998: 194ff), the global economy that is emerging is a result of the world-wide spread of new technologies, not the spread of free markets. The outcome is 'not a universal free market but an anarchy of sovereign states, rival capitalisms and stateless zones'. He argues that global free markets fracture societies and weaken states. Where there are weak governments, states have collapsed or ceased to be effective and societies have been desolated by market forces, over which governments have no control. His prognosis is that only a framework of global regulation, involving currencies, capital movements, trade and environmental conservation, 'can enable the creativity of the world economy to be harnessed in the service of human needs'.

## INTERNATIONAL INSTITUTIONS

There is a range of international institutions seeking to influence patterns of international trading, national economic policies and economic development. Most of them were created at the end of the Second World War. The functions and activities of the main ones are outlined below, in alphabetical order. One critique made by some observers of these international institutions is that they are strongly free market in their economic approach and are encouraging neo-liberal economic policies, privatisation and tax-cutting initiatives, rather than Keynesian, interventionist policies.

## General Agreement on Tariffs and Trade (GATT)

The GATT came into existence in 1948 and proved to be a useful body for international tariff bargaining. Its articles of association pledged its member states to expand multilateral trade with the minimum of trading barriers, reduce import tariffs and quotas and abolish preferential trade agreements. There have been successive negotiations among the contracting parties, aimed at reducing levels of tariffs since GATT's first meeting in Geneva in 1947. After conclusion of negotiations on the Uruguay Round of trade liberalisation in December 1993, GATT's focus shifted to 'market access negotiations'. As participants moved forward on ratifying and implementing the agreements, the Preparatory Committee discussed the issues necessary to bring the World Trade Organisation (WTO) into operation on 1 January 1995. The GATT Council of Representatives continued to meet, as did the committees overseeing the Tokyo Round Codes. The Council's other work continued in working parties established to review accessions, free trade agreements and other matters of interest to the contracting parties of the GATT.

## International Labour Organisation (ILO)

The ILO was founded in 1919 and is the only surviving major creation of the Treaty of Versailles, which established the now defunct League of Nations. In 1946, the ILO became the first specialised agency of the United Nations (UN), with the aim of promoting social justice and internationally recognised human and labour rights. It does this by formulating international labour standards, providing technical assistance to employers, workers and their organisations, and promoting development of independent employers' and workers' bodies. International labour standards are formulated through International Labour Conventions and Recommendations. These set minimum standards of basic labour rights, including freedom of association, the right to organise, collective bargaining, abolition of forced labour, equality of opportunity and treatment, and other standards regulating conditions across a spectrum of work-related issues. Technical assistance is provided primarily in the fields of technical training and vocational rehabilitation, employment policy, labour administration, labour law and employment relations, working conditions, management development, worker co-operatives, social security, labour statistics and occupational health and safety. The ILO also provides training and advisory services to employers' and workers' organisations.

The ILO operates with a unique tripartite structure, with employers and workers participating as equal partners with governments in its governing organs. The ILO carries out its work through three main bodies: the International Labour Conference (ILC), its Governing Body and the International Labour Office. Member states of the ILO meet annually in Geneva at the ILC during June and are represented by two government delegates, an employer delegate and a worker delegate, accompanied by technical advisers. The ILC establishes and adopts international labour standards and acts as a forum where social and labour questions affecting the world are discussed. The Governing Body, consisting of 28 government members, 14 employer members and 14 worker members, meets three times a year in Geneva, determines ILO policy, adopts its budget and elects the Director-General for a five-year period. The International Labour Office acts as the ILO's permanent secretariat and is the focal point for its overall activities. Staff are drawn from over 100 nationalities and are employed in Geneva and in field offices around the world.

### International Monetary Fund (IMF)

The International Monetary Fund (IMF) was created in 1945, when 29 countries signed its Charter at the Bretton Woods Conference, New Hampshire. Today, over 180 countries are members of the IMF, which has resources available totalling some US$ 195 billion (IMF 1999). The IMF was established:

• to promote international monetary co-operation

• to facilitate the expansion and balanced growth of international trade

- to promote exchange rate policy

- to assist in establishing a multinational system of payments

- to make its general resources available, under adequate safeguards, to members experiencing balance of payments difficulties

- to shorten and lessen disequilibrium in the international balance of payments of member states.

The IMF, which is located in Washington DC, is involved in three main activities: surveillance, financial assistance and technical assistance. Surveillance is the process by which the IMF appraises the exchange rate policies of its members, using comprehensive analyses of the general economic situations and policies of member states. The IMF does this through annual bilateral consultations with individual countries and multilateral surveillance twice a year in its World Economic Outlook. It is also done through precautionary arrangements, enhanced surveillance and programme monitoring, which provide members with close examination from the IMF. Precautionary arrangements serve to boost international confidence in the economic and financial policies of a member country, while programme monitoring may include setting benchmarks under a shadow programme.

Financial assistance includes credits and loans provided to member countries having balance of payments problems, to support policies of adjustment and reform. In mid-1998, the IMF had financial arrangements with 60 countries for an approved amount of US$ 63 billion. Technical assistance consists of expertise and aid provided to member states in: designing and implementing fiscal and monetary policy; institution building; collecting and refining statistical data; and training officials at the IMF Institute and with other international organisations.

The IMF makes its financial resources available through a variety of financial facilities. Members obtain these by purchasing the currencies of other member countries, or special drawing rights, with equivalent amounts of their own currencies. The IMF levies charges on these and requires that members repay their own currencies over a specified time. Regular IMF facilities are provided out of Standby Arrangements, which provide short-term balance of payments assistance for 12 to 18 months, and the Extended Fund Facility (EFF). EFF supports medium-term programmes running for three years and aims to overcome balance of payments difficulties stemming from macro-economic and structural problems. A concession IMF facility, called the Enhanced Structural Adjustment Facility (ESAF), was established in 1987 and extended in 1994. ESAF is designed for low-income member countries, with protracted balance of payments problems. ESAF drawings are loans, not purchases of other members' currencies, carrying low interest rates.

## Organisation for Economic Co-operation and Development (OECD)

The Organisation for Economic Co-operation and Development (OECD 1999: 1) 'has been called a think tank, monitoring agency, rich man's club, an unacademic university. It has elements of all, but none of these characteristics captures the essence of the OECD'. Created in 1961, in succession to the Organisation for European Economic Co-operation, its mission has been to build strong economies in its member states, improve efficiency, hone market systems, expand free trade and contribute to development in industrialised as well as in developing countries. After more than three decades, the OECD is moving beyond issues concerning only its own member countries. It is using its accumulated experience to service emerging market economies in countries making the transition from centrally planned to capitalist market systems, and in policy dialogue with dynamic economies in Asia and Latin America.

The OECD consists of some 30 member countries and provides a setting in which governments discuss and develop economic and social policies. It enables experiences to be compared, answers to common problems to be discussed and work to be undertaken in co-ordinating domestic and international policies, in an increasingly global economy.

Such exchanges can lead to formal agreements but, more often, discussion makes for better information within their own governments on a spectrum of public policy, as well as clarifying the impact of national policies on the international community.

The OECD is a club of like-minded countries. It is rich, with OECD countries producing about two-thirds of the world's goods and services, but it claims not to be an 'exclusive club'. Essentially, membership is limited only by a country's commitments to having a market economy and pluralistic democracy. The core of original members has expanded beyond Europe and north America to include Japan, Australia, New Zealand, Finland, Mexico, the Czech Republic, Hungary, Poland and South Korea. And there are contacts with the rest of the world, including the former Soviet bloc, Asia and Latin America.

Member countries meet and exchange information in some 200 committees, working groups and committees of experts. The overriding body is the Council, which has decision-making powers and is composed of one representative from each member country. Specialist committees meet to advance ideas and review progress in areas such as trade, public management, development assistance or financial markets. About 2,000 staff are employed by the OECD Secretariat in Paris and some 700 economists, scientists, lawyers and other professional staff, mainly based in 12 substantive directorates, provide research and analysis. The OECD operates in two official languages, English and French, and its staff are citizens of OECD member countries, employed as international civil servants.

The main activities of the OECD are organised through the following Directorates and Committees:

• The Economics Department monitors and analyses macroeconomic issues and structural or microeconomic matters. An economic survey of each member country is published annually. Economists in other branches focus on balance of payments and foreign trade, the international monetary system and the impact of policy instruments on agriculture, industry, energy, the environment, regional development, labour markets and fiscal policy.

- The Statistics Directorate collects economic statistics from across the OECD. Other publications cover foreign trade, national accounts, employment and unemployment, and changes in consumer prices, as well as indicators for specialised sectors.

- The Environment Directorate examines the interplay between the environment and trade policy, energy and agriculture, as well as analysing economic aspects of climate change and how cleaning up the environment can create jobs. Pollution prevention, and control through waste management and clean technology, are other parts of the Directorate's responsibilities.

- The Development Assistance Committee encourages and harmonises OECD aid to developing countries, monitors aid budgets, how they are spent and whether they conform to the priority of economic growth. The Development Centre is a research-oriented body aiming to help OECD countries understand the economic and social problems of the developing world.

- The Public Management Service (PUMA) addresses how governments manage their public sectors, including human resources management, regulation, budgeting and financial management, accountability and policy-making structures. It also analyses routes to reform. A joint initiative with the European Commission – Support for Improvement in Governance and Management (SIGMA) – helps newly democratised countries in central and eastern Europe establish public management systems.

- The Trade Directorate examines multilateral rules and the disciplines needed to keep order with the broadening of international trade, by analysing and preparing for future trade negotiations covering trade rules, the environment, competition policy, industry policy and technology.

Other major policy areas covered by the OECD are organised through:

- the Directorate for Financial, Fiscal and Enterprise Affairs works to create a relevant environment for business by encouraging efficient markets, setting a fair and predictable framework for international investment and finance, and promoting open international investment, capital movements and trade in services.

- the Directorate for Science, Technology and Industry (STI) examines how STI produce economic growth and employment. It undertakes international comparisons of innovation systems and specific policies promoting small and medium size enterprises, as well as conducting analyses of safety and intellectual property rights relating to biotechnology.

- the Directorate for Education, Employment, Labour and Social Affairs oversees work in these areas, in the belief that high unemployment, unstable and poorly paid employment, poverty and inadequate education tear at the fabric of societies and unravel their economies.

- the Agriculture Directorate monitors policy reforms and the outlook for agricultural markets and trade. It considers policies for making agricultural production and marketing more efficient and looks at links with the environment and rural development. It also monitors policies for the efficient managing of fisheries.

- the International Energy Agency, which co-ordinates energy policy and the Nuclear Energy Agency, works for safe use of nuclear energy for peaceful purposes.

- the Centre for Co-operation with Non-Members, established in 1998, was created to take charge of activities concerning non-members. One type of programme is based on policy themes such as trade, investment, taxation and the environment, bringing OECD and groups of non-members together. The other type of programme is country or region based, including Russia and China.

Other projects recently undertaken by the OECD cover:

- ageing populations – to address the fiscal and labour market implications of ageing

- combating bribery and corruption – to prevent such practices

- corporate governance – to formulate 'core principles' and 'best practices' in this area

- education and training – to support life-long learning

- electronic commerce – to examine its implications for business

- jobs – to improve labour market performance, through more employment and better living standards.

## World Bank

The World Bank is the largest provider of development assistance in the world, committing some US$ 20 billion per year in new loans. In an increasingly interconnected global economy, the World Bank offers loans, advice and customised resources to more than 100 developing countries, and countries in transition. Its main focus is helping the poorest people and countries to develop, emphasising the need for:

- investing in people, particularly through basic health and education provision

- protecting the environment

- supporting and encouraging private-sector development

- strengthening the ability of governments to deliver quality public services, efficiently and transparently

- promoting reforms to create a stable macroeconomic environment, conducive to investment and long-term planning.

The Bank also plays a vital role in working with other organisations – private, governmental, multilateral and non-governmental – in supporting the development agenda of the poorest countries.

Formed in March 1946, the World Bank has been in existence for over 50 years, with the purpose of reducing poverty and improving living standards through sustainable growth and investing in people. Its mission statement is (http://www.worldbank.org – 10/04/99):

> To fight poverty with passion and professionalism for lasting results.
>
> To help people help themselves and their environment by providing resources, sharing knowledge, building capacity, and forging partnerships in the public and private sectors.
>
> To be an excellent institution that is able to attract, excite, and nurture committed staff with exceptional skills who know how to listen and learn.

The Bank is owned by more than 180 member countries, whose views and interests are represented by a Board of Governors and a Washington-based Board of Executive Directors. An executive director represents each member country of the World Bank Group – which consists of five sub-groups (see below) – in Washington DC. The five largest shareholders – France, Germany, Japan, the UK and US – each appoint an executive director, with other member states being represented by 19 executive directors elected by groups of countries. The Bank's president, who is responsible for the Bank's overall management, is traditionally a national of the largest shareholder, the US, elected for a five-year term.

The main activities of the World Bank Group are:

• investing in people: the World Bank targets assistance where its impact is greatest – basic social services, such as reproductive and maternal health, nutrition, early childhood development programmes, primary education and support for the rural poor and women. It also helps client governments restructure social security and pension systems and establish economic safety nets to protect the poor.

• protecting the environment: environmental concerns are included in all World Bank activities, because it is more cost effective to prevent environmental damage than to clean it up later. The World Bank also helps client governments assess their environmental problems and priorities, through national action plans and regional studies.

- educating girls: the World Bank believes that an educated, skilled, socially cohesive society is crucial to sustainable development. It therefore encourages governments to educate girls because, as adults, educated women are an important economic resource, less likely to die in childbirth, more likely to have fewer children and more likely to raise well-nourished, nurtured children.

- stimulating private-sector growth: the World Bank believes that the private sector is the 'engine of long-term economic growth'. World Bank technical assistance and policy advice are helping client governments in Latin America, China, Russia and east Africa to establish good business climates through: putting in place basic laws and state agencies needed by private investors; investing in infrastructure, such as transportation and communications; and privatising state-owned enterprises and dismantling monopolies.

- strengthening government capacity: with World Bank support, governments are privatising productive state-owned enterprises and closing down unproductive ones. The Bank is helping to create a political climate conducive to greater efficiency and competition, and one less open to corruption.

- promoting economic reform: the World Bank supports client governments in their drives to improve economic and social policies so as to increase efficiency and transparency, promote stability and bring about equitable economic growth. These reforms are aimed at helping attract foreign private capital, generate domestic savings and stopping people slipping into poverty.

- leveraging investment: the World Bank's unique partnership with its client governments, and its role in helping them shape their plans and priorities, equip it to play a strong co-ordinating role in getting leveraging funds for development. The Bank finances activities aiming to improve people's lives and reduce poverty, earn an economic rate of return and promote economic growth.

- replicating success at low cost: the World Bank believes that one way to reduce poverty is to increase poor people's access to capital for investment in small businesses. Building on demonstrated success, the Bank, in partnership with other donors, is helping to expand the resources available for micro-financing the very poor in developing countries.

The component parts of the World Bank Group and their basic financial approaches are:

- the International Bank for Reconstruction and Development (IBRD), which provides loans and development assistance to middle-income countries and credit-worthy poorer countries. The IRBD obtains most of its funds through the sale of bonds in international capital markets.

- the International Development Association (IDA), which provides interest-free loans to the poorest countries, by contributions from its wealthier members.

- the International Finance Corporation (IFC), which promotes growth in developing countries by providing support to the private sector. In collaboration with other investors, the IFC invests in commercial enterprises through loans and equity financing.

- the Multilateral Investment Guarantee Agency (MIGA), which encourages foreign investment in developing countries by providing guarantees to foreign investors against losses caused by non-commercial risks. The MIGA also provides advisory services to help governments attract private investments.

- the International Centre for Settlement of Investment Disputes (ICSID), which helps promote international investment through conciliation and arbitration of disputes between foreign investors and host countries.

### World Trade Organisation (WTO)

The WTO, which is located in Geneva, Switzerland, was established in 1995, following the Uruguay Round of trade negotiations between 1986 and 1994. It has over 130 members, and its main functions are:

- administering WTO trade agreements

- acting as a forum for trade negotiations

- handling international trading disputes

- monitoring national trade policies

- providing technical assistance and training for developing countries

- seeking co-operation with other international organisations.

The WTO claims to be the only international body dealing with rules of trade between nations. WTO agreements provide the legal ground rules for international trading and commerce between countries and are the foundation of the multilateral trading system. They have three main objectives: to help international trade flow as freely as possible; to achieve further trade liberalisation, gradually through negotiation; and to set up an impartial system for settling trading disputes.

A number of fundamental principles run through WTO agreements, including: non-discrimination or 'most favoured nation' treatment between countries, freer international trade, predictable rules encouraging international competition and extra provision for less developed countries. One of the WTO's main goals is to reduce protectionism. Its creation in 1995 marked the biggest reform of the international trading system since the formation of the GATT in 1948. It was the Uruguay Round of trade negotiations that brought about a basic overhaul in international trading rules. In the process, the GATT was effectively replaced by the WTO. The GATT was amended and incorporated into WTO agreements. But whereas the GATT dealt only with trading in goods, WTO agreements also cover trading in services and intellectual property rights.

The WTO is run by its member governments, with all major decisions being made by the membership as a whole, by either ministers or officials. Decisions are normally taken by consensus. The highest authority is the Ministerial Conference, which meets every two years, while the General Council supervises routine work. New members enjoy privileges given by other member countries. Once they are members, countries find themselves in groups, some regional – such as the European Union or Association of South East Asian Nations – some dealing with specific issues. Special attention is given to six policies supporting the WTO's main functions:

- assisting developing and transition economies

- providing specialised help for export promotion

- facilitating regional trading arrangements

- encouraging co-operation in global economic policy-making

- reviewing members' trade policies

- notifying when members introduce new trade measures or alter old ones.

WTO agreements cover goods, services and intellectual property, and spell out the principles of liberalisation and permitted exceptions. They also include individual countries' commitments to reduce customs tariffs and trade barriers, and open up markets for services. In addition to setting up procedures for settling disputes, the agreements prescribe special treatment for developing countries and require governments to make their trade policies transparent. The bulkiest part of the Uruguay Round is the 20,000 plus pages listing the commitments of individual countries on specific categories of goods and services. These include commitments to cut and bind their customs duty rates on imports of goods. In some cases, tariffs are being cut to zero. There is also a significant increase in the number of 'bound' tariffs or duty rates that are committed in the WTO and are difficult to raise.

The original GATT did not apply to agricultural trade, and allowed countries to use non-tariff measures such as import quotas and subsidies. Some observers argued that agricultural trade had become distorted, especially with the use of export subsidies, which were not normally allowed for industrial products. The WTO believes that the Uruguay Round agreement is a significant step towards order, fair competition and a less distorted agricultural sector. Textiles, like agriculture, are one of the hardest-fought issues in the WTO, as it was in the former GATT system. They are now going through fundamental change, under a 10-year schedule agreed in the Uruguay Round.

The General Agreement on Trade in Services (GATS) is the first ever set of multilateral, legally enforceable rules covering trade in services. GATS has four elements:

- the main text containing general principles and obligations

- annexes dealing with rules for specific sectors

- specific commitments of individual countries to provide access to their markets

- lists showing where countries are temporarily not applying the 'most favoured nation' principle of non-discrimination.

These commitments are, like tariff schedules under GATT, an integral part of WTO agreements.

The Uruguay Round brought intellectual property rights, such as copyrights, trademarks and patents, into the GATT-WTO system for the first time. The new agreement tackles five broad issues:

- how the principles of the trading system can be applied to intellectual property rights

- how best to protect intellectual property rights

- how to enforce protection of intellectual property rights

- how to settle disputes

- what should happen while the system is being introduced.

## MULTINATIONAL BUSINESSES

Major business corporations are increasingly becoming global institutions, operating on a multinational or transnational basis across regions and continents. Multinational corporations (MNCs) are firms producing or distributing goods or services in two or more countries; transnational corporations (TNCs) are MNCs with over two-thirds of their business activities outside their home bases. Both MNCs and TNCs are adopting strategies transcending the influence of small and medium-size industrialised nations. According to Rugman and Verbeke (1988), by the late 1980s the largest 500 MNCs conducted over a half of all world trade. In the late 1990s, of the world's largest 500 MNCs, 88 per cent came from the US, EU and Japan. Of these, 32 per cent were American-owned, 31 per cent from the EU and 25 per cent from Japan. The remaining 12 per cent were from Switzerland, South Korea, Canada, Brazil, Australia and China (Fortune 1997). Of the world's top 20 TNCs, four were Swiss-owned; Canada, Sweden and the UK each had three; and Belgium and the UK/Netherlands each had two (UNCTAD 1997).

Lazar (1996) says that an MNC is created when a firm adopts a global strategy to leverage its ownership-specific advantage by combining this advantage with country-specific, locational advantages under a common governance structure. The firm or ownership advantage relies on the ability to create a competitive advantage. Country-specific advantages include: market access, its size and potential growth; availability of low cost resources, whether labour, capital or materials; a favourable policy environment; and proximity and access to other large markets. There are several options for benefiting from locational advantage: foreign direct investment, licensing, joint ventures and sub-contracting. 'The direct investment route (common governance structure) is selected if it minimizes transaction costs, taxes and/or best protects proprietary rights' (Gray 1998: 63). Gray goes on to argue that, in the broad sense, MNCs emerged with the development of European colonialism but the role of modern MNCs is on a different scale. They are able to divide the production process into discrete operations and locate them in different countries around the world. In this way, they can choose the countries whose labour markets, tax and regulatory regimes and infrastructures are the most congenial to them. 'The promise of direct inward investment, and the threat of its withdrawal, have significant leverage on the policy options of national governments.'

Factors driving the growth and increasing importance of global companies in the world economy include:

- an increasing number of countries are embracing the free-market ideology, including those in eastern Europe, Russia and the Far East, such as China, Taiwan and Malaysia

- the economic centre of gravity is shifting from developed countries to developing ones: it is estimated by the OECD (1997) that between 1999 and 2002 annual growth rates of the 28 advanced economies will average some 2.9 per cent, compared with 6.5 per cent for 127 developing economies and 5.4 per cent for 28 transition economies

- technological advances, and their declining real costs, are continuously improving business communications

- the opening up of borders to trade, investment and technology transfers not only creates new market opportunities for MNCs but also enables competitors from abroad to enter home markets

- declining trans-continental transportation costs facilitate the transfer of goods across the world economy

- as market competition intensifies, MNCs seek wider markets for their goods and services, want to exploit the cost-reducing (or quality-enhancing) potential of optimal locations, and expect to tap technological advances to serve their global customers

- in the 1990s, the major international organisations responsible for the world order, such as GATT, OECD and the World Bank, aggressively supported the reorganisation of MNCs on a worldwide basis.

With accelerating globalisation, companies are adapting to these changes, with those doing so having the best chances of turning change into competitive advantage.

The globalisation of business corporations, then, has emerged out of growing economic interdependence among countries, as reflected in increasing border flows of goods, services, capital and knowledge. Govindarajan and Gupta (1998) show that:

- between 1986 and 1996, cross-border trade in goods and services grew at an annual rate of over 6 per cent, twice the average annual growth rate of world GDP during the same period

- from 1984 to 1994, direct foreign investment grew from some 4 per cent to almost 10 per cent of world GDP

- in 1970, cross-border transactions in bonds and equities, as a ratio of GDP, was under 5 per cent in Germany, US and Japan; by 1996 the figures had risen to 197 per cent, 152 per cent, and 83 per cent, respectively.

In their view, companies have a simple but important choice arising from these developments: get on board the global train or get left behind in the global market place.

MNCs dominate international production in automobiles, consumer electronics, chemicals, pharmaceuticals and petroleum, because of their economies of scale, extensive production networks, and their products and services selling across national borders, often through well-developed networks of subsidiaries, partner firms or corporate alliances. It is also estimated that as much as two-thirds of trade and investment in these sectors is on an intra-firm basis. Of that trade and investment, the largest 500 MNCs conduct over three-quarters of the world's stock of foreign direct investment and over half its total trade. What has intensified the concentration of economic power in the hands of MNCs is cheap ICTs, which enable companies to improve their manufacturing and distribution processes, raise productivity, increase efficiency and expand profits.

To what extent MNCs are fully global, however, is a matter of debate. Free market Utopians, such as Ohmae (1995), have no doubts about the hegemony of MNCs and their pivotal role in the world economy, certainly compared with national governments, hence his 'homeless big business', 'powerless countries' and 'borderless world' vision. Also, as Bryan and Farrell (1996: 1) write: 'increasingly, millions of global investors, operating out of their own economic self-interest, are determining interest rates, exchange rates, and the allocation of capital, irrespective of the wishes or political objectives of national political leaders.' Reich (1991), in turn, has spoken of the growing irrelevance of corporate nationality. In his view, as corporations of all nations become 'transformable global webs', it is not 'which citizens own what' that matters from the standpoint of national wealth; it is 'which citizens learn how to do what' that counts. This makes a country's human resources capable of adding value to the world economy and therefore increasing their own potential worth.

Writers such as Rugman (1998), however, while seeing MNCs as vehicles of increasing global interdependence, argue that most of these firms remain firmly rooted in their native economic regions. He claims that one reason for this is the presence of non-tariff barriers to trade and investment. These are designed to limit access to internal markets in these regions or give preferential access to certain partners in return for reciprocal advantages. The barriers include rules of origin, health and safety codes, exemptions from trade agreements for certain sectors, poorly administered anti-dumping laws, and so on. Many US restrictions are aimed at European and Japanese competitors, and vice versa. This is why this strong triad of regional trading and investment blocks, in north America, Europe and the Far East, arose in the first place. The situation is advantageous for triad-based MNCs but makes life difficult for non-triad MNCs, since they have to gain access to triad markets in order to pursue a full global strategy.

In north America, for example, trade and, more importantly, investment barriers have been lowered dramatically by the NAFTA and the latest GATT agreement, thus strengthening the bargaining position of highly mobile capital and the power of large MNCs. Under the NAFTA, businesses have greater latitude to invest, divest and locate in new production sites in Mexico, Canada or the US. North American MNCs are moving from one country to another looking to compete on labour costs and seeking national jurisdictions where employment standards are lowest. Thus modern MNCs are well placed to benefit from the NAFTA's inability to define common social standards and are able to win trade concessions directly from Washington.

The prominent role that MNCs appear to play in globalisation is by acting as 'flagship firms'. Rugman (1998) describes flagship firms as those operating at the hub of an extensive business network or cluster of firms. He identifies four kinds of long-term partners that MNCs nurture: suppliers, customers, competitors and non-business infrastructure. The latter includes network partners in research and education, transport, financial services, and branches of government. MNCs, therefore, help build bridges for big business with the public and services sectors. Some of the key partners of MNCs are other MNCs, driven into alliances by costs of research and development and the difficulty of accessing new markets. These alliances tend to be less stable than relationships with key suppliers and customers. Key suppliers and flagship MNCs are mutually dependent and therefore invest more trust in their long-term managerial relationships than is normally the case between MNCs and other suppliers.

Despite the rhetoric calling for less state involvement in regulating the private sector, MNCs require certain levels of government support and public services to compete and survive in the market place. These include:

• covering the costs of basic infrastructure, such as funding high risk research, universities and vocational training systems, promoting dissemination of scientific information and facilitating technology transfers

• providing tax incentives needed for investment in industrial research and development, and in technological innovation

• guaranteeing that national MNCs have a sufficiently stable home base by providing privileged access to the internal market via public contracts such as in defence, telecommunications and transport

- guaranteeing basic scientific and technical competence, as well as protecting designated sectors of the internal market upon which national businesses may depend

- providing the necessary support and assistance – regulatory, commercial, political and diplomatic – to national businesses in their objective of surviving in international markets.

MNCs also press the state to introduce policies favouring their freedom of action in labour market regulation, so that they can reduce labour standards in order to further their competitiveness.

The Western 'flagship' model of MNCs, with its four types of partners, mirrors Japanese *keiretsu*, Korean *chaebols* and Chinese clans. In all four systems, MNCs adopt a flagship role and link with strong partners, although governments and banks play more active roles in Asian networks. In Western countries, MNCs provide a global strategic perspective for their four sets of partners, so that each one does not need to develop its own separate global strategy, except to be a key partner of an MNC. This raises questions about the claimed overriding powers of MNCs and the extent to which they contribute to a homogenised global business culture. The evidence is that MNCs are law-abiding institutions, with distinctive regional differences, and are:

- preoccupied with survival, growth and profitability, rather than interfering with non-economic areas of national activity

- spread around north America, Europe and the Far East

- not able to generate excess profits, because global competition forces them to compete with one another and to concentrate on operational efficiency and strategic planning in order to survive, rather than to pursue political goals

- able to enhance economic efficiency in their national economies

- helping to develop their national economies

- having to compete with one another, and the existence of triad economies effectively erodes any global market power by individual MNCs

- exerting their influences regionally rather than globally

- not creating cultural homogenisation in the face of persistently strong national differences, even within each of the triad economies

- adapting their products and services strategically to different political, cultural and religious systems.

## REGIONAL ECONOMIC GROUPINGS

Paralleling the growth of MNCs is the emergence of regional economic groupings around the world. This is the triad of regions covering the Association of South East Asian Nations (ASEAN), EU and North American Free Trade Agreement (NAFTA).

### Association of South East Asian Nations (ASEAN)

ASEAN was established in August 1967 in Bangkok, Thailand. The initial signatories of the Bangkok Declaration were Indonesia, Malaysia, the Philippines, Singapore and Thailand. Brunei Darussalam was admitted in 1984 and Vietnam joined in 1995, followed by the Lao People's Republic and Myanmar in 1997. The Bangkok Declaration sets out the objectives of the Association of South East Asian Nations as (http//:www.asean.org – 11/04/99):

1 To accelerate economic growth, social progress and cultural development in the region through joint endeavors in the spirit of equality and partnership in order to strengthen the foundation for a prosperous and peaceful community of South-East Asian Nations;

2 To promote regional peace and stability through abiding respect for justice and the rule of law on the relationship among countries of the region and adherence to the principles of the United Nations Charter;

3 To promote active collaboration and mutual assistance on matters of common interest in the economic, social, cultural, technical, scientific and administrative field;

4 To provide assistance to each other in the form of training and research facilities in the educational, professional, technical and administrative spheres;

5 To collaborate more effectively for the greater utilization of their agriculture and industries, the expansion of their trade, including the study of the problems of international commodity trade, the improvement of their transportation and communications facilities and the raising of the living standards of their peoples;

6 To promote South-East Asian studies; and

7 To maintain close and beneficial cooperation with existing international and regional organizations with similar aims and purposes, and explore all avenues for even closer cooperation among themselves.

In addition to its nine members, ASEAN has 12 'Dialogue Partners': Australia, Canada, China, the EU, India, Japan, Korea, New Zealand, Pakistan, Russia, US and the United Nations Development Programme.

Since its inauguration, ASEAN has produced a number of key agreements and decisions including:

• an Agreement on ASEAN Preferential Trading Arrangements in 1977, providing co-operation through mutual assistance regarding basic commodities, particularly food and energy, and provision of market support for ASEAN industrial projects, expansion of intra-ASEAN trade and an increase in utilising raw materials in the contracting states

• an Agreement on ASEAN Industrial Projects in 1980, providing the framework for co-operation in establishing large-scale industrial projects meeting regional requirements for essential products

• an Agreement on ASEAN Industrial Complementation in 1981, providing schemes for manufacturing different products within industries in ASEAN countries and their subsequent exchange

• the ASEAN Industrial Cooperation Scheme Agreement in 1996, promoting the sharing of industrial activities between ASEAN-based companies which minimises tariff dissimilarities and offers participating companies benefits of common preferential tariffs

- a decision in 1992 to establish an ASEAN Free Trade Area (AFTA) within 15 years, later reduced to 10 years

- an Agenda for Greater ASEAN Economic Integration in 1995

- an ASEAN Regional Forum inaugurated in 1994, as a consultative body for discussing regional and political security. The participants were the foreign ministers of ASEAN, the dialogue partners, three observers from Vietnam, Laos and Papua New Guinea and China and Russia, as guests.

**European Union (EU)**
The EU comprises the largest and one of the richest economic regions in the world. It has a population of some 370 million, its GDP accounts for almost two-fifths (38 per cent) of all OECD countries and its share of total world trade is about a fifth (20.9 per cent). It currently has 15 member states but negotiations are under way with another 11 central and east European countries, of which six have already had their applications accepted. This will bring another 100 million people into the Union, early in the twenty-first century. The EU is more than a free trade area. The four freedoms of its founding Treaty of Rome in 1957 are to ensure free movement of goods, services, capital and people. Despite its Single Market, the Economic and Monetary Union project and the Treaty of Amsterdam 1997, however, the EU remains 15 separate, sovereign states, speaking at least 11 different languages and enjoying very different historical and cultural traditions. Although EU citizens are free to move around to live and work in 'Europe', few actually do so. EU businesses continue to face a range of trade barriers in the Union, but these are gradually being reduced. Euro-business has been restricted for many years by internal monopolies, which EU member states have allowed in order to manage their national infrastructures, but these are gradually being dismantled under the twin pressures of privatisation and trade liberalisation.

The EU's common commercial policy means that tariffs and other import restrictions apply to all member states. For trade in goods, the EU acts as a single market dealing with the rest of the world, and the European Commission negotiates on its behalf in the WTO, but it is less united regarding trade in services. The EU is now extending its trading influence through agreements with its trading neighbours. Each of the countries in central Europe negotiating access to the EU has an 'association agreement', known as a 'European agreement', which will result in free trade for manufactured goods of the applicant states. But membership of the EU is their ultimate aim. The EU also has association agreements with its neighbours on the south and east coasts of the Mediterranean. The EU has policies too, backed by substantial funds, to encourage regional development, especially of poorer regions. There are still, from the business sector's perspective, continued restrictive social policies in the EU. Nearly all of them affect areas dealt with by individual states, such as payroll taxes, which vary from about a quarter (25 per cent) in the UK to over a half (56 per cent) in Sweden.

Competition policy regulates relations between large businesses, polices mergers and acquisitions, and seeks to avoid abuses of market power by the largest MNCs. It is an area in which the European Commission can act directly, and proven abuses can result in heavy fines. The Commission is also trying to control and diminish state aid in the Union, including in the controversial area of farming policy.

The EU is not just an inward-looking institution, however, and is adjusting its trade policy to the rapid changes taking place in the world economy and to the needs of European business. The European Commission has adopted a positive market access strategy resting on two pillars. The first is to pursue fresh market openings from Europe's partners around the world through bilateral, sectoral and global negotiations. The second rests on a proactive approach to identifying current problems, so as to ensure that the EU's partners comply with existing international commitments. The main kinds of action being taken by the European Commission include:

- recourse to the consultation and dispute settlement mechanisms of the WTO, covering instances of customs levies in excess of WTO-bound rates, discrimination in government procurement, discriminatory rates of taxation and unnecessarily burdensome standards

- accession of new members to the WTO

- consultations under bilateral preferential trade agreements, covering all countries of western and central Europe, Turkey, the Middle East and north Africa, with plans for free trade agreements with other partners

- bilateral consultations and diplomatic pressures

- negotiations involving new mutual trading concessions.

## North American Free Trade Agreement (NAFTA)

The NAFTA between the governments of Canada, the United Mexican States and the US came into force on 1 January 1994, essentially extending the US-Canada Free Trade Agreement. The 15 stated purposes of the NAFTA are to:

- strengthen the special bonds of friendship and co-operation among these nations

- contribute to the harmonious development and expansion of world trade and provide a catalyst to broader international co-operation

- create an expanded and secure market for the goods and services produced in their territories

- reduce distortions to trade

- establish clear and mutually advantageous rules governing their trade

- ensure a predictable commercial framework for business planning and investment

- build on their respective rights and obligations under the GATT and other multilateral and bilateral instruments of co-operation

- enhance the competitiveness of their firms in global markets

- foster creativity and innovation and promote trade in goods and services that are the subject of intellectual property rights

- create new employment opportunities and improve working conditions and living standards in their respective territories

- undertake each of the preceding in a manner consistent with environmental protection and conservation

- preserve their flexibility to safeguard public welfare

- promote sustainable development

- strengthen the development and enforcement of environmental laws and regulations

- protect, enhance and enforce basic workers' rights.

The Agreement contains 22 detailed chapters and seven annexes covering issues such as trade in goods, technical barriers to trade, government procurement, investment, and intellectual property. The overall objective of the NAFTA is to promote trade, investment, economic growth and, most importantly, jobs in the three countries. Its signatories support further multilateral trade liberalisation and welcome trade liberalisation in the hemisphere. Since the NAFTA's creation, it is estimated that trade within north America has grown by nearly two-thirds. In 1993, trilateral trade between Canada, Mexico and the US stood at less than US$ 300 billion but had reached almost US$ 500 billion in 1997 (http://www.nafta.org – 11/04/99). Supporters of the Agreement argue that the NAFTA, with the opportunities it creates for new trade and investment, brings benefits to companies, workers and consumers in the US.

The attractive feature of the Agreement is that Mexico is at a different stage of economic development to Canada and the US. Because of this, its supporters argue, the potential gains from economic specialisation should be relatively large. One would expect that the US would specialise in more complex products that are intensive in using knowledge, technology and capital equipment. The available evidence seems to indicate that this is what is happening. Thus, US exports of electronic goods and transport equipment to Mexico have increased substantially. However, the scale of change induced by the NAFTA is probably quite small relative to other factors impinging on the US economy, such as technological change and reductions in defence spending. On the other hand, the trade diversion impacts are not likely to be very large and the costs of administering the Agreement may be fairly important, because of the resources being expended to implement and monitor the new trading structure. To the extent that the NAFTA is promoting a trend towards economic regionalism, the complexity of the trade rules under which it operates may increase in the future.

The NAFTA may also reduce incentives for broader trade liberalisation, since companies that have made strategic commitments based on the Agreement may be reluctant to support further changes in the rules of the game. Responsibility for lessening the risks of regionalism falls to the business community, especially the MNCs standing to gain from a world market in their goods and services, and which have the resources to organise and lobby governments. Like all regional trade agreements, the NAFTA is a system of preferential trade arrangements (PTAs). A few countries adopt PTAs with each other but retain barriers with the rest of the world; trade discrimination is not allowed within the group but is permitted against outsiders. Paradoxically, the end result may be less free trade, rather than more, because MNCs trading within regional economic groupings may be content to keep the international trading *status quo* rather than do business globally.

## CONCLUSION

Global markets have become an increasingly significant part of the business context over the past two decades. Globalisation is not an uncontested phenomenon, however. It is a problematic one, which is difficult to objectify, define and categorise with precision. Some commentators emphasise its benevolent consequences for people, organisations and societies; others highlight its dysfunctional aspects. For some, globalisation is a neutral phenomenon, rooted in the pragmatic behaviour of those engaged in mutually beneficial business exchanges in the market place. Others see it as an ideological construct, associated with the search for hegemony in the international economy by the developed world – especially the US. Not all economic life is affected by world markets, however, since local, geographically discrete markets persist. Nor does it mean the inevitable convergence of national cultures and withering away of sovereign states, since globalisation affects different types of market economy in different ways. The Anglo-Saxon model of capitalism is not the only one. But national governments have to reinvent themselves to adapt to global market forces and political change.

In the private sector, globalisation encourages companies to search continuously for new products and new markets to remain competitive. Faced with increased uncertainties and change in the market place, the corporate sector invests heavily in information and communication technologies. Further, in seeking more 'added value' for their shareholders and investors, companies engage in take-overs, mergers and joint ventures, and look for investment opportunities overseas. There are continued pressures to raise productivity, improve the quality of their products or services, and increase profits. The public sector, in turn, becomes more like the private sector in the ways in which it is organised and managed, with demands by politicians and taxpayers for increased efficiency, more effectiveness and greater value for money. The emphasis becomes one of 'good management' rather than adherence to standardised rules and procedures. The boundaries between the public and private sectors become blurred and are redrawn.

The implications of globalisation for governments are equally far-reaching. One is that the redistributive functions of the welfare state are challenged and weakened. In order to promote business opportunities, governments deregulate labour, product and financial markets and encourage market flexibility. A more limited notion of citizenship emerges, rooted in what Galbraith (1993) calls 'a culture of contentment'. And, in Anglo-Saxon states, demands for lower taxation and a strong individualist culture become entrenched.

# 8 Social responsibility and business ethics

Various attempts have been made to classify complex, formal organisations and to whom they are accountable. A traditional approach is provided by Blau and Scott (1963: 42f) whose classification is based on the criterion of who the 'prime beneficiary' of the organisation is. They identify four basic categories of 'stakeholders' with relationships in any organisation: owners or managers; workers or rank-and-file participants; 'clients'; and 'the public-at-large'. On this basis, four types of organisation are identified: business concerns; mutual benefit concerns; service organisations; and 'commonweal organisations' eg co-operatives or trade unions. The prime beneficiaries in each case are: the owners, membership, client groups, and 'public-at-large' respectively. This simple typology is by no means a definitive one but it illustrates the complexity of analysing exactly who are an 'organisation's stakeholders' and whose interests an organisation primarily or otherwise serves. It also implies that: most organisations have multiple 'stakeholders' (ie those parties with interests in an organisation); different types of organisation have different types of stakeholders; some stakeholders are more influential and powerful than others; and stakeholder interests sometimes conflict with one another in the same organisation. For example, if a business's prime legal accountability is to its 'shareholders', then paying 'extra' wages to its workforce may adversely affect its shareholders' interests, because 'more' money going to its workers can result in 'less' money going to its shareholders, and *vice versa*. Similarly, if one objective of a public service organisation, such as a local authority, is keeping taxes (ie its council rates) down, then this could result in poorer services being provided to its citizens or clients. These and similar issues raise a number of questions about the social responsibilities of organisations. These include: who are an organisation's stakeholders? To whom is an organisation accountable, legally and morally? How can differing stakeholder interests be reconciled? What are some of the ethical problems arising out of such dilemmas? And is there any 'ideal' solution to these issues?

By the end of this chapter, readers should be able to understand and explain:

- the relevance of business ethics and social responsibility for organisations and managerial decision-taking.

In addition, readers should also be able to:

- evaluate the ethical issues facing organisations in dealing with their stakeholders.

## ORGANISATIONAL STAKEHOLDERS

Stakeholders are those individuals, groups or organisations that have interest in a particular enterprise and depend on it to fulfil their own goals, and upon whom, in turn, the enterprise depends in order to carry out its business or public service functions. Lynch (1997: 810) defines stakeholders as 'the individuals and groups who have an interest in the organisation, and, therefore, may wish to influence aspects of its mission, objectives and strategies'. He lists the typical stakeholders in large businesses as: employees; managers; shareholders; banking institutions; customers; suppliers; and government. This concept of stakeholding extends beyond just those working in the organisation. Thus, in a limited public company, several stakeholders have legitimate interests in the company and the ways in which it conducts its business affairs. These include shareholders who have invested in it, employees and managers working in it, banks lending it money, governments concerned about employment, investment and trade, and its customers and suppliers. These interests may be informal, such as in the case of a football supporters' club and its influence in and on a privately owned football club. In the case of a Plc football club with quoted shares, it may be formal, such as through official shareholding by individual supporters in the club. Unless an organisation's stakeholders remain satisfied with it, or at a minimum 'satisficed' (ie not fully satisfied, but not dissatisfied either), then employees and managers are likely to leave, shareholders sell their shareholdings, banks stop providing credit, customers go elsewhere and suppliers look for other outlets of their products or services. Stakeholder theory says that business organisations exist for the benefits of all those with a stake in them. This contrasts with 'stockholder theory' which states that companies exist to serve the interests of their shareholders and that the sole, or at least the overriding, duty of executives is to serve that interest.

Cannon (1994) provides another model of stakeholders. He distinguishes between owners, employees, customers, creditors, suppliers, community and government. Each of these, he argues, has 'primary' and 'secondary' expectations about a business. Owners want a financial return on their invested capital and added value for their investments. Employees want good pay, followed by good working conditions, work satisfaction and proper training opportunities. For customers, the primary expectation is the effective supply of required goods and services and, secondarily, that these are of sufficiently high quality and standard. Creditors want creditworthiness and payment on time; suppliers want payment for items received and long-term relationships with the purchasing organisation; and the community wants jobs, a safe environment, and the firms located in their community to make a contribution to it. Government, in turn, wants employment for people, compliance with its regulations, laws and taxation rules, and improved competitiveness of firms. Clearly, satisfying these divergent needs is a major issue facing most organisations, each with their multiple stakeholders.

Lawton (1998) uses a different classification of organisational stakeholders in the 'new' public sector. He identifies six sets of key stakeholders: customers, citizens, clients, colleagues, ministers and contractors. Customers are characterised as having 'purchasing power', citizens 'rights and duties', and clients 'lack of power and information'. Ministers, in turn, are characterised by having 'authority', colleagues 'equal status' and contractors 'specifications'. Thus, dealing with customers, citizens and clients involves different sets of relationships. Customers are concerned with purchasing power, protected by a legal framework providing consumer protection and rights. The language of citizenship, on the other hand, is that of general rights and solidarity. Clients, in contrast, are interested in ensuring that they receive their entitlements and that their interests are protected. Colleagues in public service organisations normally have expectations about being managed 'collegially', which means being involved in the decision-making processes affecting them, being treated equitably by their managers, and being promoted on the basis of merit. Ministers and contractors are external stakeholders and they too have interests in the ways in which public organisations are managed. Ministers are concerned with all aspects of public organisations, because they are accountable to Parliament for any matters that have aroused public interest. Contractors are concerned with how contracts are specified and monitored, and want payments made on time. Managing such diverse stakeholders in public organisations, therefore, means that different interests need to be balanced, common ones need to be identified and conflicting ones reconciled.

What role stakeholders actually play in organisations depends partly on their legal status and partly on their power in or over the organisation. The prime legal responsibility of the boards of UK Plcs, for example, is to their shareholders, but they also have certain statutory obligations to their employees, customers and suppliers, as well as having to pay their taxes to government and protect the environment. An organisation's system of governance plays a key function here but there are different models of corporate governance internationally and, in the UK, between private and public organisations, with the latter, for example, being more likely to have some element of employee involvement imposed on them. In Germany, for example, large public companies have two-tier boards, a supervisory board and a management board. The supervisory board has shareholder, employee and third-party representatives sitting on it and the management board is responsible to it. Thus, the legal accountability of German companies is both to their shareholders and employees. The strengths of this European model of corporate governance are that it promotes long-term business growth, has strong governance procedures and sustains a highly stable system of capital formation and accumulation. The major weakness is its vulnerability to global economic pressures. The Anglo-Saxon model of corporate governance, in contrast, while providing a dynamic market orientation and fluid capital resources, promotes short-term business policies, mainly concerned with corporate profits rather than long-term investment and growth in the company. The strength of the Asian model of corporate governance, in turn, is its promotion of long-term industrial strategies and overseas investment. Its weaknesses include: financial speculation; activism among institutional investors; and, sometimes, corrupt internal procedures.

Few individuals unilaterally have sufficient power personally to influence the direction, policies and their own personal interests within an organisation – even chief executives need to carry influential groups of senior managers, and even their staff, with them. Influence arises because particular individuals share similar expectations with others in the same stakeholder group. Here external stakeholders can be important, such as bankers, customers, suppliers, shareholders and trade unions. These may seek to influence what is happening in the company through their links with internal stakeholders such as managers and others working in the organisation. Thus, individuals are more likely to identify themselves with the aims of specific stakeholder groups, such as the corporate board, institutional investors or even the trade unions, which have members within the organisation. There have been several examples in the public sector recently, for example, where internal employee pressure groups, organised and co-ordinated by the trade unions, have produced 'votes of no confidence' in an organisation's chief executive. As a result, the person in question has resigned, vacated his post and been replaced by a new incumbent.

Power is the ability of individuals or groups to persuade or coerce others to follow certain courses of action. Johnson and Scholes (1999) classify a number of sources and indicators of power within organisations and power for external stakeholders. Sources of power within organisations include: formal hierarchical power; informal power, such as charismatic leadership; control of strategic resources; possession of strategic knowledge; and skills such as IT and negotiating. Internal indicators of power are visible signs that internal stakeholders have been able to get their own way. One is the status of the individual or group, such as position in the hierarchy or reputation within and outside the organisation. The second is the individual's or group's claim on organisational resources, as measured by size of budget, number of employees in the group, and so on. The third is representation in powerful positions, which might be assessed in terms of the corporate governance arrangements for the organisation, or who is represented on its important committees. The fourth indicator is 'symbols of power', such as size, location and fittings of offices, amount of support services that the group has, and so on. As Johnson and Scholes (1999: 222) conclude: 'No single indicator of power is likely to uncover the structure of power within a company. However, by looking at all four indicators, it may be possible to identify which people or groups appear to have power by a number of these measures.'

Sources of power for external stakeholders are similar to, but also different from, those for individuals and groups within organisations. The sources of power of external stakeholders are: control of strategic resources, such as materials, labour and money; involvement in the organisation, such as distribution outlets and agents; and possession of specialist knowledge such as that possessed by sub-contractors. Another is through internal links and informal influence in the organisation and organised pressure groups. Indicators of power for external stakeholders are, first, the status of the external party. The status of suppliers, for example, is normally indicated by the way that they are discussed among employees and whether the company responds quickly to the suppliers' demands. A second indicator is 'resource dependence' or the extent to which the organisation depends on the resources of particular external stakeholders to conduct its affairs successfully. This could include the relative sizes of shareholdings, loans by banks, proportion of the business linked with particular customers or suppliers, and so on. The key indicator here is the ease with which shareholders, financiers, customers or shareholders can switch their resources out of the organisation at short notice. A fourth indicator is negotiating arrangements, including whether external parties are treated at arm's length or are actively involved in negotiations with the company in doing business with it. Thus, customers or suppliers invited to negotiate over the price of a contract are in more powerful positions than those treated on a fixed-price or a take-it-or-leave-it basis. Last, symbols provide clues about the power of external stakeholders. This includes how the organisation treats its customers, suppliers or bankers, as well as the level of person dealing with its stakeholders.

## OBLIGATIONS OF ORGANISATIONS AND THEIR ACCOUNTABILITIES

The distinctive feature of private-sector businesses is that they are market-driven and market-led organisations. This means that the ways in which private businesses are managed reflect the market environment in which they operate. They buy their factor inputs in the market (ie land, labour, capital etc), sell their products or services in the market and are ultimately judged in the market by their ability to create a surplus of profits over costs, if they are to survive, prosper and grow as organisations. 'Unless, over time, private organisations are able to satisfy customer demand in the market, provide a surplus of revenues over costs and ensure capital investment programmes for the future, they cease to trade as viable organisations' (Farnham and Horton 1996: 28). In satisfying the demands of the market place, business organisations are ultimately responsible through their governing bodies for the actions they take. They have a duty to use responsibly the resources they employ, taking into account their obligations to a variety of organisational stakeholders, including shareholders, employees, suppliers, customers, the community and government. A mixture of market, legal, social and moral imperatives enforces the multiple accountabilities of business organisations.

Private businesses are held accountable in a number of ways but, legally, are accountable to their shareholders who may attend meetings and vote on issues affecting company policy. Shareholders, which are increasingly other companies, also have rights to appoint and remove directors, receive annual reports, examine their accounts and share in corporate profits. To those supporting the stockholder perspective of businesses, this is the norm and incontestable. For them, companies exist solely or primarily to serve the interests of their shareholder owners. There are certainly interests other than shareholders, whose fortunes are tied up with the company, but this is beside the point. These other interests do not own the company. The essential point from the stockholder perspective is that the company is simply a piece of property, no different, in principle, from other property such as land, houses and other artefacts that people own. From the stakeholder perspective, in contrast, corporate status transforms a business into something closer to 'public' property, ie something for which just and fair property ownership rights must be recognised. From both stockholder and stakeholder perspectives, this is nothing to do with being private or public in the legal sense of whether shares are on public sale or not. What is crucial is being incorporated. For stockholder theory, which places organisations more in a moral context, this does not lift a business out of the merely private property category. For stakeholder theory, which places organisations more in a moral context, it does.

In practice, however, private organisations are also legally accountable to their employees, suppliers and consumers in terms of the minimum standards expected of them by the state. Employees, for example, have a series of common law and statutory employment rights, preventing them from being exploited by 'bad' or exploitative employers. Some employees, the low-paid, have a statutory right to a legally enforceable minimum wage. All employees, except those derogated by the law, have statutory rights to maximum working hours per week and paid holiday entitlements. The legal obligations of private businesses to their suppliers are embodied in the law of contract, which provides a legal framework around which business organisations build their mutual commercial activities together. Corporate legal accountability to consumers is largely through consumer protection laws, while the Office of Fair Trading publishes information, proposes new laws and takes action on behalf of consumers who think that their rights have been infringed by offending businesses.

Legal accountability of private businesses to the community incorporates a variety of measures. These relate to controls over land use, building development, pollution control and noise abatement. The law relating to land use, for example, seeks to achieve a balance between the interests of people within their communities and those of business organisations. Pollution control is aimed at minimising the potentially hazardous impacts of effluents and noxious substances released into the air, land or waterways. Legislation also exists to prevent damage to individuals and households by excessive noise levels from factory machinery, motor vehicles and aircraft.

The social and moral accountabilities of private businesses have become more important in recent years, as businesses have increasingly accepted that they have extra-legal responsibilities, in response partly to pressure group lobbying and partly to changes in public opinion. These have to be taken into account when managements take decisions about issues of production, pricing, resource utilisation and distribution of profit. Businesses are also becoming increasingly customer aware and environmentally conscious. Failing to satisfy these obligations can result in fines, loss of customer loyalty and damage to their corporate reputation. Ultimately, however, the accountability of business organisations is to the market. If they do not satisfy the market place, they eventually go bankrupt and out of business.

Public organisations in contrast, since they are political bodies created by government, are ultimately accountable to the 'public' whom they serve. The public is particularly interested in public organisations, first, because public bodies are often monopoly providers, leaving the public no choice but to take what they provide. Second, public bodies exercise power to ensure compliance with public laws and can fine people or ultimately deprive them of their liberty if they break the law. Third, they provide merit goods or public goods (ie goods that everyone contributes to or benefits from), which directly affect the quality of people's lives. Fourth, they levy compulsory taxation to fund government activities. Fifth, they regulate many areas of social life, including licensing alcohol, providing street lighting and highways, checking building designs and monitoring building plans. As citizens, taxpayers and consumers, therefore, the public is obviously interested in the use of public power, the efficiency with which public money is spent, and the quality of public services provided.

It is this exercise of public power that necessitates public organisations being held accountable in a democratic society. Public officials are expected to act as stewards of the public interest and public purse, as well as being responsible for ensuring that public organisations provide the goods and services to those entitled to them. The forms that public accountability take vary according to type of public agency, level of government and its particular functions. Lawton and Rose (1991: 17) state that it is difficult to generalise about accountability in the public sector. 'The mechanics of accountability in local authorities are different from those in central government, which in turn vary from those in the NHS.' In practice, it is arguable that there are four main types of public-sector accountability: legal, political, consumer and 'professional'. All public bodies operate within a strict legal framework. Unlike private businesses, which can do anything that the law does not specifically forbid or prevent them from doing, public ones can do only what the law permits and prescribes for them. This legal rule, known as *ultra vires*, means that public officials must have legal authority for all the actions that they perform. Failure to exercise their legal responsibilities, or actions which exceed their legal authority, means that public officials can be mandated or restrained by the courts. Unlike in most other European countries, there is no system of public law courts in the UK and it is ordinary courts that hold public organisations to account, both for their actions and the procedures they use. Public officials are required to demonstrate that they have complied with substantive law, procedural law and the rules of natural justice.

Political accountability manifests itself in a number of ways. All public officials are accountable directly or indirectly to a political person or body. Civil servants are accountable to a minister, local government officers to elected councillors, and the boards of public corporations to appropriate ministers. This model assumes that powers are vested in ministers who are responsible for what public servants do, and who are accountable, in turn, to Parliament for their actions. Similarly, power is vested in elected local authority councils that are responsible to the public for the actions of their officials. The reality of ministerial responsibility has long been disputed, however, and civil servants are now more directly accountable to Parliament, through its specialist committees, than they were in the past (Drewry 1989). Local officials also deal with the public. In both cases, ultimate accountability to the public, as the electorate, is through periodic elections and the ballot box. Between elections, the press and pressure groups keep public organisations alert, and inform the public what is going on inside them.

Accountability to users and clients of public organisations is through institutions established for dealing with complaints and grievances. Various tribunals deal with appeals against administrative decisions. The Parliamentary, Health Service or Local Government Commissioners each deals with complaints about maladministration and, in addition, each public body has its internal complaint procedure. Since the 1980s, the rights of public consumers have come to the fore and all public organisations have had to look at ways in which they are responsive and accountable to the public. The

*Citizen's Charter* (Prime Minister's Office 1991) and more recently *Service First* (Cabinet Office 1998) set down standards that users of services can expect. This took accountability to consumers from the administrative and political realm into the legal one. Many public organisations now have their own charters or charter standards, eg Patients Charter, which provide mechanisms for holding them to account (Farnham and Horton 1999).

Professional accountability is particularly pertinent to the public sector, since it employs many professional workers, such as doctors, nurses, teachers, social workers, engineers, and so on. Public service professionals seek, where they can, not only to control entry into their occupations but also to determine how they work and how to police their fellow professionals. They claim professional autonomy, clinical freedom or academic freedom, as the case may be. This is because professionals see themselves as being primarily accountable to their professional colleagues and their internal codes of ethics. The Law Society deals with complaints against lawyers and the British Medical Association hears complaints against doctors. However, counter to this, public-service professional workers are increasingly being held accountable to public managers, who may or may not be drawn from among the ranks of the professionals they supervise.

## SOCIAL RESPONSIBILITY AND BUSINESS ETHICS

Creating, exchanging and distributing wealth in market economies like that of the UK is full of moral ambiguities. In the private sector, for example, it is claimed that businesses exist primarily to make profits. To earn profits, businesses produce goods or services and engage in the buying or selling of goods, services and factor inputs. If profit making is the first claim on business activities, therefore, supporters of stockholder theory argue that there is no need for businesses to act ethically with their stakeholders, other than with shareholders, because the prime responsibility of business is not to act ethically but to make money. Others argue, in contrast, that producing goods like tobacco and alcohol for profit, for example, is explicitly unethical, especially in a market economy driven by the profit motive. This is largely because of the inherent dangers of some people abusing such substances, so endangering their health, that of others, and being unable to support themselves and their families if they become ill. Some might also argue that it is unethical for top business executives to receive excessive reward packages (the 'fat cats' syndrome) while groups of their company's employees are on low wages, non-permanent contracts, and are doing what many would perceive as demanding, stressful low-quality work. Those arguing for social responsibility in business organisations, therefore, say business is not exempt from ethical concerns but must recognise, respond to and manage them.

Extreme supporters of the market, on the other hand, say that businesses and people in business should not be concerned with ethical issues. This is because the market itself is 'amoral' and exists merely to satisfy those economic wants that people demand and businesses are prepared to supply, within the framework of the law. They feel that any form of social responsibility or any ethical considerations are inappropriate in business and market transactions, because it is the law that is the final arbiter of morality, not the business sector itself. Ethical language is simply not the language of business. Thus, Friedman (1970), a major apologist of the free market, argues that there is only one responsibility of business; it is to use its resources as efficiently as possible and undertake its business activities to increase profits, so long as it stays within the rules of the game. For him, this means free competition, without deception or fraud. In his view, when business people talk of social responsibility in terms of environmental protection or employment protection, they are guilty of 'pure and unadulterated socialism' and are 'unwilling puppets of the intellectual forces that have been undermining the basis of the free market society' (Chryssides and Kaler 1993: 249).

Most people would not nowadays accept the free market 'amoral' model of management and management decision-making articulated by commentators like Friedman. Indeed, it is increasingly accepted that issues of moral responsibility do impinge on the private and public corporate sectors and on the ways in which their decisions affect organisational stakeholders, each with their own particular interests. These moral responsibilities have to be examined in terms of how corporate decisions impact not only on shareholders (or taxpayers) but also on employees, suppliers, creditors, customers, communities, government and the environment – just as individuals in their everyday lives have to consider how their actions affect others. Such matters involve, in short, issues of moral responsibility, which take two basic forms: 'duties' and 'causal responsibility'. Duties are owed explicitly to other people, groups, organisations or communities and mean 'having responsibilities' to or for others. They require the party concerned to behave morally, because of legal, social or personal constraints on them, so that they fulfil those moral duties in an appropriate way. Causal responsibility means 'being responsible' and bearing responsibility for actions that did or did not happen.

Moral responsibility in business is largely concerned with considerations of duty. First, there are the duties that people in business owe to each other, such as managers to workers, workers to managers and managers to shareholders. Second, there are duties that each of these groups owes to the business organisation as a whole. Third, there are the duties which, as organisations, businesses owe to their customers, suppliers, creditors and so on. Fourth, there are the duties of businesses to the environment. Fifth, there are duties that business organisations owe to society as a whole. The last is to some extent the most fundamental issue in business ethics, as it is asking the question: what is the 'social responsibility' of business? To explain the duties of business organisations in society is to prescribe their function in society. This specifically social role sets the moral standards against which business may be judged, and it identifies the ultimate ends towards which businesses ought to be directed and steered. In the US context, for example, De George (1999: 7ff) argues that the American business system incorporates the values of 'freedom', 'profit, money, and goods', 'fairness and of equal opportunity', 'pragmatism' and 'efficiency'. In his view, the American business value system is, consequently, a mixture of both good and bad. And he asks:

> Should freedom be emphasized more than security, or competition more than equality? ... Is the value system changing? Are some of the values ... obsolete? Many people ask these questions, as our society struggles with the realities of limited resources ... Which values are morally justifiable? And is the system of free enterprise itself morally justifiable? If so, under what conditions?

There are a number of approaches to business ethics. One is what Chryssides and Kaler (1996) call the 'business is business' view of business ethics. This assumes that a firm's aims are purely commercial and that it is the responsibility of its stakeholders to determine whether the firm is acting ethically and how the firm's actions affect their interests. It is not the firm's and its leaders' duty to do this. Chryssides and Kaler go on to identify a second view of business ethics, namely that legislation provides a floor of ethical standards below which firms should not fall. They call this the 'act consistently with the law' view. By this approach, firms must at least fulfil their legal obligations regarding their customers, suppliers, bankers, government, the community, the environment, and their employees. Further, since regulatory legislation applies to all companies, it is reasonable to suppose that one's competitors, in accepting the same constraints on their corporate behaviour as one's own firm, face the same pro rata costs as those covered by the legal requirements. A third view of business ethics is the 'good ethics coincides with good business' approach or what is called 'coincidence theory'. This argues that if companies behave ethically in relation to their stakeholders, then virtue is its own reward. Firms selling high-quality goods, rather than defective ones, for example, are likely to retain their customers. Similarly, ethical employment policies are more likely to benefit both staff and the company than are unethical ones. A fourth view of business ethics, called 'conventionalism', is that business people should act in accordance with conventional standards of morality (ie the prevailing standards accepted by the public) or those standards typically associated with good business practice. A fifth view of business ethics is called 'no difference theory'. This argues that business people should maintain the same standards in business life, as they do in their private lives. Just as we do not expect neighbours to dispose of their garden rubbish in our gardens, then neither should we expect firms to pollute the environment.

There is, then, no universal model of business ethics. Business ethics, or ethical business practices, are both subjective and contingent upon those pursuing or evaluating them. Business ethics raises questions about how firms *should* deal with those business issues that have implications for their stakeholders, but it does not produce universalistic answers to these questions. Chryssides and Kaler (1996: 3) claim that business ethics has two aspects. 'One involves the specific *situations* in which ethical controversy arises; the other concerns the *principles* of behaviour by which it is appropriate to abide.' Some examples where ethical controversy arises include the following (though this list is neither inclusive nor exhaustive):

- the ethics of employment, including pay, unions, workers' rights, equal opportunities and non-discrimination

- the ethics of accounting, finance, corporate restructuring and investing

- the ethics of marketing, truth and advertising

- the ethics of information technology

- the ethics of intellectual property, corporate disclosure and insider trading

- the ethics of safety, risk and environmental protection

- the ethics of whistle-blowing

- the ethics of international business.

Central to the study of business ethics, then, is the assumption that 'moral rules' apply to business behaviour, just as they do to individual behaviour, and that certain actions are wrong and others are right or moral. Thus, it would be generally agreed that: employers expect their employees not to steal from them; parties to a contract expect each other to honour it; and suppliers expect the businesses dealing with them to pay them promptly. The problem is that there is no universal benchmark of morality. Different people resolve moral dilemmas in business using different approaches and frames of reference.

There are at least six perspectives on morality. One is 'moral subjectivism'. This suggests that there is no objective answer to moral dilemmas and that it is up to individuals to choose between what is right and what is wrong. Thus existentialists, for example, would argue that the important thing in ethics is not *what* you decide but *that* you decide. A second approach is based on 'cultural relativism', where what is right and wrong is relative to the circles in which you move. By this view, moral 'truth' varies according to time, place and circumstances and it acknowledges that environments shape people's moral values and beliefs. A third approach, based on religious morality, suggests that there are absolute answers to moral questions and what is right and what is wrong. Fundamental moral principles do not vary but stand for all time and in all places. The fourth approach, based on Kantian principles, says that human reason is the arbiter of truth. The essence of morality on this view is that it is the process of rational deduction that determines the basis of right and wrong, implying that morality is not the same as self-interest, and reason demands that one's duty is to be done for duty's sake. A fifth approach is the utilitarian one. This argues that in making moral decisions it is necessary to balance one person's welfare against someone else's, and to reach a decision based on the course of action achieving the greatest good. Utilitarianism finds the seat of morality in humankind, not in religion or God. Moral acts result in human happiness, while immoral ones harm people by causing them pain. A sixth approach to solving moral dilemmas is based on universal human rights and 'natural law'. According to this view, rights rather than duties are the basis of moral choice and moral decisions. In recognising rights, natural law sets limits to the degree to which the law may intrude upon people. Not all laws are just laws, however, and when the state – or even businesses – deprives people of any of their fundamental natural rights, this is contrary to natural law (Singer 1995).

De George (1999) says that business ethics, defined as the interaction of ethics and the business community, can be analysed at four levels. The first is at macro-level or the level of the economic system and possible modifications of it. The second is concerned with the study of the business system but also includes moral evaluation of the public sector, trade unions, voluntary bodies, small businesses, consumerism, and so on. The third focuses on the moral evaluation of individuals and of their actions in economic and business transactions. Last, because business is becoming more internationalised, a fourth level of analysis is global or international, including the actions of multi-national corporations, use of natural resources and other activities affecting humankind generally. The study of business ethics, in turn, typically involves five kinds of activities:

- applying general ethical principles to particular cases or practices in business

- investigating whether terms used to describe moral individuals, and the actions that they take, can also be applied to businesses and other organisations

- analysing the moral presuppositions of business

- going beyond the field of ethics into other areas, such as philosophy, economics or organisation theory to resolve problems in business ethics

- describing morally praiseworthy and exemplary actions of either individuals or organisations.

According to De George (1999: 25f), 'business ethics can help people approach moral problems in business more systematically and with better tools than they might otherwise have'. And it can help them see issues which they might typically ignore and impel them to make changes that they might not otherwise make. 'But business ethics will not, in and of itself, make anyone moral.'

An interesting development in the private sector is the creation of codes of written ethical policies. Schlegelmilch and Houston (1999: 39) define these codes of conduct as statements 'setting down corporate principles, ethics, rules of conduct, codes of practice or company policy concerning responsibility to employees, shareholders, the environment or any other aspect of society external to the company.' An example of a formal ethics policy is provided by an American company, Johnson Controls, whose stated corporate ethical 'creed' is that: 'We believe in the free enterprise system. We shall consistently treat our customers, employees, shareholders, suppliers and the community with honesty, dignity, fairness and respect. We will conduct our business with the highest ethical standards' (Johnson Controls 1999: 3ff). The company goes on to say that it is an organisation where honesty and integrity are essential to the ways in which it does business and how it interacts with people. It believes that customer satisfaction is the source of employee, shareholder, supplier and community benefits and it will 'exceed customer expectations through continuous improvement in quality, service, productivity and time compression'. The company also states that it is committed to the fair and effective selection, development, motivation and recognition of employees and that it will provide them with training and support 'to achieve excellence in customer satisfaction'. In addition to seeking improvements and innovations in its business, the company claims that its products, services and workplaces 'reflect our belief that what is good for the environment and the safety and health of all people is good for Johnson Controls'.

Thirteen detailed issues are covered by the code:

- reporting risks
- promoting the health and safety of its employees and reporting deficiencies
- providing equal opportunity and diversity in all its employment and purchasing practices

- protecting the environment, including waste management, recycling and energy conservation

- protecting the company's information that is critical to its competitive position and reputation

- avoiding conflicts of interest, and building trust in the company

- using corporate funds properly and honestly

- upholding the integrity of the company's record-keeping and accounting systems

- not making any political or governmental contributions

- upholding the rule of law

- complying with the laws relating to the protection and disclosure of classified information

- not acting with competitors to fix prices or violate anti-trust laws

- complying with laws restricting the company to where it can do business and with whom.

Additionally, all employees of the company are expected to carry out their work, in accordance with its business standards of conduct, and are expected to report any violations of the ethics policy to the company.

The ethical beliefs and values associated with what is considered to be justifiable behaviour in public organisations are somewhat different from those of the private sector, although there are overlaps. Indeed, it is argued by some that the very essence of public organisations is their need to act socially and responsibly to all their stakeholders at all times. Indeed, enduring themes recurring in describing the values and ethics of the public sector are those of accountability, responsibility, acting in the public interest, integrity, financial probity and responding to citizen, client and user needs. Thus, one of the arguments favouring nationalisation was that the 'commanding heights' of the economy, such as public utilities, needed not only to be controlled by and accountable to government but also socially responsible to their plural stakeholders. How this was to be done was not always spelt out in practice. Yet there was an assumption underpinning the actions of public officials in nationalised industries, as in other parts of the public sector, that they would be fully accountable, be beyond financial reproach, and would treat their users, suppliers and employees fairly and reasonably and in accordance with best practice. One example of this was the idea of public employers being 'good practice', 'model' employers, acting as an example for private employers to follow (Beaumont 1992, Farnham 1997). It was also a legislative requirement for boards of nationalised industries to recognise appropriate unions and negotiate and consult with their representatives on terms, conditions, health and safety, and related issues. In the 1970s, there were even experiments in worker directors appointed to the boards of some nationalised industries, such as in iron and steel (Brannen *et al* 1976).

These features of public service organisations are associated with what has been called the 'public service ethos', which is traditionally characterised as comprising honesty, integrity, impartiality, recruitment and promotion on merit, probity and accountability, and is associated with a notion of 'acting in the public interest'. In the UK, it has its roots in the Northcote-Trevelyan report (1854) on the civil service and can be found in the workings of public services elsewhere. Pratchett and Wingfield (1994), in their research on the public service ethos in local government, describe the generic ethos as comprising accountability, bureaucratic behaviour, a sense of community, motivation and loyalty. An assumption is that there is something distinctive about the public service ethos, since there are differences between the ways in which public and private organisations are managed. Factors inducing the public sector ethos are claimed to be: the statutory framework within which most public services operate; the public sector's concern with equitable outcomes; and the processes and structures that they adopt to achieve a complexity of goals. Others factors are that recipients of public services are citizens or clients, as opposed to being market-driven customers, and that public services are uniform services, provided nationally. Pratchett and Wingfield (1994: 14) question whether there is a generic public service ethos, even in local government. For them, it is a concept 'only given meaning by its organisational and functional situation, and may be subject to very different interpretations over both time and location'. They argue that different local authorities adopt a differing ethos, varying between a community-based approach and a commercial one.

Another way of examining ethical issues in public organisations is by identifying the 'principles of public life', which are taken to be guidelines for action based on ethical values. They were identified by the Nolan committee (1995) in its report on standards in public life. The committee's objectives were to examine concerns about standards of conduct of public office holders in the UK, to ensure the highest standards of propriety in public life. Nolan identified seven principles of public life. These were:

- selflessness: public office holders should take decisions solely in terms of the public interest

- integrity: public office holders should not put themselves under financial obligations to outside individuals or organisations

- objectivity: in carrying out public business or making appointments, public office holders should make choices based on merit alone

- accountability: public office holders are accountable for their decisions and actions to the public and must submit themselves to scrutiny for this

- openness: public office holders should be as open as possible about the decisions and actions they take, giving reasons for their decisions

- honesty: public office holders have a duty to declare any private interests relating to their public duties and take steps to resolve any conflicts arising from this

- leadership: public office holders should promote and support these principles by leadership and example.

In an interesting observation about why people join the public service, a former senior civil servant, in his evidence to the Nolan committee, recorded his view. It is 'because they want to serve ... They have some consciousness of what it means in serving the public ... I think that the continuation of the desire to serve, that almost ethical view of the thing, will continue' (Nolan 1995: para 194).

In international and comparative contexts, it is observable that a number of OECD countries are responding to general concerns about public confidence in ethical standards in public organisations, by integrating ethics into new ways of managing public sector organisations (Hondeghem 1998). Three key values have been identified in guiding the behaviour of contemporary public servants. First, there is 'responsibility', with public servants being expected to behave in responsible ways involving personal judgement and being aware of the consequences of their behaviour on others. A second important set of values is transparency, openness and service to the public, with all public servants being expected to do what they can to inform and serve the public. Third, there is the value of integrity, which means that the general interest, not personal interests, must determine the behaviour of public servants. Maguire (1998) identifies four main tendencies in recent ethical initiatives in OECD countries:

- countries like the UK, US, Finland, the Netherlands and Norway, where the primary focus is checking for gaps in existing ethical infrastructures and reinforcing them, rather than completely overhauling them

- countries like Australia, Canada and New Zealand, where a great deal of attention is being given to refocusing ethical management in relation to overall public management reforms and redefining the nature of accountability

- countries like Spain, Portugal and Mexico, where ethical frameworks are being included in the modernisation programmes of public administration

- countries, such as in the transition economies of eastern Europe, where ethical infrastructures are being created from the 'bottom up', as part of their development of new democratic systems.

Maguire (1998: 33) concludes that regardless of where a country may wish to situate itself regarding managerial reforms, ongoing attention to ethics will remain essential to retain public confidence. And 'governments will be judged by their citizens not only on how efficient and effective they are, but on how well they safeguard the public trust invested in them'.

## ETHICS AND PROFESSIONALISM

Ethical statements in private and public organisations are concerned with establishing agreed normative principles as guidelines to right or 'moral' actions by those managing enterprises and those employed by them. Thus, organisations have formal and informal rules, aiming to ensure consistency, continuity, control and accountability within their boundaries. These rules can embrace ethical principles, or even incorporate explicit ethical policies, and individual managers and employees are expected to adhere to them as a contribution to good ethical practice. In the post-industrial economy, however, increasing numbers of professional workers are employed in both private and public organisations. These include diverse professional groups such as architects, accountants, computer and IT specialists, doctors, engineers, nurses, scientists, social workers, teachers, technologists and personnel professionals. As professional workers, these groups often belong to professional associations which have their own professional codes of practice and good conduct. This is because professionals often look to their own profession for a professional ethos, rather than to the organisations employing them. Belonging to an appropriate professional association normally involves being bound by its professional code of conduct, which regulates the activities of the group's members and sets out its ethical position and professional standards of behaviour to the public.

Various models of professionalism have been proposed. Trait models of professionalism, for example, list the attributes said to represent the common core of professional occupations. Millerson (1964) lists 23 elements incorporated within definitions of professions. These include: skills based on professional knowledge; provision of training and education; testing the competence of members; altruistic service to clients; and adherence to professional codes of conduct. A weakness of trait approaches is that they tend to incorporate the professionals' own definition of what it means to be a professional. Functionalist models of professions make no attempt to present exhaustive lists of traits. Instead, the components of professionalism are limited to those said to have functional relevance for society and the professional–client relationship. Thus, Barber (1963) claims that professional behaviour may be defined in terms of four essential attributes. These are: a high degree of generalised and systematic knowledge; primary orientation to community rather than personal self-interest; a high degree of control of behaviour through internalised codes of ethics, operated by the professionals themselves; and a system of rewards that are mainly symbols of work achievement. Like the trait model, the functional one excludes from consideration the power dimension of professionalism (ie potential conflicts between professionals and their clients), which suggests that there are variations in the institutionalised ways in which occupational activities are controlled.

Johnson (1972: 45) responds to this omission by arguing that professionalism can be defined as 'a peculiar form of occupational control rather than an expression of the inherent nature of particular occupations'. For him, a profession is not an occupation 'but a means of controlling an occupation'. He provides a three-fold typology of institutionalised forms of professional control. The first is where the professionals define the needs of their clients and the manner in which these needs are to be catered for. This is 'collegiate control', based on either occupational authority or a guild system, as in the medical profession. A second form of control is 'patronage', where clients define their own needs and the manner in which they are to be met. This may be 'oligarchic' patronage (as in the patron–artist relationship) or 'corporate' patronage (such as how some large organisations recruit and promote professional staff). The third form of professional control is 'mediation', which is where a third party (either business or the state) mediates the relationship between the professionals and their clients (such as between government and professional nurses or schoolteachers).

Abbott (1988: 20) has developed a 'jurisdictional' model for understanding professionalism. He proposes an approach for analysing the development of professions in terms of the link between a particular profession and the nature of work undertaken by that profession. He uses the term 'jurisdiction' to denote the link between a profession and the tasks constituting the work it does.

> The central phenomenon of professional life is thus the link between a profession and its work, a link I shall call jurisdiction. To analyse professional development is to analyse how this link is created in work, how it is anchored by formal and informal structure, and how the interplay of jurisdictional links between professions determine the history of individual professions themselves.

He argues for a scheme that examines how professions develop jurisdictional control by filling in 'jurisdictional gaps', and that there is no reason for expecting that the process of professionalisation follows any particular pattern of development. This analysis has led Holmes (1998: 10) to conclude that the functionalist approach of the IPD to developing the skills and competencies of the personnel profession is flawed. This, in his opinion, is particularly a problem with the 'Core Management' and 'Core Personnel and Development' fields. Using Abbott's framework, in his view, would enable the profession to reframe its 'jurisdictional claims'. He argues that the currently dominant managerialist orientation of the scheme, which reduces the personnel profession to managerial definitions of the personnel or human resources function, can be shown 'to place the profession in a vulnerable position likely to lead to its withering or decline'. He believes that the personnel and development profession should lay claim to a broader jurisdiction than solely the management and development of employees within organisations.

Professional codes of conduct concentrate on the individual behaviour of professional workers, and serve to regulate the behaviour of professionals with their clients and other stakeholders. Clients, for example, may want some guarantees that they are being treated with due professional care and attention, with sanctions being invoked where this is lacking. Lawton (1998: 88) suggests that professional ethical codes serve a number of purposes:

- to promote ethical behaviour and deterrence of unethical behaviour

- to provide a set of standards or written benchmarks against which to judge behaviour

- to act as guidance when faced with difficult decisions

- to establish rights and responsibilities

- to provide a statement of principles indicating what the profession stands for

- to create a contract between professionals and their clients

- to act as a statement of professional development

- to legitimise professional norms and justification for sanctions, when those norms are ignored, or unethical conduct occurs

- to enhance the status of the profession

- to provide a statement of professional conduct, identifying client expectations.

A code of professional conduct, then, can function as a public statement of ethical principles and inform others of what to expect. Kernaghan (1975) reported that such codes lie on a continuum. At one end is the short, '10 commandments' approach that provides general statements of broad ethical principles, with few if any administrative arrangements. At the other extreme is the 'Justinian Code' approach. This provides a comprehensive coverage of principles and administrative arrangements in some detail.

In terms of personnel and development professionals, Winstanley *et al* (1996: 5ff) argue that 'the relationship between ethics and human resource management is emerging as a subject of serious academic enquiry'. They identify three main issues in the area: ethical concerns, ethical frameworks and putting ethics into practice. They raise concerns about the lowering of employment standards, for example, where several types of undesirable change are identified. These are, first, insecurity and risk in terms of jobs and employment opportunities. Second, new forms of work organisation and management control are giving rise to surveillance and control of employees at work. Third, deregulation of management decision-making in firms is leaving little scope for employee participation in the workplace, and this element in contemporary HRM 'is at best unsympathetic to the exercise of democratic rights by employees or to stakeholder models of corporate governance'. Fourth, the rhetoric of HRM, with its themes of commitment and identification, fits poorly with the trend towards less secure employment and evidence of diminished employer commitment to employees, with 'a relentlessly instrumental orientation to the employment relationship on the part of employers'.

Winstanley *et al* (1996: 9ff) also argue that the prevailing common sense ethical framework justifying contemporary HRM policies based on its utilitarianism to organisations is a weak principle for ethical action. They identify a number of alternative ethical frameworks lending themselves to analysing HRM. These are:

• basic human, civil and employment rights, by seeking greater job security, openness, and transparency and avoiding scapegoating at work

• social and organisational justice, by providing procedural principles for evaluating current employment practices

• universalism, by emphasising the Kantian principle of

treating individuals as ends in themselves and not just means to ends

- community of purpose, by adopting a stakeholder and more communitarian view of the firm rather than just a stockholder one.

Another level of engagement with ethics is for human resources writers to utilise appropriate ethical frameworks helping to explain and analyse the nature of changes taking place in the employment relationship and to use the frameworks 'more prescriptively in action'.

In seeking ways of putting ethical principles into practice in the personnel and development area, Winstanley *et al* (1996: 11) propose the use of employment charters, legal regulation, innovation in good practice and challenging 'the inevitability thesis' on the demise of job security. They are unconvinced that the 'ethical stewardship' role of personnel professionals in raising awareness of ethical issues is a viable one. 'There is the risk that assuming ownership of the "ethical" issues and conscience in the organization might yet again serve to decrease their status' (p 11). Drawing on Connock and Johns (1995), they conclude that ethical leadership must come from the top of organisations, 'not be part of the ghetto of human resource management'. In their view, growth in interest in stakeholding, ethical consumerism and international labour standards are some of the developments putting ethics and HRM on the political agenda.

## CONCLUSION

Issues of stakeholding, accountability, social responsibility and business ethics are becoming increasingly important, in both private and public organisations. Those leading organisations are recognising, responding to and managing the multiple interests making demands on organisational resources and policies. Because of mass communications, greater public awareness and the activities of external pressure groups, business leaders and public managers are finding it steadily more difficult to ignore these conflicting power-centres and pressures acting on them. Also, with the shift towards free markets in recent years, and the internationalisation of business, more people are questioning the market's ability to deliver real progress and quality of life, rather than just economic growth. It is also becoming increasingly difficult for the business sector to define its role solely in the narrow sense of the 'business is business' approach. As a result, some business leaders are redefining their leadership roles in organisations. This means placing responsibility on top management – not just on the state, the market or technology – for dealing with the multiplicity of morally-ambiguous problems associated with the emerging business context of the twenty-first century. These include issues of justice and equity in organisations, maintaining environmental sustainability, creating jobs, narrowing social cleavages in organisations, managing technological change and developing corporate ethical policies, as well as making profits. This sort of leadership sees the organisation as a learning system, where an ethical perspective can provide a valuable insight for determining both rational and moral choices in times of exponential change.

# Bibliography

ABBOTT, A. *The System of the Professions*. Chicago: University of Chicago Press.

ALDCROFT, D. H. (1993) *The European Economy 1914–1990*. London: Routledge.

ALLEN, T. *and* SCOTT MORTON, M. (eds) (1994) *Information Technology and the Corporation of the 1990s*. Oxford: Oxford University Press.

ANDREWS, K. (1987) *The Concept of Corporate Strategy*. Homewood, ILL.: Irwin.

ANSOFF, I. (1965) *Corporate Strategy*. Harmondsworth: Penguin.

ARTIS, J. (ed.) (1996) *The UK Economy*. Oxford: Oxford University Press.

ARTIS, M. *and* LEE, N. (eds) (1994) *The Economics of European Union*. Oxford: Oxford University Press.

ATKINSON, J. (1984) *The Flexible Firm*. Brighton: Institute of Manpower Studies.

BACON, R. *and* ELTIS, W. (1976) *Britain's Economic Problem*. London: Macmillan.

BALL, A. (1993) *Modern Politics and Government*. London: Macmillan.

BALL, A. *and* MILLARD, F. (1986) *Pressure Group Politics in Industrial Society*. Basingstoke: Macmillan.

BARBER, B. (1963) 'Some problems in the society of professions'. *Daedalus*. Fall issue.

BARCLAY REPORT (1995) *Joseph Rowntree Foundation Inquiry into Income and Wealth*. London: Joseph Rowntree Foundation.

BARNATT, C. (1995) *Cyber Business: Mindsets for a wired age*. Chichester: Wiley.

BARTLETT, C. *and* GHOSHAL, S. (1989) *Managing across Borders.* Boston, Mass.: Harvard Business School Press.

BEATSON, M. (1995) *Labour Market Flexibility.* London: Employment Department.

BEAUMONT, P. (1992) *Public Sector Industrial Relations.* London: Routledge.

BELL, D. (1973) *The Coming of Post-Industrial Society.* New York: Basic Books.

BELL, D. (ed.) (1985) *The Conservative Government 1979–84.* London: Croom Helm.

BENN, T. 1980. *Arguments for Socialism.* Harmondsworth: Penguin.

BERESFORD, P. *and* BOYD, S. (1999) *The Sunday Times Rich List 1999: Britain's richest 1,000.* London: *Sunday Times.*

BIENEFELD, M. (1996) 'Is a strong national economy a Utopian goal at the end of the twentieth-century?' In: Boyer, R. and Drache, D. *States against Markets.* London: Routledge.

BIMBER, B. (1990) 'Karl Marx and the three faces of technological determinism'. *Social Studies of Science.* 20. 331–51.

BJIKER, W. E. *and* LAW, J. (eds) (1992) *Shaping Technology/Building Society: Studies in socio-technical change.* Cambridge, Mass.: MIT Press.

BLACKABY, F. (ed.) (1979) *De-Industrialisation.* London: Heinemann.

BLAIR, T. (1998) *The Third Way.* London: Fabian Society.

BLAKEMORE, K. *and* DRAKE, R. (1996) *Understanding Equal Opportunities Policies.* London: Harvester Wheatsheaf.

BLAU, P. *and* SCOTT, W. (1963) *Formal Organisations.* London: Routledge.

BLAUNER, R. (1964) *Alienation and Freedom: The factory worker and his industry.* Chicago: University of Chicago Press.

BODDY, D. *and* BUCHANAN, D. (1986) *Managing New Technology.* Oxford: Blackwell.

BOOTH, A. (1995) *British Economic Development since 1945.* Manchester: Manchester University Press.

BORRIE, J. (chair) (1994) *The Report of the Commission on Social Justice.* London: Vintage.

BOWMAN, C. (1996) *The Essence of Strategic Management.* London: Prentice Hall.

BOYER, R. *and* DRACHE, D. (eds) (1996) *States against Markets.* London: Routledge.

BRADLEY, H. (1996) *Fractured Identities, Changing Patterns of Inequality.* Oxford: Blackwell.

BRANNEN, P. *et al* (1976) *The Worker Directors.* London: Hutchinson.

BRAVERMAN, H. (1974) *Labour and Monopoly Capital.* New York: Monthly Review Press.

BRAVERMAN, H. (1974) *Labor and Monopoly Capitalism: The degradation of work in the twentieth century.* New York: Monthly Review Press.

BRITTON, A. (1991) *Macro-Economic Policy in Britain 1974–1987.* Cambridge: Cambridge University Press.

BRYAN, L. *and* FARRELL, D. (1996) *Market Unbound.* New York: Wiley.

BRYSON, A. *and* McKAY, S. (1997) 'What about the workers?'. In Jowell *et al* (see below).

BRYSON, C. (1997) 'Benefits claimants: villains or victims?'. In Jowell *et al* (see below).

BUCHANAN, D. *and* BODDY, D. (1983) *Organisations in the Computer Age: Technological imperatives and strategic choice.* Aldershot: Gower.

BUCHANAN, D. *and* HUCZYNSKI, A. (1997) *Organizational Behaviour: An introductory text.* 3rd edn. Hemel Hempstead: Prentice Hall.

CABINET OFFICE (1997) *Service First: The New Charter Programme.* London: The Stationery Office.

CABINET OFFICE (1998) *Improving Management in Government.* London: HMSO.

CABINET OFFICE (1998) *Public Bodies 1997.* London: The Stationery Office.

CAIRNCROSS, A. (1992) *The British Economy since 1945.* Oxford: Blackwell.

CALLENDER, C. (1996) 'Women and employment'. In Hallet, C. *Women and Social Policy.* Hemel Hempstead: Prentice Hall Europe.

CALLON, M. (1986) 'Some elements of a sociology of translation: domestication of the scallops and the fishermen of St. Brieuc Bay'. In Law, J. (ed.) *Power, Action and Belief.* London: Routledge.

CAMERON, I. (1993) 'Formulating an Equal Opportunities Policy'. *Equal Opportunities Review,* 47 January/February.

CAMPBELL, A. and GOOLD, M. (1987) *Strategies and Styles.* Oxford: Blackwell.

CANNON, T. (1994) *Corporate Responsibility.* London: Pitman.

CHRYSSIDES, G. and KALER, J. (1993) *An Introduction to Business Ethics.* London: Chapman and Hall.

CHRYSSIDES, G. and KAYLER J. (1996) *Essentials of Business Ethics.* London: McGraw-Hill.

CLARK, J., MCLOUGHLIN, I., ROSE, H., KING, J. (1988) *The Process of Technological Change: New technology and social choice in the workplace.* Cambridge: Cambridge University Press.

CM 3807. *The New Modern Dependable NHS.* London: Ministry of Health.

COATES, D. (ed.) (1995) *Economic and Industrial Performance in Europe.* Aldershot: Elgar.

COCKBURN, C. (1991) *In the Way of Women.* Basingstoke: Macmillan.

COHEN, G. (1978) *Karl Marx's Theory of History: A defence.* Princeton, NJ: Princeton University Press.

COHEN, M. (1996) *Democracy and the Future of Nations.* In: Boyer, R. and Drache, D. *States and Markets.* London: Routledge.

COMMISSION ON CITIZENSHIP (1990) *Encouraging Citizenship.* London: HMSO.

CONNOCK, S. and JOHNS, T. (1995) *Ethical Leadership.* London: Institute of Personnel and Development.

CONSTABLE, J. and MCCORMICK, R. (1987) *The Making of British Managers.* London: BIM.

COOMBS, R. *and* HULL, R. 'The politics of IT strategy and development in organisations', in Dutton, W. (ed.), (see below).

COOPER, A. (1989) 'Theorizing Gender'. In Reid, I. and Stratta, E. (eds). *Sex Differences in Britain*. Aldershot: Gower.

CRICK, B. (1964) *In Defence of Politics*. Harmondsworth: Penguin.

CROMPTON, R. *and* JONES, G. (1989) 'Clerical "proletarianization": myth or reality?'. In McDowell, L., Sarre, P. and Hamnett, C. *Divided Nation: Social and cultural change in Britain*. London: Hodder and Stoughton.

CROSSMAN, R. H. S. (1963) *Introduction to the English Constitution by Walter Bagehot*. London: Fontana.

CURTICE, J. *and* JOWELL, R. (1998) 'Trust in the political system'. In Jowell *et al* (see below).

CURWEN, P. (ed.) (1994) *Understanding the UK Economy*. London: Macmillan.

DAHRENDORF, R. (1982) *On Britain*. London: BBC.

DAHRENDORF, R. (1987) 'The erosion of citizenship and its consequences for us all'. *New Statesman*, 12 June.

DAVID, F. (1997) *Strategic Management*. London: Prentice Hall International.

DAVID, R. *and* BRIERLEY, J. (1978) *Major Legal Systems in the World Today*. London: Stevens.

DAVIDSON, M. *and* COOPER, C. (1992) *Shattering the Glass Ceiling*. London: Paul Chapman.

DAWSON, P. (1996) *Technology and Quality: Change in the workplace*. London: International Thomson Press.

DE GEORGE, R. (1999) *Business Ethics*. New Jersey: Prentice Hall.

DE GEUS, A. (1988) 'Planning is learning'. *Harvard Business Review*; March–April.

DE WIT, B. *and* MEYERS, R. (1998) *Strategy: Process, content, context*. London: International Thomson Business Press.

DEVLIN, LORD. (1978) 'Judges, government and politics'. *Modern Law Review*; 41.

DREWRY, G. (ed.) (1989) *The New Select Committees*. Oxford: Clarendon.

DUTTON, W. (ed) (1996) *Information and Communication Technologies: Visions and realities*. Oxford: Oxford University Press.

EDGE, D. (1995) 'The social shaping of technology'. In Heap, N., Thomas, R., Einon, G., Mason, R. and Mackay, H. (eds) *Information Technology and Society*. London: Sage.

ELCOCK, H. (1996) 'Strategic Management'. In: Farnham, D. and Horton, S. *Managing the New Public Services*. London: Macmillan.

EVANS, G. (1998) 'How Britain views the EU'. In Jowell *et al* (see below).

FARNHAM, D. (1990) *The Corporate Environment*. London: Institute of Personnel Management.

FARNHAM, D. (1997) *Employee Relations in Context*. London: Institute of Personnel and Development.

FARNHAM, D. *and* HORTON, S. (eds) (1996) *Managing the New Public Services*. London: Macmillan.

FERGUSON, P. *and* FERGUSON, G. (1994) *Industrial Economics: Issues and perspectives*. Maidenhead: Macmillan.

FIELD, F. (1996) 'Britain's underclass: countering the growth'. In Lister, R. (ed.) *Charles Murray and the Underclass*. London: IEA.

FINEGOLD, D. *and* SOSKICE, D. (1988) 'The failure of training in Britain: an analysis and prescription'. *Oxford Review of Economic Policy*. Vol. 4. Autumn.

FLECK, J. (1993) 'Configurations: Crystallising contingency'. *International Journal of Human Factors in Manufacturing*. 3, 1:15–36.

FORTUNE (1997) 'The Fortune global 500'. *Fortune Magazine* (4 August).

FRIEDMAN, M. (1970) *The Counter Revolution in Monetary Theory*. London: Institute of Economic Affairs.

FRIEDMAN, M. *and* SCHWARTZ R. (1963) *A Monetary History of the United States.* Princeton: Princeton University Press.

FUKUYAMA, F. (1992) *The End of History and the Last Man.* New York: Free Press.

GALBRAITH, J. (1993) *The Culture of Contentment.* Harmondsworth: Penguin.

GAMBLE, A. (1988) *The Free Economy and the Strong State.* Basingstoke: Macmillan.

GIDDENS, A. (1973) *The Class Structure of the Advanced Societies.* London: Hutchinson.

GIDDENS, A. (1989) *Sociology.* Cambridge: Polity Press.

GIDDENS, A. (1990) *The Consequences of Modernity.* Cambridge: Polity.

GIDDENS, A. (1998) *The Third Way.* Cambridge: Polity Press.

GOVINDARAJAN, V. *and* GUPTA, A. (1998) 'Setting a course for the new global landscape'. *Financial Times: Mastering Global Business.* Part one.

GRAY, J. (1998) *False Dawn.* London: Granta.

GRIFFITH, J. (1991) *The Politics of the Judiciary.* (2nd edn) London: Fontana.

GRINT, K. *and* WOOLGAR, S. (1992) 'Computers, guns and roses: what's social about being shot?'. *Science, Technology and Human Values.* 17, 3: 366–80.

GRINT, K. *and* WOOLGAR, S. (1997) *The Machine at Work: Technology, work and organization.* Cambridge: Polity Press.

GUEST, D. (1987) 'Human resource management and industrial relations'. *Journal of Management Studies.* 24 (5).

HALL, S. *et al* (1978) *Policing the Crisis.* London: Macmillan.

HALSEY, A. (1988) *British Social Trends 1900–1986.* Basingstoke: Macmillan.

HAMEL, G. *and* PRAHALAD, C. (1989) 'Strategic intent'. *Harvard Business Review.* May–June.

HAMEL, G. *and* PRAHALAD, C. (1993) 'Strategy as stretch and leverage'. *Harvard Business Review*; March–April.

HAMEL, G. *and* PRAHALAD, C. (1994) *Competing for the Future*. Boston: Harvard Business School Press.

HAMMER, M. *and* CHAMPY, J. (1993) *Re-engineering the Corporation: A manifesto for business revolution*. London: Nicholas Brealey.

HAMNETT, C., MACDOWELL, L. *and* SARRE, P. (eds) (1989) *The Changing Social Structure*. London: Sage.

HAMPDEN-TURNER, C. *and* TROMPENAARS, F. (1995) *The Seven Cultures of Capitalism*. New York: Piatkus.

HANDY, C. (1987) *The Making of Managers*. A report on management education and development in the US, West Germany, France, Japan and the UK. London: NEDO.

HANNAN, N. *and* FREEMAN, J. (1989) *Organisational Ecology*. Boston, Mass.: Harvard University Press.

HARALAMBOS, M. (1995) *Sociology: Themes and perspectives*. Slough: University Tutorial Press.

HARRIS, P. (1993) *An Introduction to Law*. London: Butterworth.

HARRIS, P. *and* BUCKLE, J. (1976) 'Philosophies of the law and the law teacher'. *The Law Teacher*.

HAX, A. (1990) 'Redefining the strategy concept'. *Planning Review*, May/June.

HEARN, J. *and* PARKIN, W. (1995) *'Sex' at 'Work'*. London: Harvester Wheatsheaf.

HEATH, A. *and* PARK, A. (1997) 'Thatcher's children'. In Jowell *et al* (below).

HEATH, A. *and* SAVAGE, M. (1994) *Middleclass Politics*. In: Jowell, R. Curtice J., Brook L. and Ahrendt D. *British Social Attitudes: Eleventh report*. Aldershot: Social and Community Planning.

HEATH, A., JOWELL, R. *and* CURTICE, J. (1985) *How Britain Votes*. Oxford: Pergamon.

HELD, D., GOLDBLATT D., McGREW A. *and* PERRASTON J. (1997) *Global Flows, Global Transactions*. Cambridge: Polity Press.

HIGGINS, J. *and* VINCZE, J. (1993) *Strategic Management: Text and cases.* Fort Worth: The Dryden Press.

HIRST, P. *and* THOMPSON, G. (1996) *Globalisation in Question.* Cambridge: Polity Press.

HOBBES, T. [1651] (1946) *Leviathian.* Oxford: Blackwell.

HOLLOWAY, D., HORTON, S. *and* FARNHAM, D. (1999) 'Education'. In Horton, S. and Farnham, D. *Public Management in Britain.* Basingstoke: Macmillan.

HOLMES, L. (1998) 'W(h)ither the personnel profession'. IPD Professional Standards Conference; July. University of Warwick.

HORTON, S. (1997) 'The Employee Relations Environment'. In Farnham, D. *Employee Relations in Context.* London: IPD.

HORTON, S. *and* FARNHAM, D. (eds) (1999) *Public Management in Britain.* London: Macmillan.

HREBINIAK, L. *and* JOYCE, W. (1984) *Implementing Strategy.* New York: Macmillan.

HUGHES, A. (1995) 'Employment in the public and private sectors'. *Economic Trends*; 495, January.

HUTTON, W. (1995) *The State We're In.* London: Cape.

INTERNATIONAL MONETARY FUND (1999) *An Introduction to the IMF.* Washington, DC: IMF.

ISAAC-HENRY, K. (1999) In: Horton, S. *and* Farnham D. *Public Management in Britain.* London: Basingstoke.

JACKSON, P. (1997) 'Information systems as metaphor: innovation and the 3 Rs of representation'. In McLoughlin, I. and Harris, M. (eds), (see below).

JACKSON, P. *and* VAN DER WIELEN, J. (eds) (1998) *Teleworking: International perspectives, from telecommuting to the virtual organisation.* London: Routledge.

JEWELL, B. (1993) *The UK Economy and Europe.* London: Pitman.

JOHNSON CONTROLS (1997) *Ethics Policy: The cornerstone of customer satisfaction.* Milwaukee, Wis.: Johnson Controls.

JOHNSON, G. *and* SCHOLES, K. (1999) *Exploring Corporate Strategy*. Hemel Hempsted: Prentice Hall Europe.

JOHNSON, T. (1972) *Professions and Power*. London: Macmillan.

JONES, B. (1997) *Forcing the Factory of the Future: Cybernation and societal institutions*. Cambridge: Cambridge University Press.

JOWELL, R. *et al* (1992) *British Social Attitudes: 9th report*. Aldershot: Ashgate.

JOWELL, R. *et al* (1997) *British Social Attitudes: The end of Conservative values? 14th Report*. Aldershot: Ashgate.

JOWELL, R. *et al* (1998) *British and European Social Attitudes: How Britain differs: 15th Report*. Aldershot: Ashgate.

KAHN-FREUND, O. (1977) *Labour and the Law*. Stevens: London.

KANTER, R. M. (1984) *The Change Masters*. London: Allen and Unwin.

KAY, J. (1993) *Foundations of Corporate Success*. Oxford: Oxford University Press.

KEENOY, T. (1990) 'HRM: a case of the wolf in sheep's clothing'. *Personnel Review*; 19 (2).

KERNAGHAN, K. (1975) *Ethical Conduct*. Toronto: Institute of Public Administration.

KEYNES, J. M. (1936) *The General Theory of Employment, Interest and Money*. London: Macmillan.

KILBRANDON REPORT. (1973) *The Royal Commission on the Constitution*. Cmnd 5460. London: HMSO.

KING, D. (1987) *The New Right*. Basingstoke: Macmillan.

KNIGHTS, D. *and* MURRAY, F. (1994) *Managers Divided: Organisation politics and information technology management*. Chichester: Wiley.

KOTLER, P. (1994) *Marketing Management*. New York: Prentice Hall.

KUMAR, K. (1995) *From Post-Industrial to Post-Modern Society*. Oxford: Blackwell.

LABOUR PARTY (1988) *Democratic Socialist Aims and Values*. London: Labour Party.

LABOUR PARTY (1995) *Constitution and Rules*. London: Labour Party.

LATOUR, B. (1987) *Science in Action*. Milton Keynes: Open University Press.

LATOUR, B. (1988) 'Mixing humans and non-humans together: the sociology of the door closer'. *Social Problems*. Vol. 35, 298–310.

LAW, J. (1987) 'Technology and heterogeneous engineering'. In Bijker, W., Hughes, T. P. and Pinch, T. J. (eds) *The Social Construction of Technological Systems*. Cambridge, Mass.: MIT Press (1987).

LAWTON, A. (1998) *Ethical Management for the Public Services*. Buckingham: Open University Press.

LAWTON, A. *and* ROSE A. (1991) *Organisation and Management in the Public Sector*. London: Pitman.

LEFTWICH, A. (1984) *What is Politics?* Oxford: Blackwell.

LEGGE, K. (1993) 'The role of personnel specialists: centrality or marginalization?'. In Clark, J. (ed.) *Human Resource Management and Technical Change*. London: Sage.

LENZ, R. *and* LYLES, M. (1985) 'Paralysis by analysis: is your planning system becoming too rational?'. *Long Range Planning*; 18 August.

LOCKE, J. [1690] (1947) *An Essay concerning the True Original, Extent and End of Civil Government*. Oxford: Oxford University Press.

LOCKWOOD, D. (1958) *The Blackcoated Worker*. London: Allen and Unwin.

LYNCH, T. (1997) *Corporate Strategy*. London: Pitman.

MACKENZIE, D. *and* WAJCMAN, J. (eds) (1985) *The Social Shaping of Technology*. Milton Keynes: Open University Press.

MAGUIRE, M. (1998) 'Ethics in the public service'. In: Hondeghem, A. (ed.) *Ethics and Accountability in a Context of Governance and New Public Management*. Amsterdam: IOS Press.

MARSHALL, J. (1984) *Women Managers: Travellers in a man's world*. Chichester: Wiley.

MARSHALL, T. H. (1950) *Citizenship and Social Class*. Cambridge: Cambridge University Press.

MASON, D. (1995) *Race and Ethnicity in Modern Britain.* Oxford: Oxford University Press.

MCLOUGHLIN, I. (1999) *Creative Technological Change: Shaping technology and organisation.* London: Routledge.

MCLOUGHLIN, I. and CLARK, J. (1994) *Technological Change at Work.* 2nd edn. Milton Keynes: Open University Press.

MCLOUGHLIN, I. and HARRIS, M. (1997) Introduction: 'Understanding innovation, organizational change and technology'. In McLoughlin, I. and Harris, M. (eds) (see below).

MCLOUGHLIN, I. and HARRIS, M. (eds) (1997) *Innovation, Organizational Change and Technology.* London: International Thomson Press.

MCLOUGHLIN, I.(1997) 'Babies, bathwater, guns and roses'. In McLoughlin, I. and Harris, M. (eds) (see below).

MCVICAR, M. (1996) 'Education'. In Farnham, D. and Horton, S. *Managing the New Public Services* (2nd edn). Basingstoke: Macmillan.

MILL, J. S. (1972) *Utilitarianism, Liberty and Representative Government.* London: Dent.

MILLER, D. and FRIESEN, P. (1984) *Organisations: A quantum view.* New York: Harper.

MILLERSON, G. (1964) *The Qualifying Associations.* London: Routledge and Kegan Paul.

MINTZBERG, H. (1987a) 'The strategy concept I: the five P's for strategy'. *California Management Review*; Fall.

MINTZBERG, H. (1987b) 'Crafting strategy'. *Harvard Business Review*; 65 (4).

MINTZBERG, H. (1994) *The Rise and Fall of Strategic Planning.* London: Prentice Hall.

MINTZBERG, H., QUINN J. B. and GHOSHAL, S. (eds) (1995) *The Strategy Process.* London: Prentice Hall.

MURRAY, C. (1989) 'The emerging British underclass'. *Sunday Times Magazine.* November. This is reproduced in Lister, R. (ed.) *Charles Murray and the Underclass: The developing debate.* London: IEA.

MURRAY, C. (1996) *The Underclass: The crisis deepens.* London: Institute of Economic Affairs.

NEGROPONTE, N. (1995) *Being Digital.* London: Hodder and Stoughton.

NOLAN COMMITTEE (1995). *Standards in Public Life: Vol 1.* London: HMSO.

NORTHCOTE-TREVELYAN REPORT (1854) *Report on the Organisation of the Permanent Civil Service.* London: HMSO.

NUGENT, N. (1999) *The Government and Politics of the European Union.* Basingstoke: Macmillan.

OHMAE, K. (1995) *The End of the Nation-State.* London: Harper Collins.

ORGANISATION FOR ECONOMIC CO-OPERATION AND DEVELOPMENT (1999) *What is the OECD?* Paris: OECD.

ORLIKOWSKI, W. (1992) 'The duality of technology: rethinking the concept of technology in organizations'. *Organisational Science.* 3, 3, 398–427.

OULTON, N. (1995) 'Supply side reform and UK economic growth: what happened to the miracle?'. *National Institute Economic Review*; 154.

PAINE, T. [1791–2] (1984) *The Rights of Man.* Harmondsworth: Penguin.

PAINTER, C. *and* ISAAC-HENRY, K. (1999) 'Local government'. In: Horton, S. and Farnham D. *Public Management in Britain.* London: Macmillan.

PAINTER, R., PUTTICK, K. *and* HOLMES, A. (1998) *Employment Rights.* London: Pluto Press.

PATEMAN, C. (1979) *Participation and Democratic Theory.* Cambridge; Cambridge University Press.

PETRELLA, R. (1996) 'Globalisation and internationalisation'. In: Boyer, R. and Drache D. *States against States.* London: Routledge.

PETTIGREW, A. *and* WHIPP, R. (1991) *Managing Change for Competitive Success.* Oxford: Blackwell.

PETTIGREW, A. M. (1973) *The Politics of Organisational Decision-Making*. London: Tavistock.

PINCH, T. *and* BIJKER, W. (1987) 'The social construction of facts and artifacts: or how the sociology of science and the sociology of technology might benefit each other'. In Bijker, W., Hughes, T. and Pinch, T. (eds), *The Social Construction of Technological Systems*. Cambridge, Mass: MIT Press.

PIORE, M. *and* SABEL, C. (1984) *The Second Industrial Divide: Possibilities for prosperity*. New York: Basic Books.

POLANYI, K. (1944) *The Great Transformation*. Boston: Beacon Press.

POLLARD, S. (1969) *The Development of the British Economy 1914–1967*. London: Allen and Unwin.

POND, C. (1989) 'Wealth and the two nations'. In McDowell, L., Sarre, P. and Hamnett, C. (eds) *Divided Nation: Social and cultural change in Britain*. London: Hodder and Stoughton.

PORTER, M. (1980) *Competitive Strategy*. New York: Free Press.

PORTER, M. (1985) *Competitive Advantage*. New York: Free Press.

POULANTZAS, N. (1975) *Classes in Contemporary Capitalism*. London: New Left Books.

PRATCHETT, L. *and* WINGFIELD, M. (1994) *The Public Service Ethos in Local Government*. London: Commission on Local Democracy.

PREECE, D. A. (1995) *Organizations and Technical Change: Strategy, objectives and involvement*. London: Routledge.

PREECE, D., STEVEN, G. *and* STEVEN, V. (1999) *Work, Change and Competition: Managing for Bass*. London: Routledge.

PRIME MINISTER'S OFFICE (1991) *The Citizen's Charter*. London: HMSO.

QUINN, J. B. (1978) 'Strategic change: "logical incrementalism"'. *Sloan Management Review*. Fall.

QUINN, J. B. (1980) *Strategies for Change*. Homewood, Ill.: Irwin.

RAMSAY, H. *and* BEIRNE, M. (1992) 'Manna or monstrous regiment? Information technology, control and democracy in the workplace'.

In M. Beirne and H. Ramsay (eds), *Information Technology and Workplace Democracy*. London: Routledge.

REICH, R. (1991) *The Work of Nations*. New York: Alfred A. Knopf.

ROCHE, M. (1987) 'Citizenship, social theory and social change'. *Theory and Society*; 16.

RONEY, A. (1998) *EC/EU Factbook*. London: Kogan Page.

ROUSSEAU, J. J. [1762] (1972) *The Social Contract*. Oxford: Clarendon.

RUGMAN, A. (1996) *Selected Papers, Volume 1: The Theory of Multinational Enterprises and Volume 2: Multinationals and Trade Policy*. Cheltenham: Edward Elgar.

RUGMAN, A. (1998) 'Multinationals as regional flagships'. *Financial Times*: Mastering Global Business. Part one.

RUIGROK, W. *and* VAN TAULDER, R. (1995) *The Logic of International Restructuring*. London: Routledge.

RUSSELL, H. (1998) 'The rewards of work'. In Jowell, R. *et al British and European Social Attitudes*. Aldershot: Ashgate.

SARLVIK, B. *and* CREWE, I. (1983) *Decade of Dealignment*. Cambridge: Cambridge University Press.

SAUNDERS, P. (1989) 'Beyond housing classes: sociological significance of private property rights in means of consumption'. In McDowell, L., Sarre, P. and Hamnett, C. (eds) *Divided Nation: Social and political change in Britain*. London: Hodder and Stoughton.

SCARBROUGH, H. *and* CORBETT, M. (1992) *Technology and Organisation: Power, meaning and design*. London: Routledge.

SCHLEGELMILCH, B. *and* HOUSTON, J. (1990) 'Corporate codes of ethics'. *Management Decision*; 28 (7).

SCOTT MORTON, M. (ed.) (1991) *The Corporation of the 1990s: Information technology and organizational transformation*. New York: Oxford University Press.

SCOTT, J. *et al* (1998) 'Partner, parent, worker: family and gender roles'. In Jowell, R. *et al British and European Social Attitudes: 15th Report*. Aldershot: Ashgate.

SCOTT, R. (1995) *Institutions and Organisations*. London: Sage.

SCRUTON, R. (1980) *The Meaning of Conservatism*. Harmondsworth: Penguin.

SELDON, A. (1990) *Capitalism*. Oxford: Blackwell.

SENGE, P. (1990) 'The leader's new work: building learning organisations'. *Sloan Management Review*; Fall.

SEWELL, G. *and* WILKINSON, B. (1992) ' "Someone to watch over me": surveillance, discipline and the just-in-time labour process'. *Sociology*. 26, 2, 271–289.

SMART, B. (1993) *Postmodernity*. London: Routledge.

SMITH, A. [1776] (1976) *The Wealth of Nations*. Oxford: Clarendon.

SMITH, D. (1987) *The Rise and Fall of Monetarism*. Harmondsworth: Penguin.

SOCIAL AND LIBERAL DEMOCRATS (1989) *Our Different Vision*. London: Social and Liberal Democratic Federation.

*SOCIAL TRENDS 23* (1993) London: HMSO.

*SOCIAL TRENDS 27* (1997) London: Office of National Statistics.

*SOCIAL TRENDS 28* (1998) London: Office of National Statistics.

SOROS, G. (1995) *Soros on Soros*. New York: Wiley.

STACEY, R. (1993) *Strategic Management and Organisational Dynamics*. London: Pitman.

THOMAS, L. *and* WORMALD, E. (1989) 'Political participation'. In Reid, I. and Stratta, E. *Sex Differences in Britain*. Aldershot: Gower.

THOMASON, G. (1991) 'The management of personnel'. *Personnel Review*; 20 (2).

THOMPSON, P. *and* MCHUGH, D. (1995) *Work Organisations: A critical introduction*. 2nd edn. London: Macmillan.

TOMKINS, C. (1987) *Achieving Economy, Efficiency and Effectiveness in the Public Sector*. London: Routledge.

TOWNSEND, P. (1979) *Poverty in the United Kingdom*. Harmondsworth: Penguin Books.

TRIST, E. L., HIGGIN, G. W., MURRAY, H. *and* POLLACK, A. B. (1963) *Organizational Choice*. London: Tavistock.

Twining, W. *and* Miers, D. (1982) *How to Do Things with Rules.* London: Weidenfeld and Nicolson.

United Nations Conference on Trade and Development (annual). *World Investment Report.* New York and Geneva: United Nations.

Van De Wee, H. (1987) *Prosperity and Upheaval.* Harmondsworth: Penguin.

Veljanovski, C. (ed.) (1991) *Regulators and the Market.* London: Institute of Economic Affairs.

Waterson, M. (1988) *Regulation of the Firm and Natural Monopoly.* Oxford: Blackwell.

Weber, M. (1968) 'Status groups and classes'. In Roth, G. and Wittich, C. (eds) *Economy and Society.* New York: Bedminster Press.

Weber, M. (1971) 'Class, status and party'. In Thompson, K. and Tunstall, J. (eds) *Sociological Perspectives.* Harmondsworth: Penguin.

Webster, D. (1981) *The Labour Party and the New Left.* London: Fabian Society.

Whittington, R. (1993) *What Is Strategy and Does It Matter?* London: Routledge.

Wilkinson, B. (1983) *The Shopfloor Politics of New Technology.* Oxford: Heinemann.

Williams, R. *and* Edge, D. (1996) 'The social shaping of technology'. In Dutton, W. (ed.), (see below).

Williamson, O. (1991) 'Strategising, economising and economic organisation'. *Strategic Management Journal*; 12.

Winner, L. (1977) *Autonomous Technology: Technics-out-of-control as a theme in political thought.* Cambridge, Mass.: MIT Press.

Winner, L. (1985) 'Do artefacts have politics?', *Daedalus.* 109: 121–36.

Winstanley, D., Woodhall, J. *and* Heery, E. (1996) 'Business ethics and human resource management'. *Personnel Review*; 25 (6).

WITZ, A. (1992) *Professions and Patriarchy.* London: Routledge.

WOMACK, J., JONES, D. and ROOS, D. (1990) *The Machine that Changed the World.* New York: Rawson Associates.

WOOD, S. (1982) (ed.) *Degradation of Work: Deskilling and the labour process.* London: Hutchinson.

WOODWARD, J. (1958) *Management and Technology.* London: HMSO.

WOODWARD, J. (1965) *Industrial Organization: Theory and practice.* Oxford: Oxford University Press.

WOODWARD, J. (ed.) (1970) *Industrial Organization: Behaviour and control.* Oxford: Oxford University Press.

WOODWARD, J. (ed.) (1980) *Industrial Organisation: Theory and practice.* 2nd edn. Oxford: Oxford University Press.

WOOLGAR, S. (1994) 'Rethinking requirements analysis: some implications of recent research into producer-consumer relations in IT development'. In Jirotka, M. and Goguen, J. A. (eds) *Requirements Engineering: Social and technical issues.* London: Academic Press.

WOOLGAR, S. (1996) 'Technologies as Cultural Artefacts'. In Dutton, W., *op cit.*

WORLD BANK (1998) *World Development Report.* Geneva: World Bank.

WRIGHT, E. (1985) *Classes.* London: Verso.

ZUBOFF, S. (1988) *In the Age of the Smart Machine: The future of work and power.* Oxford: Heinemann.

# Professional Standards Index

The indicative content of the module is covered in the eight chapters of the book, mainly sequentially, as follows:

- Chapter 1: The Strategic Framework [sections 1(a) and 1(b)]

- Chapter 2: The Economy [section 2(a)]

- Chapter 3: The Political System [section 2(b)]

- Chapter 4: Social Structure [section 2(c)]

- Chapter 5: Legal Framework [section 2(d)] (including The Legislative Process under 2(b))

- Chapter 6: Technology [section 2(e)]

- Chapter 7: International Factors [section 2(f)]

- Chapter 8: Social Responsibility and Business Ethics [sections 1(c) and 3(a), 3(b) and 3(c)]

The learning outcomes of the professional standards, in turn, are set out at the beginning of each chapter.

# Index

Chartered Institute of Personnel and Development

# Customer Satisfaction Survey

The more feedback we get, the better our books can be! We will send you a
**FREE CIPD MOUSE MAT** (UK addresses only) as a thank you for completing this card.

Name and address: ...................................................................................................

................................................................................................................................

CIPD membership number: ☐ ☐ ☐ ☐ ☐ ☐ ☐ ☐

1   Title of book...................................................................................................

2   Date of purchase: month ............................................... **year** ........................

3   How did you acquire this book?
    ☐ bookshop   ☐ Plymbridge   ☐ CIPD website   ☐ other (specify) ...........................

4   If ordered from Plymbridge, when did you receive your book?
    ☐ 1 week          ☐ 2 weeks          ☐ more than 2 weeks

5   Please grade the following according to their influence on your purchasing
    decision, with 1 as least influential: (please tick)

|           | 1 | 2 | 3 | 4 | 5 |
|-----------|---|---|---|---|---|
| Title     |   |   |   |   |   |
| Publisher |   |   |   |   |   |
| Author    |   |   |   |   |   |
| Price     |   |   |   |   |   |
| Subject   |   |   |   |   |   |
| Cover     |   |   |   |   |   |

6   On a scale of 1 to 5 (with 1 as poor and 5 as excellent) please give your impression
    of the book in terms of: (please tick)

|                       | 1 | 2 | 3 | 4 | 5 |
|-----------------------|---|---|---|---|---|
| Cover design          |   |   |   |   |   |
| Paper/print quality   |   |   |   |   |   |
| Good value for money  |   |   |   |   |   |
| General level of service |   |   |   |   |   |

7   Did you find the book:   covers the subject in sufficient depth   ☐ Yes   ☐ No
                             useful for your work                     ☐ Yes   ☐ No

8   Are you using this book to help:
    ☐ in your work   ☐ study   ☐ both   ☐ other (specify) .......................................

If you are using this book as part of a course, please give:

9   Name of academic institution.........................................................................

10  Name of course ...........................................................................................

11  Is this book relevant to your syllabus?          ☐ Yes          ☐ No

**Call 020 8263 3387 for our latest books catalogue. Don't forget, CIPD members get 10%**

**Publishing Department**

**Chartered Institute of Personnel and Development**

**CIPD House**

**Camp Road**

**Wimbledon**

**London**

**SW19 4BR**